SUPPORTIVE THERAPY
FOR BORDERLINE PATIENTS

A Psychodynamic Approach

SUPPORTIVE THERAPY

FOR BORDERLINE PATIENTS

A Psychodynamic Approach

Lawrence H. Rockland

with
Devra Braun
Harold W. Koenigsberg
Samuel Perry
Charles Swenson

THE GUILFORD PRESS

NEW YORK   LONDON

© 1992 The Guilford Press
A Division of Guilford Publications, Inc.
72 Spring Street, New York, NY 10012

Printed in the United States of America

This book is printed on acid-free paper.

Last digit is print number: 9 8 7 6 5 4 3 2 1

Library of Congress Cataloging-in-Publication Data

Rockland, Lawrence H., 1932–
    Supportive therapy for borderline patients : a psychodynamic
approach / Lawrence H. Rockland.
        p.   cm.—(Diagnosis and treatment of mental disorders)
    Includes bibliographical references and index.
    ISBN 0-89862-182-8
    1. Borderline personality disorder—Treatment.   2. Supportive
psychotherapy.   I. Title.   II. Series.
    [DNLM: 1. Borderline Personality Disorder—therapy.   2. Physician
-Patient Relations.   3. Psychotherapy—methods.   WM 190 R683s]
RC569.5.B67R63   1992
616.85′8520651—dc20
DNLM/DLC
for Library of Congress   92-1538
                                                                        CIP

*For Nancy, Harry, Tom, Peter,
Ari, Kyla, and Noah*

Foreword

My interest in borderline personality disorder and professional responsibility as head of an outpatient department has resulted in my doing a very large number of consultations on such patients (probably more than 1,500). I must be cautious in drawing any conclusions from this type of experience since my sample is so heavily biased in the direction of individuals who are having crises in their treatments. Nonetheless, I have become convinced that many borderline patients are not helped by the psychiatric treatment they receive and, even more troubling, that a fair percentage of them are made worse by it. This unhappy situation (if it is true) may be the consequence of factors within the patient that make psychiatric treatment ineffective or harmful, but I believe that some of the iatrogenic consequences of treatment result from the way it is delivered. This is why I am so delighted by Dr. Rockland's book and relieved that it is available. Dr. Rockland's approach makes sense to me at a time when much of the literature on the psychotherapy of borderline personality does not. I will briefly indicate what I mean by this and how clinicians and patients may benefit from some of Rockland's treatment suggestions.

It is ironic that the modern concept of borderline personality emerged from a realization that such individuals were more suited to a supportive than to an uncovering approach. These original observations have been obscured by a more recent literature that has espoused one or another form of uncovering psychodynamic psychotherapy for borderline personality—usually buttressed by a theoretical rationale to explain the pathogenesis of the disorder and its suggested treatment, and a description of anecdotal case examples. The writing and lecturing of a charismatic group of therapists has led to the widespread use of uncovering techniques in the treatment of borderline personality. Although the techniques vary depending on the particular perspective of the given author, they share in common a tendency toward an intense patient/therapist relationship, anxiety-provoking confrontations, and a relative abstinence in regard to practical advice giving and reality testing.

Doubtless, uncovering techniques can be useful in the hands of highly talented therapists as applied to fairly well-functioning and highly talented borderline patients. I fear, however, that when either of these conditions fails to be met, the risk/benefit ratio for uncovering treatment of borderline personality becomes unfavorable. My consultation experience suggests that too many therapists with too little training are providing too many interpretations in overly intensive relationships with poorly selected borderline patients. The negative results include catastrophic self-destructive behavior in response to the therapist's real or imagined rejections, psychotic transferences, sexual indiscretions, addiction to therapy, and failure to have a life outside of the sessions.

On balance, the average expectable borderline patient treated by the average expectable therapist is, I believe, more likely to benefit and less likely to be harmed by receiving a supportive psychotherapy, supplemented when necessary by medication. The fact that this is not the community standard may reflect that I am wrong about this issue, but there is another explanation. Psychodynamic uncovering treatments have attracted an extensive and enthusiastic literature and have been spelled out in great detail. Until now supportive treatment has not received the same attention or clarity.

Fortunately Dr. Rockland's book should go far in redressing this imbalance. He presents a well-worked out and beautifully illustrated exposition of supportive therapy that should improve the clinical practice of every clinician who reads the book carefully and digests its message. Many therapists prefer uncovering therapy because they see it as more intellectually gratifying or professionally ambitious. In contrast, the available research literature, and my own clinical experience, suggest that supportive therapy requires greater skill than uncovering treatment and that the results achieved are more likely to correlate with the skill with which the treatment is delivered. Once one understands the patient's defense, it is more difficult to frame an appropriate response than merely to interpret it.

Dr. Rockland's book brings the pendulum back to center. Early authors on borderline personality emphasized the value of supportive therapy (and the danger of uncovering therapy) for these individuals. More recent authors have promoted uncovering approaches. Dr. Rockland provides the first comprehensive and systematic exposition of supportive therapy for borderline personality, while at the same time specifying when and how to integrate a more uncovering approach. I have learned a great deal from this book and feel confident that it will have a pronounced beneficial effect on clinical practice.

ALLEN FRANCES, M.D.
New York State Psychiatric Institute

Acknowledgments

A number of people helped to bring this book to publication in addition to the four authors who contributed chapters. Alan Francis initially urged me to write it, and then remained warmly supportive throughout the process. I value his friendship and I will miss him when he leaves for Duke.

Otto Kernberg was also supportive of the book, and continued to stimulate my interest and best intellectual effort. I am grateful to him and to the entire Westchester Division Borderline Psychotherapy Research Group: John Clarkin, Harold Koenigsberg, Ann Appelbaum, Steve Bauer, Lisa Gornick, Paulina Kernberg, Mike Selzer, Tom Smith, and Frank Yeomans.

The staff of Guilford Publications was very helpful, particularly Sarah Kennedy and Seymour Weingarten. My secretary, Patricia Kelly, labored long hours without complaint and made many helpful editorial and grammatical suggestions; Louise Taitt and Elaine Kensek (who, tragically, died early in the work) also helped with the endless typing.

Finally, I want to express my gratitude to my wife Charlotte, who responded to my fatigue, preoccupation, and bouts of irascibility with humor, love, and understanding.

Thank you all.

Contents

III. ISSUES IN TREATMENT

Introduction*

Patients with borderline psychopathology, whether conceptualized as Borderline Personality Disorder (BPD; DSM-III-R, 1987) or as Borderline Personality Organization (BPO; Kernberg, 1967, 1984), constitute a significant public health problem, as well as a difficult and complex treatment dilemma for their therapists. They utilize large amounts of mental health resources—inpatient, day hospital, and outpatient. The impulsivity that characterizes these patients leads to their often presenting in acute crises and frequently dropping out of treatment programs, sometimes without explanation. This impulsivity, combined with the affective instability, unstable relationships, and strong acting-out potential that characterize these patients tends to create an intense and chaotic treatment situation that is often confusing and anxiety laden for the therapist.

The higher functioning and more stable of these patients can be treated with a primarily exploratory therapy, although dropouts are very common and successful outcomes unusual (Waldinger & Gunderson, 1987). For the majority, characterized by questionable motivation, poor educational and work performance, inadequate social supports, or the potential for malignant regressions, exploratory psychotherapy is not appropriate. In fact, it can be harmful and can lead to clinical deterioration, for example, psychotic episodes or increased suicidality and self-mutilation, often requiring hospitalization. Other treatment approaches are required for most borderline patients; the alternatives prevalent in current practice are psychodynamic but *supportive*, cognitive/behavioral, or psychopharmacologic.

---

*Because a greater percentage of borderlines are female, I've chosen to use the pronoun "she" when refering to a borderline patient throughout the text.

The cognitive/behavioral approach that is receiving most interest currently is Linehan's Dialectical Behavior Therapy (DBT; Linehan, 1987a, 1987b), her treatment for "para-suicidals," most of whom meet the criteria for BPD. The treatment consists of an organized sequence of treatment/educational modules, carried out simultaneously in individual and group formats. DBT appears to be an effective therapy for borderline patients, but the requirements for compliance with the program, for example, the performance of homework assignments, in light of the negative transferences, primitive defenses and acting out potential that characterize BPD patients, limit the applicability of this treatment approach. In addition, although behaviors may change, the therapy does not address the structural pathology of BPD.

The role of psychopharmacology in the treatment of these patients remains unclear. Drugs do not appear to alter the basic psychopathology of BPD and currently are most reasonably viewed as adjunctive to psychotherapeutic approaches.

Some type of supportive psychotherapy is indicated for large numbers of borderline patients, and supportive variants are, in actuality, being delivered to many of these patients. But dynamic psychotherapists struggle with supportive, or mixed supportive/exploratory, treatments for these difficult patients with almost no help from the literature. Guidance and help are sorely needed because simple reassurance, advice, and other naive supportive interventions are generally unsuccessful. Yet it is this rudimentary version of supportive therapy that is often viewed as the only psychodynamic alternative to exploratory treatment. In fact, "psychodynamic" is often applied only to exploratory psychotherapies, as though supportive psychotherapy were not equally grounded in the same theoretical foundations, an issue discussed more fully elsewhere (Rockland, 1989).

I believe that a large percentage of borderline patients are best treated with a sophisticated supportive therapy, firmly rooted in a thorough understanding of psychodynamic principles, dynamic psychotherapy, and the subtleties of transference and countertransference. As Dewald (1971) wrote, "The majority of people with psychiatric illness . . . character problems, acute or chronic psychoses, somatic conversion symptoms etc., are not suitable candidates for a formal attempt at insight oriented psychotherapy. Instead they are more suitably and expeditiously treated by a dynamically oriented supportive approach" (p. 114). All of this, ideally, is integrated with knowledge of, and experience with, borderline psychopathology.

However, the literature is sparse regarding the entire subject of dynamically oriented supportive psychotherapy, and this is particularly true as regards the application of that modality to borderline patients. There is a moderate literature on treating borderline patients with psychoanalysis (Abend, Porder, & Willick, 1983, Giovacchini, 1984), abundant work about exploratory approaches to these patients (Adler, 1985; Kernberg, 1984; Masterson, 1976), but almost no literature on supportive approaches. Early authors (Knight, 1954; Stern, 1938, 1945; Zetzel, 1971) recommended supportive psychotherapy for these patients and proposed general treatment guidelines, but they did not elaborate a treatment methodology in any detail.

A recent exception is Kernberg (1984). He emphasizes the noninterpretive handling of negative transferences and primitive defenses as core to the supportive therapy of BPO patients. I agree generally with his views, but they are limited; the subject deserves more detailed description and greater elaboration than are possible in a single paper. This marked imbalance in the literature, and between the literature and the realities of clinical practice, clearly deserves to be redressed. This book is a step in that direction.

I (1989) have previously elaborated the general principles, goals, strategies, and techniques of Psychodynamically Oriented Supportive Therapy (POST), and that material is summarized in Chapter 3 of this book. However, some abbreviated comments on POST are usefully included here.

In brief, POST is rooted in psychodynamic theory and requires as detailed a psychodynamic understanding of the patient as do the exploratory psychotherapies. It is carried out face to face; usually on a once, sometimes twice, per week schedule; and aims at strengthening the functions of the ego, thereby improving the patient's adaptations to both inner and outer worlds. Mild to moderate positive transferences are not addressed, while negative transferences and overidealized and erotized transferences are rapidly undermined. Resistances and defenses are always evaluated regarding their adaptive/maladaptive values, and accordingly are either supported or undermined. The therapeutic alliance is a constant focus of attention, strengthening the relational and other nonspecific factors that underlie success in all psychotherapies. Regression is discouraged, and therefore so are free association, focus on dream material, and therapist anonymity. The supportive therapist listens to and processes patient material as a psychodynamic clinician, but responds as a combination of dynamic therapist and family physician. The treatment is probably more difficult to carry out skillfully than is exploratory psychotherapy and psychoanalysis. It requires more clinical hunch and intuition because of the less transparent, more defended nature of the patient material.

This book addresses the supportive psychotherapy of patients with Borderline Personality Disorder rather than Borderline Personality Organization. Borderline Personality Disorder is one of 11 personality disorders on Axis II of DSM-III-R and is defined by the presence of five of eight phenomenologic criteria. Borderline Personality Organization is one of three personality organizations (Kernberg, 1967, 1984), differentiated from Neurotic and Psychotic Personality Organizations by the structural criteria of identity diffusion and prominent "primitive" defenses, in the presence of grossly intact reality testing.

I chose BPD because (1) it currently is the more commonly accepted connotation of the term "borderline," and (2) BPO subsumes a large group of clinically discrepant patients, making it essentially synonymous with lower level character pathology (Gunderson, 1984), and thus less useful clinically. On the other hand, Kernberg's argument that the disparate surface phenomena are based in common underlying psychic structures and that, therefore, BPO is the more useful connotation, particularly for discussions of dynamic psychotherapy, is also convincing. Consistent with that argument, this treatment, though designed for patients with BPD, is applicable with minor modifications to any of the BPO personality disorders.

Psychodynamically Oriented Supportive Therapy is relevant to the treatment of the BPD patient in three ways. First, treatment of the acute crises that these patients so frequently present; major depressions, severe eating disorders, destructive self-mutilations, etc., are almost always best treated supportively. Second, a number of BPD patients are probably most appropriately treated with an initial supportive approach and a later switch to a more exploratory modality. In such cases, the same therapist can usually make the switch from supportive to exploratory therapy if he ensures that he is neither excessively supportive nor inordinately revealing of himself during the supportive phase (assuming, of course, that he is competent to conduct both treatments). Third, a large number, perhaps a majority, of BPD patients are best treated throughout by a dynamic supportive approach.

In essence, then, this book addresses a significant gap in the literature by elaborating a psychotherapy for BPD, applicable with minor modifications to other BPO Axis II disorders, that is supportive and firmly rooted in psychodynamic theory. It applies the general principles of POST (Rockland, 1989) specifically to the patient with BPD. It is relevant, in one of the three ways noted above, to the treatment of a large majority of patients with BPD.

The treatment is not presented as the definitive psychotherapy for BPD, and certainly not as a panacea. Borderline patients are too variable across multiple parameters to imagine that one psychotherapy could be most effective for all of them. The inner chaos of the BPD patient ensures that any psychotherapeutic approach will be frustrating and problematic, characterized by intense, chaotic transferences and distressing, anxiety-laden countertransference reactions.

A young resident, new to outpatient psychiatry, remarked recently, "I love treating borderline patients, it's exhilarating." Her enthusiasm was laudable, her naiveté striking, and I thought sadly, "She's got so much to learn." That evening her patient made a suicide attempt, and the now panicky resident was desperately trying to arrange a hospitalization. The patient, in turn, was adamantly refusing not only hospitalization but any further contact with the therapist. Such is the beginning of wisdom.

OVERVIEW OF THE BOOK

The first three chapters present theoretical background material. Chapter 1 traces the changes in the concept of the "borderline" from a vaguely defined psychopathology located between neurosis and psychosis to a criterion-based personality disorder on Axis II of DSM-III-R. The changes in psychotherapeutic approach over time, specifically the swing from supportive to exploratory to mixed models and differential therapeutics, are the focus of Chapter 2. Chapter 3 summarizes the general principles of Psychodynamically Oriented Supportive Therapy.

Chapter 4 is a transition between the background theoretical material and the clinical focus of the remainder of the book. It discusses the indications and contraindications for POST in BPD patients, focusing first on general criteria and then on clinical aspects that are specific to the BPD patient.

Chapters 5, 6, 7, and 8 present the 2½-year, twice weekly, dynamic supportive psychotherapy of a 24-year-old female with BPD. The chapters deal successively with Evaluation and Treatment Planning (Chapter 5), Early Phase issues (Chapter 6), Middle Phase issues (Chapter 7), and Termination (Chapter 8). Extensive excerpts of session dialogue, with accompanying commentary and discussion by the author, are provided throughout.

Chapters 9 and 10 address areas of recurrent difficulty in POST of the BPD patient. The focus of Chapter 9 on countertransference reflects the inevitability and importance of countertransference problems in the treatments of these patients, while Chapter 10 discusses treatment of the acting out and impulsivity that characterize these treatments. Dr. Perry, in Chapter 11, describes intermittent continuous therapy of a supportive type for the borderline patient and discusses the rationales for this type of treatment. In Chapter 12, Dr. Koenigsberg reviews the role of psychopharmacology in the treatment of BPD patients, focusing successively on the various psychopharmacologic agents and on the psychological aspects of introducing medication into the treatment. Dr. Swenson, in Chapter 12, takes up the many supportive aspects of extended inpatient treatment for borderline patients, and in the last chapter the author reiterates and expands on some of the key issues in the book.

PART I

THEORETICAL BACKGROUND

CHAPTER 1

The Concept
of the Borderline

Views of what constitutes a borderline patient have changed markedly since the first clinical description in 1938 by Stern (Stern, 1938). He described a heterogeneous group of patients whose pathology was neither neurotic nor psychotic and who did poorly in standard psychoanalytic treatment. Today, the borderline patient is seen as suffering from a discrete personality disorder on Axis II of DSM-III-R characterized by five of eight criteria that focus on instability of self, affects, and interpersonal relationships; impulsivity; and self-destructiveness. The earlier view that the borderline bordered on schizophrenia, "borderline schizophrenia" (Knight, 1953a), has faded and its relationship first to affective disorder, and more recently to other Axis II personality disorders, has become the current focus of interest. This chapter traces these trends over time, focusing on the major contributors, and then concentrates on present areas of interest and controversy.

PSYCHOANALYTIC CONCEPTS
Adolph Stern

Although the term had been used in a vague and inconsistent manner by several previous authors, it was Adolph Stern who provided the first organized clinical description of the borderline patient. He observed a number of patients in his office practice who shared common clinical characteristics, including a poor response to psychoanalytic treatment.

He called them "borderlines" (i.e., neither neurotic nor psychotic) and their clinical presentation consisted of

- *Severe Narcissistic Pathology.* This was the most basic aspect of the patients, and Stern viewed their other difficulties as secondary to the narcissistic problems. The narcissistic pathology was attributed to severe disturbances in the early mother–child relationship, particularly neglect, abuse, and brutalization.
- *"Psychic Bleeding."* A deficit of adaptive resiliency; patients tended to collapse under stress rather than responding realistically.
- *Inordinate Hypersensitivity.* This was reactive to the patient's narcissistic vulnerability. Critical comments tended to be viewed as destructive attacks and paranoid traits were common.
- *"Psychic Rigidity."* A stance of constant and inflexible self-protection, to guard against anxiety or other dysphoric affects.
- *Negative Therapeutic Reactions.* Patients tended to react to interpretations as reflecting criticism and lack of love or appreciation. They became depressed, angry, or discouraged, and this commonly led to negative therapeutic reactions.
- *Feelings of Inferiority.* These feelings led the patient to shy away from active adaptive behaviors and toward childlike dependency. They were sometimes held with a conviction that made the patient appear delusional.
- *Masochism.* Viewed primarily as an appeal to the therapist to take care of and protect the patient.
- *"Somatic" Insecurity or Anxiety.* The patient might present a composed and placid exterior, but this was always defensive against inner feelings of profound insecurity.
- *Widespread Use of Projective Mechanisms.* Patients tended to externalize, attributing their difficulties to forces or persons outside of themselves.
- *Difficulties in the Reality Function.* This was most marked in the patient's sense of reality; reality testing, by contrast, was generally intact.

These patients presented a superficial facade of good adaptation together with severe deep pathology. They would probably meet criteria for Kernberg's Borderline Personality Organization (BPO; Kernberg, 1984), but lacked the impulsivity, fluctuating intense relationships, and self-destructive behaviors of the DSM-III-R Borderline Personality Disorder (BPD). Stern's etiologic focus on early abuse and brutalization anticipated the similar interests in these issues today.

In the years following Stern's seminal paper, "borderline" was used by various authors to describe a wide spectrum of patients. Zilboorg's "ambulatory schizophrenia" (1941), Helena Deutsch's "as if" personality (1942), Schmideberg's "borderline" (1947), and Hoch and Polatin's "pseudoneurotic schizophrenia" (1949) all described patients who were viewed as having intermediate-level pathology between neurotic and psychotic, although many were closer to psychosis. By present diagnostic criteria, they were a mixed group; some were chronically schizophrenic, some had affective disorders, and some would meet DSM-III criteria for borderline, schizotypal, or other personality disorders. A close relationship to schizophrenia was clearly implied, and Hoch and Polatin considered their patients to be basically schizophrenic.

Robert Knight

It was not until 1954 that Knight presented a second systematic description of the borderline patient (Knight, 1954). Knight worked primarily with inpatients and therefore tended to treat a more disturbed group of patients than had Stern. He made the same treatment-related observations. Patients did poorly when treated by standard psychoanalytic procedures and some became clinically worse. He described the patients as presenting a surface facade that appeared neurotic, without a manifest loss of reality testing; but deeper psychic structures were very primitive and much closer to those of the schizophrenic patient.

Knight considered these patients to be cases of "borderline schizophrenia." (1953a) They had severe weaknesses in crucial ego functions, with difficulties in logical thinking, realistic planning, object relations, and adaptation to the environment. Primitive defenses, for example, marked projection and denial, were common, and unstructured clinical interviewing and psychological testing revealed "microscopic" evidence of schizophrenic illness.

Unenthusiastic about the terms "borderline case" and "borderline schizophrenia," Knight argued that they were vague and should be replaced by more accurate diagnoses. But more important than diagnosis ". . . is the achievement of a comprehensive psychodynamic and psychoeconomic appraisal of the balance in each patient between the ego's defensive and adaptive measures on the one hand, and the pathogenic instinctual disintegrating forces on the other, so that therapy can be planned and conducted for the purpose of conserving, strengthening and improving the defensive and adaptive functions of the ego" (1954, p. 108).

Knight's cases do appear to be closer to clinical schizophrenia than were Stern's patients, or those diagnosed today as BPD. His writings were influential at the time in locating the "borderline" in close proximity to schizophrenia.

John Frosch

Frosch, in a series of papers beginning in 1960 (1960, 1964, 1970), described a group of patients in the mid range of pathology whom he called "psychotic characters." He felt that this was a more accurate and precise diagnostic label for these patients, who previously had been diagnosed as borderlines, pseudoneurotic schizophrenics, or latent and ambulatory schizophrenics. Drawing a parallel between neurotic and psychotic characters, he stated that, like the neurotic character who need never develop a symptomatic neurosis, the psychotic character may never become clinically psychotic.

Frosch's descriptions of the symptomatology and structure of the "psychotic character" were similar to Knight's portrayal of the "borderline schizophrenic." The patients usually presented with multiple neurotic symptoms, a pan-neurosis, but these surface symptoms covered deeper structures that were basically psychotic. The psychotic character was a relatively stable pathological condition and not a transitional state on the path to more overt psychosis. On the other hand, the patients' hold on reality was tenuous, and they could easily decompensate into an acute, transient psychosis. They experienced difficulties in their relationship to reality and feelings of reality, but generally maintained the capacity to test reality, except during the acute psychotic regressions to which they were prone.

The psychotic character differed from the neurotic character in three crucial areas (Frosch, 1970).

1. *The Nature of the Danger.* Castration and narcissistic humiliation were the basic danger situations for the neurotic character, while loss of self and psychic dissolution constantly threatened the psychotic character. These omnipresent dangers resulted from the defective self-object differentiation of the psychotic character.

2. *The Nature of the Defenses.* Repression, displacement, reaction formation, and so forth characterized the defensive structure of the neurotic character. Massive projections and introjections, projective identification, splitting, and marked denial were most prominent in psychotic characters.

3. *State of the Ego Functions.* Patients with psychotic characters were vulnerable to altered states of being, to difficulties with reality in its three aspects (relation to reality, feelings of reality, and reality testing), and to

their egos being overwhelmed by overpowering drive or primitive super-ego forces. None of these were threats for the neurotic character.

Frosch viewed the "borderline" (psychotic character) as related to schizophrenia, evidenced by the term "psychotic" character and his emphasis on "psychotic" structures underlying the superficial neurotic symptomatology. Yet his clinical descriptions were very similar to Kernberg's BPO patient. The terminology is confusing because, in Kernberg's system, BPO patients are clearly distinguished from patients with Psychotic Personality Organization. In other words, Frosch's "psychotic character" patients are similar to Kernberg's "borderline organization" patients and different from Kernberg's "psychotic organization" patients. Only a small percentage of Frosch's patients would meet criteria for DSM-III-R BPD.

Otto Kernberg

Beginning 25 years ago, Kernberg (1967, 1971, 1975, 1977, 1984) elucidated the psychopathology of what he termed "BPO." Integrating the constructs of Melanie Klein with those of classical psychoanalytic theory, he described the borderline organization in terms of internalized object relations. BPO patients had intermediate-level pathology, between those with Neurotic Organization (healthier) and those with Psychotic Organization (sicker). All patients could be characterized as having one of the three personality organizations.

Kernberg delineated the BPO according to three main psychostructural constructs: (1) impaired identity integration, (2) predominance of primitive defenses centered around splitting, and (3) maintenance of reality testing (though not of the sense of reality or feelings of reality). Borderline Organization was distinguished from Neurotic Organization by the variables of identity and defenses (identity is integrated and defenses are centered around repression in the Neurotic Organization), and from Psychotic Organization by the variable of reality testing (reality testing is lost in the Psychotic Organization). In addition, BPO patients were characterized by nonspecific signs of ego weakness, such as low anxiety tolerance, poor impulse control, poor sublimatory capacities, polysymptomatic neuroses, and a shift toward primary process thinking.

Note that the diagnosis of BPO places the patient within one of only three possible levels of personality organization. Its strength is in identifying common psychostructural variables in patients with Borderline Organization, patients who otherwise can present very different clinical and symptomatic pictures. BPO encompasses most Axis II disorders plus a number of Axis I diagnoses. This is also its major weakness; that is, its diagnostic breadth encompasses patients who appear very different clinically. Thus it is of limited usefulness in treatment and outcome studies. A related problem is that terms closely tied to Kernberg's formulations, such as "splitting" and "projective identification," have been used in such widely disparate ways by different authors that their usefulness has been questioned (Meissner, 1980; Pruyser, 1975).

Although Frosch's psychotic character and Kernberg's BPO described similar patient populations, Kernberg's distinction between Borderline and Psychotic Organizations placed the borderline patient among the severe personality disorders related peripherally, if at all, to schizophrenia. Thus, he tended to move the "borderline" further away from any relationship to schizophrenia.

Thus far, contributions to the concept of the borderline were primarily from psychoanalysts, as they struggled to find effective ways to understand and to treat their patients. Beginning in the late 1960s and continuing through the 1970s, broader based investigators began to study large samples of patients and to empirically describe the clinical features of the borderline patient.

CLINICAL PHENOMENOLOGY
Roy Grinker

Grinker, Werble, and Drye (1968, 1977) studied 51 hospitalized borderline patients from both ego psychological and descriptive viewpoints. The patients were characterized by the predominant affects of anger, depression, and loneliness; by defective affectionate relationships; and by problems with consistent identity or self. The overall group, in turn, was subdivided by cluster analysis into four subgroups:

• *The Border with Psychosis.* These patients failed at human relatedness, had markedly maladaptive behaviors and affects, and reacted negatively and angrily toward other people and the world. Feelings of identity and reality sense were severely impaired. They had difficulty in feeling anything but anger and developed either isolated lifestyles or parasitic and symbiotic attachments to others. Substance abuse was common.
• *The Core Borderline Syndrome.* Patients were characterized by intense and oscillating involvements with others, anger as the predominant affect, varying degrees of depressive loneliness, and difficulties in experiencing an integrated sense of self.
• *The Adaptive, Affectless, Defended "As if" Patient.* These tended to be withdrawn and isolated, had a schizoid lifestyle but were able to

conform to usual social expectations. Relationships with others were bland and characterized by distance and withdrawal. Patients often appeared to be without much affect. They tended to base their behavior on cues from others, thus the "as if" qualities, and had a severely defective identity.

• *The Border with Neurosis.* Patients in this subgroup might be misdiagnosed as depressives because they made infantile attachments to others, reacting with whining complaints when dependency needs were frustrated. They too lacked a consistent sense of self and identity, and had little ability to engage in mutually satisfying give-and-take relationships.

The work of the Grinker group was crucial because it was the first systematic observation of a significant number of borderline patients. Their borderlines do not appear to be related to schizophrenia (with the possible exception of the first group), but might be related to affective illness (predominance of depression). Their studies moved the borderline further from Knight's "borderline schizophrenia," and toward severe character pathology and possibly affective illness. Grinker's work had a significant impact on Gunderson and, via Gunderson, on the criteria for DSM-III BPD.

John Gunderson

Gunderson and his colleagues (1975, 1977, 1978, 1984), over the past decade and a half, expanded on the work of the Grinker group, attempting to describe more precisely and more accurately the clinical phenomenology and symptoms of the borderline patient. Gunderson and Singer (1975) surveyed the literature and identified six prominent characteristics of these patients:

• Intense affects, usually anger or depressive loneliness; anxiety and anhedonia in some patients.
• A history of impulsive and self-destructive behavior, for example, self-mutilation, drug overdoses, drug dependency, promiscuity.
• Superficial social adequacy, for example, reasonable appearance, some achievement in school or work, social appropriateness; this was combined with a tendency to maladaptive regressions.
• A stable personality disorder, sometimes punctuated by brief psychotic episodes tending to occur under stress and usually reversible.
• Psychological test performance characterized by a normal WAIS combined with primitive and bizarre percepts on unstructured tests; reality testing grossly intact.

• Interpersonal relationships were either transient and superficial or intense, clinging, and manipulative, with marked alternations between the two. Patients were usually socially active, not withdrawn.

Continuing with direct clinical observation, Gunderson and Kolb (1978) demonstrated that BPD could be reliably distinguished from both schizophrenia and neurotic depression, two syndromes that might potentially offer difficulties in differential diagnosis. Their patient sample revealed seven characteristics of patients with BPD:

• Low achievement. School and work performance were similar to that of schizophrenic patients. (This finding was discrepant from the literature review.)
• Impulsivity. Drug dependency, promiscuity, and other impulsive, often self-destructive, behaviors.
• Manipulative suicide gestures, for example, wrist-cutting, burning or nonlethal overdoses.
• Heightened affectivity, particularly anger; chronic feelings of dissatisfaction.
• Mild psychotic regressions, usually stress related and short lived.
• High socialization, not "loners"; on the contrary, the patients had great difficulties being alone.
• Disturbed intimate relationships, characterized by devaluation, manipulation, and masochistic behaviors.

The studies of the Gunderson group exerted a powerful influence on the clinical criteria for BPD that were developed for DSM-III. Their work moved the "borderline" clearly into the area of the personality disorders, further from any relationship to schizophrenia. Nevertheless, in the late 1970s borderline was still a confusing construct, with conflicting and inconsistent descriptions in the literature. The extent of this confusion is illustrated by the work of Perry and Klerman.

Christopher Perry and Gerald Klerman

These authors (1978) compared the clinical features of borderline patients as described by four prominent authors: Knight, Grinker, Kernberg, and Gunderson. They compiled data from the four clinical accounts regarding history, mental status, interpersonal relations, defense mechanisms, and overall personality functioning and combined them into a list of 104 descriptors. Of these 104 items, 55 were mentioned by only one author, while only one item was present in all four descriptions (appropriate behavior during the interview). Fourteen appeared in three of the four clinical accounts and focused on the prevalence of anger, negativism, emotional shallowness, brief psychotic episodes, interpersonal difficulties, and acting out.

Perry and Klerman commented, "Reviewing our findings, we are struck by the number of different criteria proposed for borderline patients. In one way or another, it seems as if the whole range of psychopathology of personality is represented. . . . More striking, however, is the lack of overlap in the four sets of criteria in comparison to the total number of criteria" (p. 150).

DSM-III

Robert Spitzer et al.

Spitzer, Endicott, and Gibbon (1979), as part of the efforts of the DSM-III Task Force to construct a Personality Disorders Axis, reviewed the literature on the use of the term "borderline." They concluded that it is used in two major ways: (1) to describe a group of "borderline schizophrenics" and (2) to describe a second group of patients called "borderlines" or "unstable borderlines." The former group was probably genetically related to schizophrenia, as exemplified by the work of Kety, Rosenthal, and Wender (1968). The latter group was best represented by the writings of Gunderson (BPD) and Kernberg (BPO).

The goals were to operationally define both uses of the term "borderline" and to examine the relationship between them in order to determine whether they were best represented on Axis II by one or two disorders. Four thousand psychiatrists were asked to rate two patients on a 22-item list consisting of borderline/unstable and borderline schizophrenic phenomenology; 800 responded.

Eighteen percent of the patients considered borderline met criteria for borderline schizophrenia, 21% for unstable borderline; more than half met criteria for both. Nevertheless, the authors concluded, "We believe we have presented strong evidence that the borderline concept is not unitary, and is best conceptualized as consisting of at least two major dimensions that are relatively independent within a borderline group" (p. 23). They defended their conclusions (1979) by arguing that Axis II personality disorders were not meant to be mutually exclusive; overlap was common. They applied the term "Schizotypal Personality Disorder" to those previously called Borderline Schizophrenia and "BPD" (considered more acceptable than "Unstable") to the other group.

Thus DSM-III, published in 1980, radically narrowed the concept of the borderline by separating off the schizotype. Borderline became codified as BPD, characterized by five or more of the following:

- Impulsivity in at least two potentially self-damaging areas
- Unstable and intense interpersonal relationships, characterized by idealization, devaluation, and manipulation
- Inappropriately intense anger
- Identity disturbance as demonstrated by confusion regarding gender identity, goals, values, and vocational aims
- Affective instability, as revealed by marked shifts from euthymia to depression, irritability, or anxiety
- Intolerance of aloneness, combined with desperate efforts to avoid being alone
- Physically self-damaging acts, for example, suicide gestures or self-mutilations
- Chronic feelings of emptiness, loneliness, and boredom

Schizotypal Personality Disorder was characterized by at least four of the following:

- Magical thinking, superstitiousness
- Ideas of reference
- Social isolation
- Recurrent illusions, depersonalization, or derealization
- Odd speech without grossly loosened associations or incoherence
- Inadequate rapport in interpersonal relationships
- Suspiciousness or paranoid ideation
- Undue social anxiety and hypersensitivity to criticism

Both personality disorders remained substantially unchanged in DSM-III-R, although there were minor modifications in both content and order.

Let us pause for a moment and summarize the main trends up to 1980 and the publication of DSM-III.

1. The concept of the borderline patient was gradually sharpened and narrowed from the initial descriptions of a heterogeneous group of patients, not grossly neurotic or psychotic, who did poorly in standard psychoanalytic treatment to a clinical syndrome, a personality disorder, with clearly defined criteria.
2. The connection between the borderline and schizophrenia gradually faded. This reached its logical conclusion in DSM-III with the separation of Schizotypal Personality Disorder from BPD.
3. Although BPD achieved DSM-III legitimacy, Kernberg's BPO continued to be widely used, particularly by psychodynamic clinicians.

4. Defining a criteria-based BPD in place of the previous heterogeneous and vaguely defined borderline group led to enormous research interest in the disorder. BPD became the most intensely studied of the Axis II diagnoses.

THE BORDERLINE, POST-DSM-III

The further developments in the concept of the borderline patient over the past decade can be usefully discussed by focusing on six areas of continuing controversy. These are (1) Borderline Personality Disorder versus Borderline Personality Organization, (2) structural characteristics of the borderline patient, (3) psychopathogenesis of borderline pathology, (4) the relationship of the borderline to affective illness, (5) the relationship of the borderline to neurological impairments, and (6) the interrelationships of BPD and other Axis II Personality Disorders.

Borderline Personality Disorder versus Borderline Personality Organization

Borderline Personality Disorder is one of 11 personality disorders on Axis II of DSM-III-R, distinguished from the other personality disorders by specific characteristics, although overlap with other personality disorders is very common. The specific characteristics focus on pathology of the self and of relationships with others. The former include unstable identity or identity diffusion, impulsivity that is frequently self-destructive; labile and dysphoric affects, particularly anger; severe problems in being alone; and feelings of inner badness. Problems with others include unstable and intense relationships that oscillate between idealization and devaluation; frantic clinging to others to avoid being alone, frequently associated with "manipulative" suicidal gestures; and a tendency to poor performance in school or vocational function.

Borderline Personality Organization is characterized by identity diffusion resulting from marked splitting; a predominance of primitive defenses, such as splitting, projective identification, and denial; and generally intact reality testing. BPO encompasses most of the Axis II personality disorders, as well as a number of Axis I diagnoses, such as cyclothymia, most substance abuse, eating disorders, etc. Using a geographic metaphor, BPO locates the patient generally in the Midwest, while BPD more specifically places the patient in Chicago or Houston. BPO derives from psychoanalytic studies, while BPD, with its more observable behavioral characteristics, derives from traditional phenomenologic psychiatry. The former is construed as a pathology of internal object relationships and ego functions, while the latter is defined by clinical signs and symptoms.

I believe that the narrower BPD usage is preferable to the broader BPO because its greater specificity makes it more useful, for example, in treatment and outcome studies. The more broadly defined BPO remains useful because of its explication of the core dynamic and structural issues to be anticipated in the psychotherapy of these patients. However, as Gunderson (1984) argues, these patients might better be labeled "severe character disorders" or "lower level character pathology," thus decreasing terminologic confusion. "Borderline" as used in this book refers to the patient who meets criteria for BPD, as specified in DSM-III-R.

Psychostructural Characteristics of BPO

Abend, Porder, and Willick (1983) published the results of a New York Psychoanalytic Institute Kris Study Group on borderline patients. Their observations and conclusions are based on the detailed study of four patients treated in extended psychoanalyses. Although the patients fulfilled criteria for BPO, they do not meet DSM-III-R criteria for BPD, while their capacity to undergo psychoanalytic treatment suggests that they were at the healthier end of the borderline spectrum (however defined).

The authors found that

- Patients showed evidence of severe oedipal problems rather than pathology primarily in the preoedipal area.
- There were not the frequent shifts in all-bad and all-good self and object images characteristic of splitting.
- All patients had serious narcissistic pathology.
- Patients used many higher level or neurotic defenses, as well as the expected borderline or "primitive" defenses. Repression was a crucial aspect of defensive functioning, and the patients could not be distinguished from neurotic patients by patterns of defenses.
- "Primitive defenses," for example, splitting and projective identification, were not particularly useful in understanding the behaviors of these patients. The phenomena explained by splitting could as easily be accounted for by classical defense mechanisms, such as identification with the aggressor, reaction formation, isolation, and displacement. Behaviors reflecting projective identification could more usefully be viewed as instances of projection in patients with poor self-object differentiation.

Abend et al. concluded that borderline patients differed from neurotic patients quantitatively rather than qualitatively. Both neurotic and borderline patients use repression-related and splitting-related defenses; the difference is one of degree. In addition, they questioned the clinical usefulness of concepts such as splitting and projective identification.

The findings deserve attention because they derive from senior clinicians and are based on careful study of extensive analytic material, albeit only four patients. It is quite possible that, had they studied a larger sample of more representative borderline patients, including those at the more pathological end of the borderline spectrum, their findings might have been different.

Theories of Psychopathogenesis

Among current authors, there are three main theories of the psychopathogenesis of borderline psychopathology: (1) excessive aggression (Kernberg, 1984), (2) defective self-soothing internal objects (Adler, 1985), and (3) abandonment depression (Masterson, 1976). Each etiologic focus has its specific consequences for treatment.

Kernberg, using a conflict model, stresses excessive aggression of either constitutional or environmental origin as the core problem for the borderline patient. It is the excessive aggression that leads to defensive splitting, as the patient attempts to keep good internal objects uncontaminated by intense aggression. Thus, conflicts over aggression and rage produce what Kernberg views as the basic structural defect in borderline patients, the inability to integrate positive and negative self and object representations. This theoretical view leads directly to Kernberg's emphases on the mobilization of negative transferences and the identification of part-self and part-object images in the early phases of the treatment.

By contrast, Adler utilizes a deficit model that stresses defects in positive, self-soothing internal objects, the inability to evoke memories of good objects. This leads to the borderline patient's sensitivity to aloneness and to the frantic restitutive efforts to avoid abandonment. The treatment strategies resulting from this viewpoint follow Winnicott (1965) and Kohut (1971, 1977) in attempting to repair the hypothesized defect. Adler recommends a more supportive stance, and he does not stress interpretation in the early phases; rather he emphasizes the patient's need for a holding environment and a soothing self-object.

Masterson believes that borderline pathology results from mothers who are themselves borderline and who reward the child's continued attachment while withdrawing emotional support in response to the child's striving for autonomy. This leads to his focus on "abandonment depression." Like Adler, Masterson is quite supportive early in the treatment; he is fairly real, actively encouraging the patient's attempts at increasing autonomy.

The controversy between conflict and deficit models of psychopathology may well turn out to be a straw man. Conflict and deficit can be viewed as complementary rather than as contradictory (Wallerstein, 1981). In this view, the two models would interact with each other and vary in relative importance from patient to patient.

The Relationship of BPD to Affective Illness

As BPD became increasingly separate from schizophrenia, investigators became interested in its relationship to affective disorder. For example, Akiskal (1981) argued that a large percentage of borderline (BPD) patients, in fact, suffered from "subaffective disorders." Subaffective disorders differ from major affective disorders in that they are less severe and more chronic; dysthymia and cyclothymia are common examples.

Akiskal studied 100 patients diagnosed as borderline by Gunderson's DIB (1981) criteria; 16 also met criteria for Schizotypal Personality Disorder. Almost half of the patients had Axis I affective diagnoses, most falling within the atypical or subaffective group. More than half of the patients were also significant substance abusers.

Follow-up ranging from 6 months to 3 years revealed that 29 developed melancholic depressions, 11 had brief hypomanic episodes, 4 had manic psychoses, and 8 had mixed affective states. Family history data disclosed that 17 patients had first-degree relatives with bipolar disorder and another 17 had first-degree relatives treated for major depression.

Akiskal concluded that only about 20% of his BPD sample suffered from primary character pathology. The larger group consisted of chronic, atypical, and complex variants of affective illness, the personality disorder occurring in reaction to the affective illness. For example, Akiskal states that an unstable identity can result from cyclothymic mood swings. However, he is not persuasive in his argument that the personality disorder is secondary to the affective disorder, rather than vice versa. The marked substance abuse is not sufficiently taken into account. Most important, his subjects are BPD patients with a heavy Axis I overlay from the start. Given that fact, the follow-up and family history data are not surprising, and certainly cannot be generalized to all BPD patients, many of whom do not present with a prominent Axis I affective overlay.

Recent evidence suggests that major affective disorder is no more common in BPD than in other Axis II personality disorders. Barasch et al. (1985) write, "We found that forty percent of our borderline patients had had an episode of major depression during the three-year follow-up period. . . . However forty percent of our patients with other personality disorders also experienced episodes of major depression. This new finding suggests that either BPD has no special relation to affective disorders or, perhaps, all patients with personality disorders are predisposed to affective disorders" (p. 1486).

Gunderson and Elliot (1985) review current hypotheses about the relationships between BPD and Affective Disorder. They summarize studies of demography, phenomenology, course of illness, family prevalence, psychodynamics, biological issues, and response to psychopharmacology and utilize the data to evaluate a number of possibilities. They reject the possibility that Affective Disorder is primary and leads to BPD, as not consistent with the available data. The opposite sequence, BPD as primary and leading to Affective Disorder, is also dismissed for similar reasons. A third possibility is that because Affective Disorder and BPD are both common conditions, they frequently overlap simply by chance. There is some evidence to support this view, but it is not impressive.

The authors propose a fourth hypothesis that they believe best fits the available data. This views both Affective Disorder and BPD as consisting of heterogeneous subgroups, diagnosed by signs and symptoms arising from diverse sources. Thus the frequent concurrence of the two disorders results from the heterogeneity of the phenomena that define them. Both develop from a combination of constitutional and environmental factors, which later combine to produce either major depression, dysthymia, or BPD, alone or in various combinations.

The Relationship of BPD and Subtle Neurological Impairments

Andrulonis et al. (1981) studied 91 hospitalized patients who met DSM-III criteria for BPD. Eleven percent had a past history of brain trauma, encephalitis, or epilepsy; this subgroup was primarily female. Twenty-seven percent had a history of minimal brain dysfunction or learning disability, and these were primarily males. Andrulonis concluded that there is a significant overlap between BPD and episodic dyscontrol/minimal brain dysfunction syndromes.

Clinically, borderline patients with organic syndromes differed from those without such syndromes. They were more commonly males and had an early onset of difficulties such as academic problems or acting out. The nonorganically stigmatized borderlines tended to be female and had a later onset of problems, commonly during early high school years. Females were more likely to become seriously depressed, to have an affectively laden family history, and to experience more frequent episodes of brief psychosis.

Thus, it appears likely that some patients develop BPD out of a substrate of Minimal Brain Dysfunction or Attention Deficit Disorder. These impairments are probably most reasonably viewed as predisposing factors that lead to BPD, given the addition of a sufficiently traumatic environment or other relevant etiologic factors.

BPD and Other Personality Disorders

The border between BPD and the other personality disorders is becoming a subject of increasing interest and study. BPD patients frequently overlap with other personality disorders, and the typical BPD patient also meets criteria for one or more of the other Axis II diagnoses. The very significant overlap with Schizotypal Personality Disorder has already been noted. In addition, patients with BPD frequently overlap with Antisocial, Histrionic, and Narcissistic Personality Disorders.

One issue raised by these overlaps is that of categorical versus dimensional diagnoses on Axis II. The reader is referred elsewhere for a more complete discussion of this controversy (Frances, 1982). The current categorical personality disorders can be diagnosed with some modest reliability. The relationships between BPD and its neighboring personality disorders will undoubtedly be subjected to further study.

FINAL THOUGHTS

It is becoming increasingly clear that BPD encompasses patients who are different from each other in many ways. Patients can achieve five of eight BPD criteria in many different combinations and permutations, ensuring heterogeneity. For example, Hurt and Clarkin (1990) delineate three subclusters of BPD patients: (1) the identity cluster, (2) the affective cluster, and (3) the impulsive cluster. Clearly, further research is needed in this area, because these or other subgroupings will probably suggest different treatment approaches.

It is also becoming clear that patients can develop BPD via different etiologic pathways. Subtle neurological impairment, complex affective variants, and chaotic, depriving, abusive, or brutalizing environments all appear to have etiologic significance, either singly or in combination.

The rapid growth of new knowledge about BPD during the past decade is impressive. Undoubtedly, future studies will lead to new understandings of the pathology, etiology, and especially more specific and more effective treatments for these very difficult patients.

CHAPTER 2

Historical Trends in the Treatment of the Borderline: The Swinging Pendulum Between Supportive and Exploratory Therapies

DEVRA BRAUN

The historical changes in the concept of the borderline patient described in the previous chapter were paralleled by significant alterations in the conceptualizations of effective psychotherapy for these patients. The borderline patient was, from the outset, associated with severe treatment difficulties. Adolf Stern (1938) noted "This borderline group of patients is extremely difficult to handle effectively by any psychotherapeutic method" (p. 467). As Stern and other psychoanalysts began to document the clinical features characteristic of borderline patients, they simultaneously attempted to understand and explain the failure of classical psychoanalytic treatment methods, and to formulate alternative psychotherapeutic approaches.

This chapter describes the changing trends in the psychotherapy of borderline patients, again focusing on key contributors. A period during which primarily supportive treatments were advocated by Stern (1938), Knight (1953b), Zetzel (1971), and others was followed by a swing toward exploratory treatment, advocated by Kernberg (1972) and others, strongly influenced by the results of the Menninger Psychotherapy Research Project (Kernberg et al., 1972). More recently, a number of writers, including Masterson (1981a), Chessick (1982), Gunderson (1984), and Adler (1985), have described treatments with substantial supportive components, particularly in the early stages of treatment, even where the authors classify the psychotherapy as primarily expressive or exploratory.

SUPPORTIVE PSYCHOTHERAPY
Adolph Stern

Adolph Stern (1938) described a number of characteristics of borderline patients that made the establishment of a therapeutic alliance particularly difficult, including feelings of inferiority, masochism, the use of projective defenses, difficulties in reality testing, and inordinate hypersensitivity. The patient's feelings of inferiority and masochistic tendencies discouraged him from active adaptive or problem-solving behaviors, while his tendency to use projective defenses allowed him to easily attribute his problems to external causes at the expense of introspection and insight. The inordinate hypersensitivity and narcissistic vulnerability of these patients caused "inevitable" (p. 473) negative therapeutic reactions.

In "Psychoanalytic Therapy in the Borderline Neuroses" (1945), Stern described the ways in which he modified classical analytic technique for more effective treatment of the borderline patient. "In the borderline group . . . the positive transference is limited by the poor capacity for object love. Therapy in which the analyst employs the so-called passive role makes inadequate provision for the handling of such a weak transference and the patients' concomitant dependent needs" (p. 193). He concluded that, at least in the initial phases of treatment, the therapist must take an active role in bringing about "a reality-determined relationship—essentially different from the original childhood relation to the parents—from which these patients might obtain more assurance and courage to face their painful affects. To achieve these ends the analyst could not remain uninvolved in the patients' lives . . ." (p. 194).

Thus, Stern recommended a relatively reality-determined relationship between patient and therapist as a corrective for pathological early childhood experiences. He felt that patients would benefit from contrasting the real patient–doctor relationship with previous unrealistic transference-determined reactions. With these and other factors in mind, he had his patients sit up and face the therapist. This "is the accustomed position in ordinary friendly relations" (p. 194). He spoke of allowing the patient "to familiarize himself realistically with the person and personality of the physician" (p. 195) and of encouraging an atmosphere that "will prevent the patient's feeling that he lacks the analyst's respect, sincere interest, protection and support" (p. 195).

Stern's attempts to promote a more real relationship between analyst and patient inevitably downplayed the role of transference analysis. "I have learned to pay more heed to what a patient thinks, feels and says about me and to ascribe less to transference and resistance than in former years" (p. 196). "Support, assurance, understanding, respect, consideration and unflagging interest are all necessary. The assurance of being wanted, of belonging, helps materially to develop self-assurance and a strong ego structure" (p. 197). The ultimate objective, however, of Stern's supportive approach was to facilitate the patient's development so that he could become an appropriate candidate for a later classical psychoanalytic treatment.

Robert Knight

In his article "Borderline States" (1953b), Robert Knight, like Stern, described borderline patients as generally unsuitable for classical psychoanalytic treatment. Out of the very disjunction between the patients' initial relatively integrated presentations and their subsequent decompensations in the analysis, psychotherapists could take their cue as to treatment stance. He spoke of the "much better front these patients are able to present and maintain in face to face psychiatric interviews, where the structured situation and the visible, personal, active therapist per se provide an integrating force to stimulate the patient's surviving adaptive, integrative, and reality-testing capacities. Our therapeutic objective, . . ." he stated, "would be the strengthening of the patient's ego controls over instinctual impulses and educating him in the employment of new controls and new adaptive methods. . . . Our formulations will be in terms of his ego operations rather than of his id content, and will be calculated to improve and strengthen the ego operations" (pp. 10–11).

Knight described a stance of substantial deviation from technical neutrality (1953b) in which defenses and symptoms were selectively attacked or bolstered. For example, "The psychoneurotic defenses and symptoms especially are not attacked, for just these ego operations protect the patient from further psychotic disorganization" (p. 11). Therapy should be specifically "planned and conducted for the purpose of conserving, strengthening, and improving the defensive and adaptive functions of the ego" (p. 12). Elsewhere, Knight (1953a) added that the "borderline schizophrenic patient . . . needs *proofs* of emotional support . . . and of genuine human interest rather than merely detached professional interest" (p. 150).

Elizabeth Zetzel

The identification by Stern and Knight of this difficult group of patients who were resistant to or regressed excessively during psychoanalytic treatment led to an increase in literature on the supportive treatment of borderline patients. Grinker (1968) and others advocated a nonintensive psychotherapy that supported adaptive defenses.

Zetzel formulated her supportive approach to the treatment of borderline patients in 1971. She prescribed "regular but limited contact (very seldom more than once a week). . . . The treatment of these patients involves considerable activity and definite structure on the part of the therapist. It is mainly directed toward helping the patient achieve further progress and maturation through the utilization of a realistic doctor-patient relationship" (p. 870). Zetzel believed that the borderline patient's difficulties in maintaining a clear distinction between transference and reality was a barrier to his ability to benefit from either psychoanalysis or exploratory psychotherapy. In particular, she cautioned against transference interpretation directed toward insight; in fact, she argued for structuring a limit-setting, reality-based weekly treatment so as to discourage the blossoming of transference reactions.

Zetzel stressed, however, that supportive therapy should not be confused with the therapist's presentation of himself as an omnipotent figure with inexhaustible resources. The therapist should make clear to the patient the kind of supportive treatment that he can consistently offer, and then clarify and confront the regressive distortions that threatened to impair the realistic doctor–patient relationship.

EXPLORATORY PSYCHOTHERAPY

Toward the end of this period of interest in supportive therapy, data from the Menninger Psychotherapy Research Project became available (Kernberg et al., 1972). The Menninger Project was the most ambitious attempt of its era, or ever, to document differential outcomes for patients treated either with supportive psychotherapy, expressive psychotherapy, or psychoanalysis. It examined the treatment and post-treatment experiences of 42 patients with a variety of nonpsychotic diagnoses, assigned by their therapists to treatments based on clinical indications, that is, without any attempt at randomization.

In summarizing the findings of the Menninger study, Kernberg et al. stated that patients with low ego strength (Borderline Personality Organization [BPO]) improved little with psychoanalysis and less with supportive therapy. Thus, they cautioned against both psychoanalysis and supportive psychotherapy as effective treatments for these patients. Psycho-analysis tended to fail for several reasons: (1) Borderline patients could not tolerate the regression of an analytic treatment, (2) they were prone to develop transference psychoses, and (3) transference acting out gratified primitive needs, preventing analytic progress.

As for supportive therapy, negative transferences and widespread primitive defenses interfered with an effective therapeutic alliance and resulted in externalization of the negative transference. Such patients treated supportively would likely act out those transferences outside of the treatment situation while presenting sterile and emotionally shallow material in the sessions.

Kernberg (1984) concluded that "expressive psychotherapy is the treatment of choice for most patients with borderline personality organization" (p. 167). "Supportive psychotherapy," he stated, "is rarely if ever the treatment modality of choice" and is indicated only for those patients for whom both expressive (exploratory) psychotherapy and psychoanalysis are contraindicated (p. 168).

Otto Kernberg

The exploratory or insight-oriented "expressive" psychotherapy that Kernberg recommended for most patients with BPO is one that he described and developed over a period spanning more than two decades, culminating in its elucidation in manual form in 1989 (Kernberg et al.). The authors of the 1989 work described as its overall goals, "To enhance the borderline patient's ability to experience self and others as coherent, integrated, realistically perceived individuals, and to reduce the need to use defenses that weaken ego structure. . . ."(p. 8).

According to Kernberg, borderline patients are unable to integrate libidinal and aggressive aspects of internal representations of self and others. They cannot tolerate the ambivalence and conflict inherent in the knowledge that the idealized internalized maternal image is the same as the threatening, frustrating maternal image toward whom they experience rage. They rely on splitting and other primitive, ego-weakening defenses to keep separate contradictory experiences of self and others, motivated by anxiety that rage will totally overwhelm the good internal images of self and others.

Kernberg recommends the use of clarifications and confrontations to begin the education and integration of self and nonself images that the patient experiences separately. This is followed by interpretations directed toward (1) the here-and-now transference, (2) external reality, (3) the past, and (4) the patient's defenses in order to further the interpretive process; genetic interpretations are reserved for the later stages of treatment.

After a careful and complete initial evaluation, Kernberg recommends outlining realistic treatment goals and establishing a treatment contract. It is the potential of these patients for serious acting out that threatens the viability of the treatment and requires the treatment contract. In order to set the terms of the treatment contract, the therapist shows the patient how the treatment is threatened by specific acting out and introduces rules and structures to safeguard the treatment. The therapist does not deal interpretively with the patient's refusal to agree to terms of the contract; rather the contract is considered the minimum necessary condition to allow the psychotherapy to commence.

The fact that negative transferences are confronted and interpreted early in Kernberg's treatment model makes rapid recognition of, and response to, transference acting out of an especially crucial task. For example, if the patient has a history of late payment of therapy bills, it is explained how this behavior threatens the treatment and requires the introduction of a treatment-protecting structure (for example, the requirement that bills be paid in advance). The therapist structures the therapy through the initial contract setting, limit setting, and the use of environmental interventions such as hospitalization in order to limit transference acting out and other threats to the treatment.

The treatment contract contains the minimal structure necessary to protect the treatment; contract guidelines are held to firmly avoiding debates with the patient about what does or does not constitute a threat to the treatment. When the patient violates the contract, the therapist confronts and interprets the behavior and sets consistent limits, starting with less stringent levels of restriction and moving to higher levels when necessary. These limits include the threat of discontinuing the treatment altogether if the patient persistently does not fulfill his end of the treatment contract.

Technical neutrality—the therapist's position of equidistance from the patient's id, ego, superego, and external reality—is maintained as consistently as possible. (The standard definition of technical neutrality—equidistance of the therapist from id, ego, superego, and external reality—is actually slightly misstated regarding the ego. The therapist is "equidistant" from the defensive functions of the ego but not from its observing functions, with which he is hopefully in alliance.) When acting out forces the therapist's deviation from technical neutrality, the necessity for the deviation is discussed and neutrality is reinstated as soon as possible.

Kernberg's expressive psychotherapy, as described, is at the exploratory end of the supportive/exploratory continuum for borderline patients. However, as Adler (1989) has noted, "Opportunities to see videotapes of Kernberg's actual treatment of patients and to hear his discussions of them reveal that there are many elements of his everyday work in his expressive psychotherapy that would be considered to be "supportive" by others who write about the treatment of patients with borderline personality disorder" (p. 52). Kernberg's evident "basic caring and concern for his patients" (p. 52), as well as the sheer volume of words with which he anchors his patients in reality, are elements of Kernberg's personal style that appear to provide a supportive aspect to his treatment. Kernberg argues against combining supportive and exploratory techniques; in practice, as Adler points out, the boundary may not be so clear cut.

CLASSICAL PSYCHOANALYSIS
Bryce Boyer and Peter Giovacchini

Together with the increased interest in exploratory psychotherapy in the 1970s, there was a resurgence of interest in classical analysis for treating borderline patients. Volkan (1987), Boyer and Giovacchini (1967), and others adapted psychoanalytic technique and treated borderline patients with psychoanalysis, often five sessions weekly.

Boyer (1980) described a reversal of psychoanalysts' attitudes pertaining to the treatment of borderline patients. He argued that early attitudes that psychoanalysis was contraindicated for borderlines were yielding to a growing belief that psychoanalysis, with a few modifications, is the treatment of choice. It should be noted, however, that Boyer's borderlines were high-functioning outpatients; almost all were professionals, for example, educators and physicians, and in all probability would not meet DSM-III-R criteria for BPD.

In sharp contrast to the approach of Kernberg, Boyer set minimal limits on regressive acting out in the transference. In the initial phases of treatment, in particular, he describes situations in which the therapist behaved in a manner that furnished direct gratification of the primitive instinctual wishes of the patient. In one treatment he allowed a patient to come to sessions intoxicated, to physically threaten him, and to expose herself. "When I remained passive and silent, she sat at my feet, hugged my legs and eventually touched my penis" (p. 185). Only then did the therapist remove her hand and advise her to express herself in words instead of actions.

In common with Kernberg, Boyer placed emphasis on the analysis of transference and countertransference, restricted analysis of early negative transferences primarily to the here and now, avoided early genetic

interpretations, and vigorously interpreted evidence of primitive defenses in the transference. He writes of setting limits to protect the
neutrality of the therapist, although, as noted above, he set much less
stringent limits than do most therapists.

Boyer explicitly focused on the therapy as a corrective experience,
reminiscent of earlier theorists such as Alexander (1946) and Stern. The
success of the treatment depended in part on "the rectifying emotional
and cognitive experience of the patient's development of new object
relations with the therapist" (p. 175). However, he excluded the use of
supportive and nonanalytic procedures as a means to these ends.

Giovacchini (1980), writing together with and separately from Boyer,
also advocated an essentially classical analytic approach to borderline
patients. He felt that they "cannot tolerate a nonanalytic approach" (p.
359) and believed that borderline patients in supportive treatment might
show symptomatic improvement, stabilization, and social rehabilitation,
but rarely character change. He wrote that borderlines often decompen-
sated, and even suicided, when the supportive therapist, in his desire to
rescue the patient, allowed the patient to maintain a delusional belief in
the therapist's omnipotence. This led eventually to a repetition of the
bitter disappointments of childhood, with expectable results.

Abend, Porder, and Willick

Abend, Porder, and Willick (1983) reported on the psychoanalyses of
four borderline (BPO) patients. They concluded that borderline patients
differed from neurotic patients quantitatively not qualitatively. They
viewed borderlines as a heterogeneous group and wrote that their pathology originated from problems at various stages of psychic development.
Hence, they rejected what they described as the "prepatterned" or
"preplanned" treatment approaches of Masterson (1976), Rinsley (1982),
and Kernberg. They differed from Kernberg by arguing that early
genetic interpretations are useful with borderlines, while confronting
patients' contradictory attitudes or aggression may not be particularly
useful.

Unlike Masterson and Rinsley, they argued that borderline pathology
does not result from a particular type of parenting or from an arrest at a
particular stage of development. Thus, they rejected his specific suggestions for correcting such arrests.

Abend, Porder, and Willick concluded that at least some borderline
patients can be successfully psychoanalyzed without significant deviation
from the classical approach. However, it is important to recognize that
though their patients had BPO they appear to have been healthier than
the usual BPD patient.

COMBINED EXPLORATORY
AND SUPPORTIVE TREATMENTS
James Masterson's Reconstructive Psychotherapy

While Boyer and Giovacchini, and Abend, Porder, and Willick were advocating a return to classical psychoanalytic treatments for at least some borderline patients, other writers were developing treatment methods that combined exploratory and supportive features. Masterson (1976) shared Kernberg's view that exploratory rather than supportive psychotherapy should be utilized whenever feasible for treating the borderline patient. He believed that his "reconstructive therapy," in contrast to supportive therapy "offers the greatest and most enduring change" (p. 94). Yet his reconstructive therapy contained significant supportive elements, especially in the initial phases of treatment.

Masterson's Object Relations Theory focused on developmental arrest as the source of borderline psychopathology. He hypothesized that the mother of the potential borderline rewards the child for regressive, clinging behavior but withdraws when the child attempts to separate and develop increased autonomy. As a result, the child suffers a developmental arrest at the separation–individuation stage of development and experiences "abandonment depression" when he attempts further distance and autonomy from the mother. Masterson also stated that "the mother of the borderline patient usually suffers from a borderline syndrome herself" (p. 37).

Subsequently, Masterson (1978) postulated that "two interactions with the mother—that is, reward for regression, withdrawal for separation-individuation—are introjected by the child, along with their associated part-object and part-self representations, to form the essential intrapsychic structure of the borderline—the split object relations unit" (p. 128). Similar to Fairbairn's split internalized bad objects, Masterson called them the RORU (Rewarding Object Relations Part Unit) and the WORU (Withdrawing Object Relations Part Unit). These part-object and part-self representations are kept separated from each other by the defense of splitting.

Although Masterson felt that exploratory or "reconstructive" psychotherapy is the treatment of choice for the borderline patient, he also saw an important role for supportive therapy, particularly in the early stages of treatment. He believed that supportive therapy could effect lasting change (1978), although he used the term "supportive" in quotation marks in order to "emphasize that it is actually more than supportive," sometimes "bringing about dramatic changes in the life of the patient" (p. 92).

He recommended that "Most borderline patients begin treatment on a supportive basis—that is, one or two times a week" (p. 92) and envisioned both reconstructive and supportive therapies as having an initial "Testing

Phase" (p. 99), which extended from the onset of treatment to the overcoming of the initial resistance and the establishment of a therapeutic alliance. During this stage the patient's destructive and self-destructive acting-out behaviors need to be confronted.

During the "Working Through Phase" (p. 102), the patient and therapist have a collaborative therapeutic alliance. The patient experiences a transferential relationship to the therapist in which he relives the "abandonment depression" associated with earlier maternal withdrawal and may project merger wishes onto the therapist. Masterson emphasized the role of real external disturbances in the early parent-child relationship as the basis for the transference, in contrast to Kernberg's focus on distortion and fantasy, that is, internal contributions from the child. In the "Working Through Phase," as in the Testing Phase, all distortions and acting out of the transference are rigorously confronted and interpreted.

The therapist is advised to use Mahlerian "communicative matching" techniques in the therapy. In healthy parenting, the mother communicatively matches the needs of the small child by responding to the child's cues in such a way as to provide approval for further individuation. In a similar fashion, Masterson responded encouragingly to the patient's expression of his newly emerging self; this stage of the therapy was viewed by Masterson as a reliving of, as a corrective experience for, the patient's thwarted childhood attempts at separation and autonomy.

During the "Separation Phase" (p. 104), the last of Masterson's four phases of treatment, the old anxieties over separation as abandonment are reexperienced by the patient in the context of the termination of the therapeutic relationship. Masterson advised that, ideally, the patient should initiate the termination process himself and that it should be a gradual process.

Gerald Adler

Adler (1985, 1989), and Buie and Adler (1982), also stressed supportive interventions early in the treatment, with more exploratory approaches predominating as the treatment progressed. Adler viewed "deficit" rather than "conflict" as central to borderline psychopathology, a view consistent with Kohut's formulations of narcissistic pathology. Deficits of holding/soothing introjects make borderline patients unable to rely on their own inner resources to tolerate separations. He believed that patients longed for the holding and soothing qualities of the therapist and other important objects, but were unable to maintain evocative memories of these positive figures when physically separated from them.

Adler theorized that the core difficulty of borderline patients occurred prior to the splitting that Kernberg postulated. (Kernberg believes that the borderline has both good and bad images of the self and others, but that splitting defenses were necessary to keep them apart, thus avoiding intrapsychic conflict and the contamination of positive images by unacceptable rage.) By contrast, Adler believed that there was an actual deficit of good images, resulting from childhood deprivations. The borderline patient never internalized a stable image of a holding and soothing mother, and therefore is unable to soothe herself; this deficit led to the frantic attempts to avoid abandonment.

The aim of Adler's first phase of treatment was to maintain a dyadic relationship in which the therapist could be used as a stable holding and soothing self-object. For this initial phase, Buie and Adler (1982) and Adler (1985) prescribed a supportive therapeutic framework. They stated, "The amount of support may considerably exceed that involved in most psychotherapies. To some extent the therapist in reality acts as a holding self-object" (p. 67). The therapeutic task was to provide the patient with an interpersonal experience that could be gradually internalized, allowing the development of a dependable evocative memory for the soothing and sustaining relationship with the therapist. Adler recommended such early treatment supports as extra phone calls, extra appointments, or postcards during the therapist's vacation, any or all of which might be needed to keep the patient's anxieties about aloneness within tolerable bounds.

When the patient succeeded in developing dependable holding introjects after months or years of the first phase of treatment, she was no longer viewed by Adler as borderline (1989). She had progressed from dealing with the borderline issues of aloneness and annihilation to the narcissistic issues of worthlessness and incompleteness. Adler drew on Kohut's work with narcissistic personality disorders for ways of dealing empathically with this second phase of treatment. In the final phase of treatment, structures are consolidated, and therapist and patient validate the patient's gains to help permanently incorporate them in her identity.

There are elements of this process, particularly the role the therapist plays as a real, holding, and soothing "self-object" object in the initial phases of therapy, which are similar to the corrective emotional experience described by Alexander (1946) and used by Masterson (1976), Chessick (1977), and others. However, Adler also stressed the exploratory aspects of the treatment, including a detailed focus on transference and countertransference issues.

DISCUSSION

In 1980, standardization of the characteristics of the BPD in DSM-III made possible comparisons of treatment methods and outcomes with well-defined patient groups. Studies in the early 1980s provided further impressive evidence that induction into treatment, and the treatment itself, involved serious difficulties for patients with BPD.

In a study of outpatient borderlines, Skodol et al. (1983) reported that two thirds of the patients dropped out of treatment in less than 3 months. Similarly, Gunderson et al. (1989), in a prospective study of 60 borderline inpatients, found that 60% of the patients discontinued their assigned psychotherapy within the first 6 months for a variety of reasons; 43% of the total group were treatment dropouts, and over half of these left angrily after early confrontations.

Waldinger and Gunderson (1987) asked 30 experienced therapists to assess the outcomes of their treatments with borderline patients. The therapists reported that only 54% of almost 800 patients continued in treatment past 6 months. One third of the patients "completed" treatment, and of those only 10% were considered by the therapists to have been successfully treated.

Many questions remain regarding the effects of supportive versus exploratory psychotherapy on dropout rates and on overall treatment outcomes for borderline patients. The large number of interrelated variables has made it extremely difficult to design studies that accurately assess the influence of the type of psychotherapy on treatment outcome. Many of the outcome studies, including the Menninger study, have serious methodological flaws.

For example, Gunderson (1984) questioned whether the conclusions drawn from the Menninger study about the poor outcome of borderline patients treated supportively are warranted by the study data. He cited the following flaws in the study design: (1) no untreated comparison group, (2) patients not randomly assigned to treatments, (3) no blind assessments, (4) questionable diagnoses, (5) no quality control over therapy, and (6) probable confounding effects by other treatments. Gunderson argued that these methodological problems make it impossible to draw any convincing conclusions regarding the relative efficacies of the various treatments studied for borderline patients.

More recently, Wallerstein (1986) summarized the difficulties in meaningfully distinguishing the results of supportive therapies from those of the exploratory treatments that were delivered to the patients in the Menninger study. He noted that in every treatment in the study, from supportive therapy to psychoanalysis, "the treatment carried more supportive elements than originally intended, and these supportive elements accounted for more of the changes achieved than had been originally anticipated" (p. 730). "Supportive psychotherapeutic approaches, mechanisms and techniques . . . often reached the kinds and degrees of change expected to depend on more expressive and insightful conflict resolutions, and they often did so in ways that represented indistinguishably structural changes. . . . The changes predicted for the 20 patients in psychotherapy, though more often predicated to be based on the more expressive mechanisms and techniques, in fact were more often actually achieved on the basis of the more supportive mechanisms and techniques" (pp. 725-6). These findings are striking but require confirmation from further studies.

Michael Stone's (1987) long-term follow-up of more than 500 patients (approximately 300 of whom were borderline) treated at the New York State Psychiatric Institute (PI) revealed that "supportive interventions were important for all the patients and were sufficient, in many instances, to bring about significant improvement" (p. 231). Stone concluded that the experience with the PI 500 suggests that expressive therapy is effective with no more than one third of carefully selected inpatients and that many of these would do equally well with supportive forms of therapy (1990).

The absolutism of the early years—with some authors believing that psychoanalysis was absolutely contraindicated for all borderline patients and others arguing that pure expressive therapy was the obvious treatment of choice unless specifically contraindicated—has generally yielded to a more eclectic approach. As Adler stated (1989), "Apart from Kernberg's (1982) relatively clear distinctions between supportive and expressive psychotherapy, most of the literature defines a mixture of supportive and expressive/exploratory techniques" (p. 62).

Waldinger and Gunderson (1987) also noted that "a large number of borderline patients are treated with a mixture of interpretive and supportive therapeutic techniques" (p. 21). They felt that this was consistent with the widely acknowledged notion that "borderline" refers to a broad range of patients with pathologies of varying degrees of severity. They further suggested that the etiological models of conflict (Kernberg) versus deficit (Adler and Buie, Giovacchini) are not mutually exclusive but rather are "applicable to different degrees with different patients, or even to the same patients at different points in time" (p. 21). This view is interesting in light of the differentiations made by many authors of stages of treatment, each stage involving a different admixture of supportive and exploratory elements.

Waldinger and Gunderson (1987) highlighted fundamental commonalities among different clinicians in their approaches to treating the borderline patient. These included:

1. The importance of a stable frame or structure for the treatment.
2. Increased activity of the therapist.
3. Tolerance of negative transferences.

4. Establishing a connection between the patient's actions and feelings in the present.
5. Making self-destructive behaviors ungratifying.
6. Blocking acting-out behaviors.
7. Focusing clarifications and interpretations on the here and now.
8. Paying careful attention to countertransference feelings.

These basic features characterize both supportive and exploratory (expressive) therapies, and are viewed as crucial by authors whose views about etiology and effective treatment vary widely. There may be other intangible features that successful treatments have in common, for example, specific qualities in the therapists' personalities or a good patient–therapist "fit." One further point to be emphasized in this historical review is that the operative issue is not simply supportive versus exploratory therapy. Many treatments usually thought of as exploratory incorporate a number of supportive elements, both in initial and in later phases of the treatment, while supportive therapy without any gain in insight is inconceivable.

The argument that exploratory therapy is the treatment of choice for borderline patients is, historically, a relatively recent one. It was preceded by a long period in which it was believed that only supportive treatment was indicated for these patients. Some authors, for example, Waldinger and Gunderson (1987) and Stone (1990), have argued against clear superiority of one treatment model over another; instead they have looked at a variety of treatment methods that are effective and have attempted to understand why they work in particular instances with particular patients.

Other authors (e.g., Hurt & Clarkin, 1990) have suggested that borderline patients are usefully subclassified according to clusters of symptoms or behaviors. It is possible that borderlines of certain subtypes are best treated by purely exploratory psychotherapy or even psychoanalysis, while others should be treated supportively. However, the early impressions, for example, from the Menninger study, that supportive therapy resulted in inferior outcomes for borderline patients needs to be questioned. Gunderson et al. (1989) and Stone (1987) have provided evidence that a large proportion of patients are not appropriately treated with expressive therapy. Wallerstein (1986) and Stone (1987, 1990) have documented that significant and lasting clinical improvements can result from supportive treatments. It appears that many, perhaps most, borderline patients are best treated with a primarily supportive psychotherapy or a mixed supportive/exploratory model.

CHAPTER 3

Psychodynamically Oriented Supportive Therapy

The psychodynamic psychotherapies are usefully divided into two major classes: (1) exploratory (expressive, insight-oriented, or uncovering) psychotherapies and (2) supportive (suppressive) psychotherapies. Psychodynamically oriented supportive therapy, or POST, is in the latter group and is rooted in conflict theory and ego psychology. Its goals are the strengthening of ego functions and consequent improved adaptations, rather than the insight and structural change that are the aims of the exploratory therapies.

POST is as fundamentally "psychodynamically oriented" as is exploratory psychotherapy. This point deserves emphasis because frequently the terms "psychodynamic" or "psychoanalytically oriented" are applied only to exploratory therapy. Exploratory psychotherapy is more similar to psychoanalysis in methodology, but it is also true that a sophisticated dynamic supportive therapy must be as grounded in a detailed understanding of the patient's conflicts, ego and superego functions, interpersonal relations, etc., as is exploratory treatment. In fact, it is only after a careful evaluation of the patient's entire mental life that an informed decision can be made about the appropriateness of a primarily exploratory or a primarily supportive treatment for that patient.

Psychodynamic supportive and exploratory therapies in pure culture are models, useful primarily in formulating methodologies at the polar extremes of the supportive/exploratory continuum (Rockland, 1989). Actual psychotherapies are variable mixtures of supportive and exploratory interventions. The twin tasks of (1) determining the appropriate supportive/exploratory mix for the individual patient at a specific time and (2) deciding which conflictual areas are to be explored and which handled supportively, are the ultimate tests of the skill and sophistication of the dynamic psychotherapist.

It is always the ego in its various functions that is supported in POST. Supporting the ego can be accomplished directly—by focusing on specific problematic ego functions, or indirectly—by decreasing the stresses and pressures placed on the ego by the other three psychic agencies. Strengthening the functions of the ego, in turn, is in the service of improved adaptations to both inner and outer worlds, and *adaptation* is always a key construct in POST.

The significance of POST is grounded in three basic assumptions: (1) Psychoanalytic theory has no serious competitor as a system for understanding human psychology, particularly the two-person interaction called psychotherapy, and (2) neither psychoanalysis nor exploratory psychotherapy is the appropriate treatment for most of the patients who consult the dynamic psychotherapist, in public clinics or in private offices. (3) Therefore the application of psychoanalytic knowledge to increase the effectiveness of the supportive therapy that most patients require is of great value, and is a most worthwhile example of applied psychoanalysis.

CONTRASTING EXPLORATORY AND SUPPORTIVE PSYCHOTHERAPIES

In order to clarify the differences between exploratory and supportive psychotherapies, I will compare them across a number of parameters. The reader is again reminded that these are models, the polar extremes of a continuum of dynamic psychotherapies, and that all actual psychotherapies are clinically appropriate mixtures of supportive and exploratory interventions.

Goals

Although the ultimate goals of all dynamic psychotherapies are improved ego function and adaptation, the more proximal or more direct goals of exploratory psychotherapy are insight into unconscious psychic conflict and the subsequent structural change that is obtained by working through. The proximal, direct goals of POST are a return to homeostasis for the patient in crisis and the strengthening of ego functions with subsequent improved adaptations for the chronically impaired patient. In other words, the proximal goals of POST are identical to the ultimate goals of all dynamic psychotherapies, while the proximal goals of exploratory treatment are different.

Therapist Stance

In an exploratory treatment, the therapist attempts to maximize transference development by very limited gratification of transference wishes and by anonymity, the relative "blank screen." This is in contrast to the more "real" stance of the supportive therapist, who tends to be more verbally active and less frustrating. He is generally more self-revealing and may supply some of his own reality and values, *but only to the extent required by the patient's ego defects.*

The danger of countertransference acting out by the supportive therapist is a serious one. He must be more aware and more concerned about it than the exploratory therapist, who is safeguarded by the more definitive guidelines for conducting the treatment. The skillful supportive therapist furnishes advice, personal values, help with problem solving, etc., only as they are required by the particular patient's psychopathology. Tendencies to overcontrol, to rescue, to overgratify, or to "sell" a particular lifestyle are to be consistently guarded against.

The Handling of Transferences

As opposed to exploratory treatment, where all transferences are appropriate for exploration and interpretation, the therapist using POST does not usually address positive transferences; rather he uses them to maximize his influence with the patient. However, when they become extreme, for example, excessively idealized or erotized, they are serious resistances to the treatment and are responded to as are negative transferences.

Negative transferences are addressed rapidly and are not encouraged to develop fully, to "bloom." After allowing their full expression, the therapist confronts the discrepancies between the transference and the realities of the doctor–patient relationship. At times, they are usefully directed out of the office and out of the transference by pointing out parallels in the patient's relationships with other key figures in her life.

The Handling of Resistances

All resistances are systematically dealt with and interpreted in exploratory psychotherapy. In supportive therapy, however, resistances are evaluated according to their adaptive/maladaptive values. When primarily adaptive, they are supported and encouraged; when maladaptive, they are clarified, confronted, undermined, and/or discouraged.

Techniques

In exploratory psychotherapy, all classes of interventions (Bibring, 1954) are appropriate so long as they are under the primacy of, and leading to, interpretation, the crucial intervention in that modality. In POST, supportive interventions are used more freely and more frequently. Increased insight into conscious and preconscious material may occur via clarifications and confrontations, but interpretation of unconscious mental processes and conflicts is not utilized.

Attitude Toward Regression

As opposed to exploratory psychotherapy where a moderate, modulated regression is encouraged in order to reveal deeper levels of unconscious material and transferences, regression is discouraged in POST. Logical thought is encouraged, while free association is discouraged. Dreams are not a focus of attention; when presented they are responded to matter of factly with reality-oriented comments or "displacement upwards" (Werman, 1984). The reason for this is that the patient in supportive psychotherapy is usually already struggling against regressive tendencies, and further regression is not helpful and may possibly be dangerous.

GOALS, STRATEGIES,
AND TECHNIQUES OF POST

The goals and strategies of POST have already been noted above, and will simply be listed here.

1. Goals—Increased homeostasis for the patient in crisis; strengthening of ego functions, directly and indirectly, and improved adaptation to inner and outer worlds in the chronically impaired patient
2. Strategies
   - Therapist "realness"
   - Focus on conscious and preconscious material; avoidance of unconscious material
   - Encouragement of a mildly positive transference
   - Handling resistances according to their adaptive/maladaptive values
   - The discouragement of regression, and of whatever might increase it, for example, free association or dream analysis

Let us digress for a moment and examine how specific ego functions can be strengthened, either directly, or indirectly, by decreasing pressures on the ego from the other three psychic agencies.

Direct Strengthening

- The reality testing function is strengthened by clarifying, confronting, and undermining primitive defenses, thereby improving the patient's ability to distinguish between self and object representations, or internal versus external stimuli, that is, reality testing.
- The regulation of drives is strengthened by discouraging impulsivity and encouraging delay and sublimations.
- Object relations are improved by encouraging and praising healthier modes of relatedness while discouraging unhealthier modes, both inside and outside of the transference.
- Thought processes are improved by confronting vague and idiosyncratic speech, giving the patient more conscious control over her thinking processes and the opportunity to compensate for faulty logic and thinking. For example, think more before starting to speak.
- Defensive functions of the ego are strengthened by supporting adaptive defenses while undermining and discouraging those that are maladaptive.
- The synthetic function is improved by clarifying, confronting, and undermining splitting operations. Splitting leads to identity diffusion, thereby weakening the synthetic function of the ego.

Indirect Strengthening

- Pressure on the ego from drive demands is decreased by relative gratifications; for example, partial, modulated satisfaction of dependency wishes.
- Pressure from an overly punitive and demanding superego is decreased by undermining perfectionistic demands on the self and others, or by the therapist sharing more realistic values.
- External stressors are decreased by the use of environmental interventions; for example, suggesting a move away from home to a halfway house, or hospitalization.

3. Techniques

The specific techniques of psychodynamically oriented supportive therapy can be usefully divided into two groups; (1) those that are ideally utilized by a psychodynamically skilled clinician but do not require psychodynamic sophistication and (2) those that do require psychodynamic sophistication.

I. Techniques that do not absolutely require psychodynamic sophistication:
  • Encouraging the therapeutic alliance
  • Furnishing hope and reassurance
  • Giving suggestions and advice
  • Educating the patient
  • Accepting abreaction without interpretation
  • Making environmental interventions
    a. With the patient
    b. With the family or other collaterals
  • Reframing. (This refers to helping the patient view her situation in more realistic terms. For example, helping a severely depressed patient to see that although past, present, and future seem hopeless now, it has not really been so nor will it be so in the future.)
  • Giving encouragement and praise; setting limits and prohibitions
  • Emphasizing strengths and talents; encouraging sublimations
  • Prescribing somatic treatments in a matter-of-fact medical manner, without attention to the patient's unconscious fantasies about medication
  • Using clarifications
  • Making confrontations
  • Furnishing a model for identification

The techniques listed above can be utilized, for example, by family physicians or by mental health workers.

II. Techniques that do require psychodynamic training and expertise:
  • *Strengthening Adaptive Defense Mechanisms.* These tend to be higher level defenses clustered about repression. Common examples are the giving of complicated theoretical explanations to the obsessional, highly intellectualized patient, or encouraging repression and denial in the histrionic patient.
  • *Undermining Maladaptive Defense Mechanisms.* These are usually the so-called primitive defenses focused around splitting and consisting of projective identification, denial, and so forth. When used to excess these "primitive" defenses weaken ego functioning, particularly reality testing. However, no defenses, however maladaptive, are undermined if they are absolutely essential to the patient's continuing function.

• *Supplying Inexact Interpretations.* Glover (1931) described the supportive effects of inexact interpretations; they induce displacements and artificial neuroses. An example is the deliberate ignoring of obvious homosexual material and directing the patient's attention instead to "pseudo-homosexual" issues, such as dependency, fears of intimacy, and feelings of lack of masculine adequacy.

• *Using Benign Projections and Introjections.* These interventions locate the patient's difficulties outside of his psychic self. Benign projections locate the responsibility for the patient's problems in other people and other periods of time. Benign introjections locate the difficulty in the patient's physiology and biochemistry, for example, a "chemical imbalance," or a "stimulus barrier" problem. Both are variants of inexact interpretation.

• *Using Understanding of the Patient's Character and Unconscious Transferences to Determine the Nature and Style of Interventions.* For example, being more liberal with advice to a patient who is comfortable with dependency needs, while encouraging the patient with a counterphobic style and strong reaction formations against dependency that she is capable of figuring out how to resolve the problem by herself.

PSYCHODYNAMIC PRINCIPLES AND POST

Transferences in Supportive Therapy

The general strategy regarding transferences in POST is to encourage a mildly positive transference, Freud's "unobjectionable positive transference" (1912) while attempting to avoid, or dealing rapidly with, the idealizing and erotized transferences that can function as resistances and the intensely negative transferences that can destroy the treatment. The therapist does not attempt to uncover transferences that are not in the patient's conscious awareness; rather, he uses them to inform and to shape his interventions. Transference is not stimulated by therapist anonymity and abstinence, and tends to be somewhat diluted and diminished by the therapist's more real stance. The "unobjectionable positive transference" and mildly libidinized positive transferences are not commented upon; they furnish the therapist additional "clout" to influence the patient's more maladaptive behaviors.

By contrast, intensely idealized transferences, which can so easily change into marked devaluations, and erotized and negative transferences are responded to rapidly. After full expression, and after maximal abreactive value has been obtained, the patient is confronted with the reality of the doctor–patient relationship, their purposes and goals in working together, and the disparities between the transferences and the reality. At times, transferences can be usefully deflected out of the office to relationships with other important people in the patient's life, by stressing the parallels in the quality of the interaction.

The therapist's more "real" stance tends to be less stimulating of negative transferences, but this is balanced by the more pathological patients who tend to be treated supportively and who generally have particular problems with aggressive feelings. Attacks of unmodulated rage are as frequently directed at the supportive therapist as the exploratory therapist.

The supportive therapist, in common with all therapists, sets strict limits on the acting out of rageful transferences in the office. The usual prohibitions against physical acts against the therapist's person or property are rigidly enforced. If the patient cannot maintain behavioral control, the therapist can decide to end the session early, telling the patient that these issues can be addressed again in the next session, hopefully in a more modulated fashion. The supportive therapist's attitude toward the patient's ragefulness is that it is fully acceptable to him, but also that it is unrealistic and maladaptive to the realities of the treatment and their work together.

Countertransference in Supportive Therapy

Countertransference is currently used in two different, but related, ways. In its narrow sense, it refers to the therapist's irrational responses to the patient, that is, his transferences. In its broad meaning it encompasses all the feelings experienced by the therapist as he sits with the patient. In either sense, it is viewed not as a negative, but rather as inevitable in dynamic psychotherapy, and an opportunity for the therapist to learn more about the patient and about himself. The narrow definition is also called the "classic" approach, the broader concept the "totalistic" approach. The broad or totalistic approach tends to be favored by therapists who work with more disturbed patients, while those who treat primarily neurotic patients tend to use the narrow, classic view.

My preference, however, is for the narrow view because it ensures adequate attention to the problematic issues that the therapist brings to the treatment, rather than viewing his affective experiences as belonging only to the patient and the patient's transferences and projections. I proposed the term "reaction to the transference" (Rockland, 1989) to refer to the therapist's use of his emotional reactions to clarify nonverbal transferences and subtle projections from the patient. Thus, I suggest the use of three terms: (1) the patient's transferences, (2) the analyst's countertransferences (his transferences to the patient and to the patient's transferences), and (3) reactions to the transference. The countertransference in its narrow view plus the reactions to the transference (2 and 3) equal the concept of countertransference in its totalistic or broad sense. In my view, the advantage of this is its simultaneous focus on both therapist and patient distortions.

Countertransference is a particularly crucial issue in the supportive treatment of sicker patients. These patients can produce severe anxiety, confusion, and dysphoric affects in the therapist, the reading and understanding of which furnish invaluable clues to subtle and nonverbalized transferences. Attention to countertransference (narrow sense) issues is crucial because of the myriad opportunities for the supportive therapist to act out countertransference feelings. This tendency is increased by the less clear guidelines for appropriate interventions that characterize supportive therapy compared to exploratory therapy.

The supportive therapist must listen to and attempt to understand the patient's transferences and resistances, while simultaneously being prepared to offer advice, limit setting, or encouragement when appropriate and when required by the patient's pathology. Because the rules for therapist interventions are less clear cut, there is the constant danger of the therapist giving advice that is not required or setting limits that are not needed, motivated by his own irrationalities. The therapist can more easily act out wishes to rescue, to overcontrol, to masochistically submit to unreasonable patient demands, etc., all under the guise of patient need. I cannot stress too often the enormous temptation to countertransference acting out that exists in supportive psychotherapy; the therapist must be constantly sensitive to these tendencies in himself. He must make every effort to ensure that his interventions are appropriate to the patient's needs and deficits, and do not result from his own conscious or unconscious wishes.

The supportive psychotherapist should always keep clearly in mind that mental health professionals do not have special expertise on how to live, or how to solve problems, and that we are not entitled to "sell" lifestyles or values to the patient, except when his ego deficits require it. The "red flag" of countertransference acting out should be raised in the therapist's mind whenever he finds himself behaving in an atypical (for him) way with a patient. He may notice that he is prolonging or shortening sessions, or that he is more or less tolerant of telephone calls. He may be more or less verbal than usual, or more or less firm in limit setting. Because of these dangers, it is crucial that the supportive therapist have a personal psychoanalytic or intensive psychotherapeutic experience, so that he can be maximally aware of, and thereby less susceptible to the acting out of, countertransference issues.

Resistance in Supportive Therapy

Resistance refers to those forces within the patient that oppose the process of treatment, the patient's rational ego, and her wish to change. It can be conscious, preconscious, or unconscious. It is the manifestation in the interpersonal setting of psychotherapy of defensive activity in the intrapsychic frame of reference. It is not viewed in pejorative terms, but rather as an invaluable source of data about the defensive functioning of the patient's ego and therefore eminently worthy of study in its own right.

The usual statement about resistances in the supportive therapy literature is that they are to be ignored or, in some cases, strengthened. However, this ignores the fact that resistance can only be conceptualized in relation to treatment goals. Supportive therapy, with its own unique goals, requires its own specific definition of resistance. Thus, resistance in supportive psychotherapy is defined as *all patient behaviors that oppose ego strengthening, either directly or indirectly, and that oppose improved adaptation to inner and outer worlds.* For example, attention to early childhood experiences that might be seen as productive in an exploratory psychotherapy would be viewed as resistance in supportive psychotherapy when the patient is using it to avoid painful present realities. Similarly, opposition to the recovery of early memories, to increased awareness of unconscious psychic conflict, or to free association, all of which would be resistance in an exploratory psychotherapy, are not viewed as such in supportive psychotherapy; rather, they are appropriate behaviors for that treatment modality.

Many patient behaviors are correctly viewed as resistances in all psychotherapies. Missed sessions, repeated latenesses, extended silences, or excessive trivia are common examples. However, even these behaviors might not always be viewed as resistance in supportive therapy; for example, when they are understood as desperate attempts to fend off a frightening decompensation. A schizophrenic patient who attempts to stave off a threatening acute psychotic regression by silence or trivial talk could be viewed as using adaptive behavior, and thus it is accepted and supported.

The Therapeutic Alliance in Supportive Therapy

Therapeutic alliance remains somewhat of an unclear concept. It is applied to the combination of the therapist's analyzing ego and the patient's observing ego that is present in a well-functioning psychoanalysis or other dynamic therapy. It is also used by researchers to refer to measures of therapist–patient fit early in the psychotherapy. In this latter sense, the "alliance" is a positive predictor of treatment outcome (Gomes-Schwartz, 1978; Marziali, Marmar, & Krupnick, 1981), but the relationship may be more complicated (Horowitz, Marmar, Weiss, DeWitt, & Rosenbaum, 1984). The term was coined by Zetzel (1956) and is very similar to Greenson's (1967) "working alliance." Both terms are related to Freud's original description of "the unobjectional positive transference" (1912).

Whatever the unclarities of the terms "therapeutic" or "working alliance," it is clear that it is a central issue in supportive psychotherapy. Because supportive psychotherapy does not utilize the interpretation of unconscious conflict with consequent "insight," the therapeutic alliance is a more positive force for change, probably through processes of identification. In addition, because of the severity of the patient's pathology, the therapeutic alliance in supportive therapy is in constant danger of being contaminated and destroyed by primitive negative transferences. Therefore the alliance must always be a focus of attention.

The therapeutic alliance is fostered by clearly spelling out the structure of the treatment situation, including meeting times, fees, arrangements regarding missed sessions, etc. In addition, the therapist attempts to anticipate problems that might disrupt the treatment; for example, substance abuse in the recently abstinent patient or health-endangering weight loss in the anorectic. The therapist openly discusses these potential dangers with the patient, and they decide, collaboratively, how these difficulties will be handled if they arise.

There should be a detailed discussion of the goals of treatment, spelled out specifically and concretely. Finally, the therapist stresses to the patient the collaborative nature of their work together. Both have crucial roles to play, and a positive outcome depends upon the best efforts of both. The structuring of the treatment described above establishes a background of reality against which resistances, transference distortions, severe acting out, etc., can be highlighted when they occur in the therapy.

Whether borderline patients can ever develop a therapeutic alliance in the psychoanalytic sense, that is, a collaboration between the observing ego of the patient and the analyzing ego of the therapist, remains controversial. If it develops, it probably does so relatively late in the treatment. The therapist must remember that sicker patients possess inherent difficulties in observing themselves realistically, and he should not anticipate a degree of collaboration of which the patient is incapable. Otherwise he will tend to view its absence as negative transference or to become prematurely discouraged about the patient's treatability.

Working Through and Termination in Supportive Therapy

While the function of working through in exploratory psychotherapy is to enable the evolution from initial insight to structural change, its function in supportive therapy is to allow repetitive focusing on pathologic mal-adaptive defenses and on marked transference distortions. In addition, repetition and time are needed for processes of identification with the therapist to occur. The therapist repetitively confronts and undermines maladaptive behaviors from all possible standpoints, in the transference and in the patient's outside life. Since all behaviors are multiply deter-mined (Waelder, 1936), the functions and determinants of each maladap-tive behavior are confronted and clarified as each becomes activated in the treatment. Positive changes are encouraged and praised. Working through as a process can be usefully compared to unlearning and learn-ing, or deconditioning and reconditioning in other theoretical frames.

Termination is handled differently in supportive therapy than in ex-ploratory treatment. Often it is not a termination at all, but rather a gradual attenuation. For chronic schizophrenic patients and patients with recurrent affective illness, for example, maintenance medications can furnish the vehicle for a lifelong, increasingly attenuated, supportive psychotherapy.

The criteria for termination in supportive psychotherapy are the reason-able attainment of the goals set at the beginning of treatment. Resistance to experiencing feelings about termination are not explored and under-mined as actively as in exploratory treatment. For example, when the patient denies any significant reactions to termination, this might be gently questioned with an air of skepticism. Similarly, when a patient wishes to stop sooner than the agreed-upon termination date, thereby decreasing or avoiding the pain of separation and loss, the therapist might question the decision but generally does not actively oppose it. (This does not apply, of course, to the patient who requires maintenance medica-tions.) Depending on the nature of the patient's psychopathology and the adequacy of her social supports, the therapist might encourage informal contacts in the future, such as occasional meetings, letters, or phone calls.

These guidelines are not applicable to the patient who wishes to pre-maturely and unilaterally terminate a supportive psychotherapy because of blatant negative transferences. The negative transferences are dealt with as described above (see pp. 45–46). Often this is successful and will allow the patient to continue treatment without feeling humiliated or controlled.

MECHANISMS OF ACTION OF POST

Although a discussion of how any psychotherapy "works" must remain somewhat speculative, one can discuss the elements that are relevant to the therapeutic effects of supportive therapy. These would include the following.

The Nonspecific Effects of All Psychotherapies

Included here are such factors as the helping relationship between therapist and patient, a therapist who is respectful and understanding of the patient, who believes he has something useful to offer the patient, and who presents a model of reasonable personal maturity. The stimulation of hopefulness (Frank, 1974) is helpful because patients frequently begin treatment feeling hopeless and demoralized. Because the supportive therapist is more real, more verbal, and often more active in offering realistic hope and reassurance, the nonspecific positive aspects of all psychotherapies may have more powerful effects in supportive than in exploratory psychotherapy.

Unanalyzed Positive Transferences

Unanalyzed positive transferences are the main mechanisms for "transference cures," the patient's willingness to change out of love for the therapist or in an attempt to obtain the therapist's love and approval. Because positive transferences that are not overly idealized or erotized are not addressed in supportive psychotherapy, they probably have more powerful effects than in exploratory treatments.

Unanalyzed Negative Transferences

Although this mechanism of change is less common than unanalyzed positive transferences, it too can lead to positive change. In this case, the patient changes out of feelings of defiance, rebellion, or negativism toward the therapist; essentially "I will do better for myself than you can, or are willing to do."

Corrective Emotional Experiences

This is a complex and controversial concept, introduced by Alexander (1961). His view of the corrective emotional experience, with some implication of role playing by the therapist, was received very negatively by the psychoanalytic community. However, Gill (1954) used the same term in a more acceptable version. In his view, the therapist's noncomplementary responses to the patient's transference patterns are themselves corrective emotional experiences. They afford the patient new and dif-

ferent responses to her usual relationship gambits by the therapist responding objectively and with understanding, rather than in a reciprocal fashion,
to the patient's transference templates. Stated concretely, the therapist
responds similarly whether the patient communicates loving or hateful
feelings, and this is a corrective emotional experience for the patient.

Corrective emotional experiences are probably not mutative in themselves. Rather, they begin the process of change by furnishing new
internalizations and identifications, and eventually modified psychic
structures.

Identifications with the Therapist

This is probably a more powerful element in all dynamic psychotherapies than is generally appreciated, but it is particularly important in
supportive psychotherapy. It is an accepted technique, and the therapist
attempts to expedite it by being more revealing of himself and sharing
personal values, etc., when clinically appropriate. The reader is again
reminded that this powerful positive mechanism is also fraught with the
dangers of countertransference acting out.

Positive and Negative Feedback Loops

Patient behaviors outside of treatment tend to stimulate reciprocal behaviors from significant others, which lead to feedback loops that can spiral
in either positive or negative directions. For example, if the patient
becomes less paranoid and suspicious as a result of changes in the treatment, others will begin responding to her in a more trusting and supportive fashion. This, in turn, will help the patient to be less paranoid, and a
positive loop has begun. Negative loops work similarly; hostile behaviors
elicit rejection from others, leading the patient to act more hostilely, etc.
Thus, positive changes that begin in the therapeutic relationship are
transferred into outside relationships, shifting feedback loops in more
positive directions.

Maximizing the Patient's Level of Function

Every patient (person) operates within a range of behaviors depending
on factors such as dysphoric affects, external stresses, fatigue, etc. Decreasing negative affects or decreasing environmental stress will enable
the patient to function closer to the healthier end of her behavioral
repertoire. The more adaptive and healthier function that follows produces more adaptive behaviors, more positive responses from others, and
the positive feedback loops described above.

Strengthening the Patient's Ego Functions

Strengthening ego functions is the primary goal of supportive psychotherapy; the mechanisms for accomplishing this, both directly and indirectly, are described above (see p. 43).

SUMMARY/FURTHER THOUGHTS

This chapter, a condensation of my earlier book (1989), presents the basic principles of psychodynamically oriented supportive therapy. It contrasts supportive and exploratory psychotherapies across a number of parameters and then focuses on the goals, strategies, and techniques of POST. Transference, countertransference, resistance, alliance, working through, and termination in POST are reviewed. The final section examines factors that contribute to the therapeutic effects of POST.

The work needs further development in two areas. First, POST requires further refinement and development of its principles, and its technology and interventions. Second, the general principles and technology need to be applied to specific clinical syndromes, exemplified by the subject matter of this book. The application of the treatment to schizophrenia and other psychotic syndromes would be a reasonable next step.

Indications and Contraindications: Borderline Personality Disorder and the Supportive/Exploratory Continuum

This chapter addresses the issues that influence the evaluator in deciding whether the specific patient with Borderline Personality Disorder (BPD) is best treated by a primarily expressive or a primarily supportive dynamic psychotherapy. The qualifier "primarily" is used to indicate that exploratory and supportive therapies are almost never practiced in pure culture; rather, they are most usefully viewed as models for formulating overall treatment strategies and for delineating specific techniques. Actual psychotherapies for all patients, but particularly for BPD patients, are almost always mixtures of supportive and exploratory interventions. Therefore the question is more accurately stated as "Where on the supportive/exploratory continuum will the psychotherapy for this BPD patient be located?" Later shifts toward more exploration or more support will depend upon the patient's overall clinical state, particularly the levels of anxiety or regression in the overall therapy, in a session, or at any moment within the session.

The supportive/exploratory mix of the treatment often requires change as the treatment progresses. The patient may turn out to be more ill than originally appreciated, and the treatment would move in a more supportive direction. On the other hand, treatments that begin in a primarily supportive mode not infrequently move into a more exploratory mode over time as the patient develops increased ego strength, decreased acting out and impulsivity, and is able to sustain a more solid, therapeutically useful alliance.

The shift from a primarily supportive to a primarily exploratory treatment may be initially planned by the therapist, or it may result from more significant progress in the treatment than was originally anticipated. The change from a primarily exploratory to a more supportive treatment is generally not planned, but is usually due to unanticipated clinical factors. For example, patients may withhold pathologic material from the early evaluative sessions; this is revealed later, presumably when the patient is more trusting of the therapist, and it may make the initial treatment plan inappropriate. Other patients develop severe regressions in exploratory treatments that surprise the therapist by their primitive and malignant qualities, and force a move toward a more supportive treatment. Wallerstein (*Forty-Two Lives in Treatment*, 1986) noted that most of the psychoanalyses and exploratory psychotherapies in the Menninger Psychotherapy Research Project became more supportive over time, due to related developments.

CASE EXAMPLES

Case Example 1

A 43-year-old woman with the diagnoses of Narcissistic and Borderline Personality Disorders was in a two times per week mixed supportive/exploratory treatment. There was no history of severe affective disorder, either in the patient or in her family. Although there were marital difficulties, the marriage appeared relatively stable. During an unusually stressful period, the husband unexpectedly left, and the patient developed a first manic episode with marked paranoid trends.

The therapist immediately became more reality oriented and more active. He consistently supported the patient's reality testing, particularly undermining the marked projections; in addition, lithium and haloperidol were started. However, the patient rapidly became more psychotic and took the medications only sporadically; hospitalization became necessary.

In the hospital, the lithium and haloperidol were continued and the psychosis resolved within 10 days. The acute psychosis and hospitalization led to the husband's return and to a recommendation for marital treatment. The mixed supportive/exploratory treatment continued, with the patient on prophylactic lithium and without any further psychotic disruptions. However, the therapist noted a tendency in himself to become more supportive whenever the patient was experiencing unusual stresses.

Case Example 2

A 32-year-old female accountant with the diagnosis of BPD was being treated in a twice a week primarily exploratory treatment. Following a traumatic reorganization at her job, the patient revealed that she was experiencing ideas of reference, of near-delusional proportion, and further that she had experienced these symptoms many times in the past under stress. This information had been omitted from the initial evaluation and had been specifically denied when asked about. This new information led the therapist to shift toward a more supportive psychotherapy.

Case Example 3

A 39-year-old physician was being treated in a primarily supportive, twice a week psychotherapy for BPD with marked paranoid trends. The patient was extremely intelligent and highly motivated. Systematic attention to, and the undermining of, splitting and projective defenses led to a significant mastery of these issues with associated behavioral changes. Simultaneously, the patient's wife also made changes as a result of her psychotherapy, and there was a marked improvement in the marital relationship.

These changes, in his intrapsychic state and in the marriage, made it possible to begin a gradual shift toward a more exploratory treatment. The therapist made exploratory interventions hesitantly at first and paid careful attention to their impact. The patient developed some increased anxiety, but no regression in function. Therefore, the therapist continued the gradual shift toward a more exploratory treatment, and the patient was well able to tolerate the change.

The supportive/exploratory continuum is arbitrarily divided into five areas, each suggesting a particular ratio of supportive and exploratory interventions. This is diagrammed below:

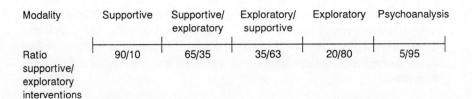

Modality	Supportive	Supportive/ exploratory	Exploratory/ supportive	Exploratory	Psychoanalysis
Ratio supportive/ exploratory interventions	90/10	65/35	35/63	20/80	5/95

SUPPORTIVE PSYCHOTHERAPY:
INDICATIONS AND CONTRAINDICATIONS
Indications

The literature (Alexander, 1954; Wallerstein, 1975) suggests two main indications for supportive psychotherapy. The first is an acute crisis in a fairly healthy patient; examples are those who have suddenly lost jobs or have suffered traumatic marital upheavals. The second applies to patients with severe and persistent ego deficits and defects, such as psychotic patients or those with severe borderline pathology. These patients generally cannot tolerate an exploratory psychotherapy, particularly the regressive potential implied by such treatment. They are in danger of suffering a psychotic, suicidal, or other acute affective decompensation, frequently requiring hospitalization. It is this second group of patients that primarily concern us here; of course, they too often present in acute crisis. In addition to most BPD patients, most other Axis II personality disorders of borderline personality organization, for example, schizoid, paranoid, schizotypal, primitive histrionic, and many narcissistic patients, are probably best treated with a primarily supportive psychotherapy.

However, clinical diagnosis is only one factor influencing treatment choice, and other variables are often more important in the decision about whether to utilize a primarily exploratory or primarily supportive psychotherapy. Other factors that play major roles in psychotherapy treatment planning are discussed below.

Motivation

Exploratory treatment requires some desire for basic character change, as opposed to the demand for immediate symptom relief; in addition, it demands the willingness to invest the time, energy, and finances that are necessary. There are many patients of varying severities and qualities of psychopathology who are simply not interested in learning about their unconscious mental life; this attitude does not necessarily stem from psychopathology. They come for symptomatic relief, preferably as quickly as possible, and have no interest in the self-scrutinizing and autoplastic change processes of exploratory therapy.

However, this presenting attitude does not totally rule out exploratory treatment. It can be tactfully explored during the initial evaluation, and sometimes, if the therapist deals skillfully with the patient's anxieties and other resistances, an exploratory treatment may become possible. Other patients who initially have no interest in exploratory treatment may feel otherwise after the resolution of an acute crisis, or after some strengthening of ego functions has been accomplished in a supportive treatment. However, in general, the patient who is lacking in motivation to understand herself and to change basic internal structures and conflicts is better treated supportively.

Psychological Mindedness

This quality, too, is highly desirable for patients to engage successfully in an exploratory treatment, and it also cuts across the spectrum of psychopathology. There are many patients whose usual way of dealing with stress and dysphoric affects is with projection, denial, somatic symptoms, or acting out, and it is difficult to engage such patients successfully in an exploratory treatment. Patients from cultural groups that customarily use alcohol, promiscuity, or similar behaviors for the relief of psychological discomfort are less likely to have the psychological interest or the talent to engage in an exploratory treatment. Therefore, they are appropriately treated supportively, when they are willing to participate in psychotherapy at all.

Intellectual Ability, Organicity

Exploratory psychotherapy requires at least an average IQ, and ideally one well above average. Intellectual limitations represent a strong contraindication to exploratory treatment, and these patients are more successfully treated supportively.

Similarly, patients with various organic deficits are better treated with a supportive therapy.

Patients with Pharmacologically Responsive Syndromes

Patients with BPD may present with Bulimia Nervosa, the bulimic symptoms sufficiently dramatic to demand the initial treatment focus. The symptoms of bulimia generally respond favorably to behavioral interventions and/or antidepressants, a generally supportive treatment context. As the symptoms of the eating disorder recede, the characterological difficulties will become more central, at least for the therapist.

Some of these patients will insist that the eating disorder be the only treatment focus, minimizing any BPD-related difficulties. Thus, the successful response to the behavioral/pharmacologic treatment makes it impossible to engage the patient in a psychotherapy for the personality disorder.

Others, more open to the view that they suffer from a personality disorder as well as an eating disorder, or that the eating disorder is part of a larger clinical picture, are amenable to psychotherapy for the BPD. The appropriate supportive/exploratory mix for those patients will depend on the whole clinical picture, the many factors, both general and specific to BPD, discussed in this chapter.

Likability

The influence of patient "likability" on treatment outcome has been discussed by Stone (1990). It is a somewhat vague concept, partly dependent on idiosyncratic factors within the therapist. However, some patients are likable to most therapists, while others are generally "unlikable." Likability is positively related to ego strength and therefore a factor favoring exploratory treatment. The individual therapist's positive reaction to a specific patient is an element in patient–therapist "fit" and therefore tends to favor a better outcome. There is the danger, however, that the therapist's "liking" a particular patient contains significant countertransference elements, and these need to be guarded against to avoid their being acted out.

Patients under Severe and Chronic Environmental Stress

It is very difficult to undertake the self-exploration required by an exploratory treatment while one is experiencing severe and chronic environmental stresses. Examples are poverty, unemployment, a psychotic spouse, or a severely damaged child. Most of these patients should be treated supportively. This is necessarily relative and does not minimize the fact that many patients unconsciously produce their own environmental stresses or handle realistic stresses so poorly that a more ambitious, exploratory treatment should be considered.

Patients Treated under Pressure from Others or Whose Goal is to Change Others

These patients are generally poor candidates for exploratory treatments, but other modalities beside supportive individual treatment should be seriously considered. Family treatment, couples treatment, group treatment, or no treatment at all (Frances, Clarkin, & Perry, 1984) may be most appropriate.

Patients with Poor Tolerance for Anxiety, Depression, and Other Dysphoric Affects

Exploratory treatment can transiently increase dysphoric affects or symptomatology as part of the change process. The therapist should have some trepidation about beginning an exploratory treatment with patients whose histories reveal severe decompensations, major acting-out episodes, or other self-destructive behaviors. Supportive psychotherapy would be the conservative choice. In addition, intolerance for dysphoric affects is a nonspecific sign of ego weakness (Kernberg, 1984) and thus another relative indication for supportive treatment.

Patients with Several Failed Attempts at Exploratory Psychotherapy

Repeated failures in previous exploratory therapies are relative contraindications to more of the same. However, these patients must be distinguished from those who have been in treatment with inadequate or poorly trained therapists and from those who have made significant gains in past treatments but nevertheless continue to have significant symptoms or other difficulties.

This distinction requires a very careful and skillful evaluation of the patient and of the past treatment episodes. In general, however, repeated failures in past exploratory treatments should lead the therapist to seriously consider alternative approaches. Supportive psychotherapy is one possibility; family or group therapies are others, as are cognitive and behavioral approaches.

Contraindications

Patients who should be in exploratory, not supportive, psychotherapy are characterized by the positive aspects of the qualities discussed above. Such patients are typically intelligent, likable, psychologically minded and psychologically talented, motivated for basic characterologic change, and so on, in short, the YAVIS patient.

There are other patients who should not be in a psychodynamically oriented individual treatment at all, and who will do better in other modalities, such as family or couple treatment, various group therapies, or other individual supportive modalities, such as cognitive or behavioral therapies. This leads into the complex field of differential therapeutics, which is beyond the scope of this chapter (see Frances, Clarkin, & Perry, 1984).

Some patients should probably not be in any psychotherapy. Those with secondary gains that outweigh any motivation for change usually make for impossible treatments. Patients who repetitively engage in severe ego-syntonic acting out, have severe antisocial personality disorders, or for whom chronic lying is a comfortable way of life are generally impossible candidates for any treatment modality.

Patients who are currently involved in legal proceedings are more effectively treated after the legal issues are settled. However, this is not always practical because the patient may require psychiatric treatment while the legal struggles drag on. At the very least, the therapist is extremely careful about treating patients requesting psychiatric help at the advice of their lawyers. When such treatment is clinically indicated, the therapist can both test the patient's motivations and safeguard the treatment by insisting on a clear distinction between the roles of psychotherapist and of expert witness, and their assignment to separate professionals.

A history of repeated failures of supportive treatment should lead the therapist to consider a different treatment recommendation, whether heroic exploratory treatment, aggressive psychopharmacology, family treatment, or no treatment at all.

There are other patients who become "psychotherapy addicts," and often the most helpful treatment recommendation for such patients is to not pursue any further psychotherapy. For example, one patient had the chief complaint "I've been out of psychotherapy for 14 months," a presentation of himself as addicted and deprived of his supplier.

Shifts Toward More Support or More Exploration During an Ongoing Psychotherapy

The decision about the locus of the psychotherapy on the supportive/exploratory continuum and tentative decisions regarding which conflict areas are to be handled supportively and which in an exploratory fashion, are the *macro* decisions of dynamic psychotherapy planning. The *micro* decisions involve factors in the patient's clinical state and/or in the treatment process that influence the therapist to move in a more supportive or a more exploratory direction from session to session, or from moment to moment within a given session. These micro decisions and the clinical factors that influence them are discussed elsewhere (Rockland, 1989) and therefore they are only listed here.

The following developments in the patient would lead the therapist to move in a more supportive direction:

- Intense, uncontrolled regressions
- Severe depressions, or serious threats of suicide, homicide, or self-mutilation
- Massive anxiety, either subjectively or manifested by the sudden and atypical appearance of primitive defenses or other regressive phenomena
- Dysfunctional observing ego
- Severe intercurrent stressors

These patient behaviors *may* incline the therapist to become more supportive:

- Serious threats to the treatment
- Excessive acting out, including substance abuse
- Chronic lying and withholding of information (if any psychotherapy is possible)
- Excessive prolonged silences

Indications for a *possible* shift in a more exploratory direction include:

- The patient rejects, or is threatened by, support
- The treatment becomes stilted and superficial; one or both participants seem to be losing interest and not valuing the treatment
- Increased self-awareness in the patient
- Increased ego strength in the patient
- Decreased acting out in the patient
- An increasingly stable and clinically useful therapeutic alliance

Borderline Personality Disorder and the Supportive/Exploratory Decision

The personal biases of the author should be noted here. I believe that most patients who meet criteria for BPD are most effectively treated with a primarily supportive psychotherapy, because the majority of these patients do not possess the combination of ego strength, motivation, and psychological mindedness necessary to undertake and to complete a successful exploratory treatment. This view is based on personal experience, supported by the high dropout rates in traditional exploratory psychotherapies (Waldinger & Gunderson, 1987) and by the low dropout rates in structured, behaviorally oriented supportive treatments (Linehan, 1987b).

I view exploratory psychotherapy as appropriate for a minority of BPD patients. However, I also believe that a significant number of these patients can become candidates for an exploratory therapy after extended work, months to years in duration, in a primarily supportive mode. This is a personal view and does not accord with the beliefs of some highly esteemed writers in the field (Kernberg, 1984).

The choice of primarily supportive versus primarily exploratory psychotherapy for the patient with BPD is influenced by all of the general factors above. In addition, however, there are issues specifically related to the patient with BPD that significantly influence the supportive/exploratory decision. In summary they comprise: (1) the severity of the

BPD pathology, (2) the quality of the BPD symptomatology, and (3) the presence and severity of associated Axis I and Axis II conditions. These issues are discussed below.

GAF Score. This factor is listed first because of its encompassing nature and its focus on function; consequently, it is influenced by most of the more specific elements that follow. The GAF score comprises Axis V of DSM-III-R (American Psychiatric Association, 1987), and consists of a 0 to 90 scale that rates the patient's psychological, social, and occupational functioning from a mental health or psychopathology standpoint; impairments due to physical or environmental limitations are specifically excluded.

The clinician is encouraged to make two GAF ratings. The first rates the patient's functional level at evaluation, and the second rates the patient's highest level of function for at least a few months of the previous year. The evaluation GAF is most pertinent to immediate treatment planning; for example, is the patient suicidal or psychotic requiring consideration of hospitalization? The past-year GAF is relevant to longer range treatment planning and to prognosis, because it measures the patient's more usual level of function to which he will probably return when the immediate crisis is resolved. To illustrate, a BPD patient with a past-year GAF score of 50 presents acutely depressed and moderately suicidal; she receives an evaluation GAF of 18. The immediate treatment attention is to the depression and suicidality. After successful treatment with antidepressants, the patient returns to a GAF of 50, and it is this rating that is most relevant to long-range treatment planning.

The GAF rating at evaluation in the BPD patient can reach almost zero because persistent and serious suicidality ensures a rating below 10. On the past-year rating, BPD patients would be expected to fall between about 30 and the low 60s. In general, BPD patients with past-year GAF scores below 45 probably should be treated supportively, while those above 50 are likely to include the minority appropriate for exploratory treatment. However, these are rough guidelines, and the decision about the appropriate supportive/exploratory mix can only be made by a total integration of all of the relevant factors.

Severity of BPD Symptomatology, Quantitative Factors. This refers to whether the patient meets five, six, seven, or eight of the DSM-III-R diagnostic criteria for BPD. Generally, the patient who meets eight of eight criteria is more disturbed than the patient who meets five. Of course, each criterion can occur with varying degrees of severity, but the above usually holds. Accordingly, the patient who meets only five BPD criteria may be in the group appropriate for an exploratory approach, while the opposite applies to the patient who meets all eight criteria.

Again, this is a rough approximation. Not only can each criterion be more or less severe, but one particular criterion, for example, acting out or impulsivity, may be severe enough by itself to warrant the choice of supportive treatment.

Subtypes of BPD Symptomatology, Qualitative Factors. In addition to the quantitative aspects of BPD symptomatology, qualitative aspects, that is, which of the criteria are met and which are not, are relevant. For example, Hurt and Clarkin (1990) describe three empirically determined subsets of BPD criteria, which they label the Identity cluster, the Affective cluster, and the Impulse cluster. The Identity cluster includes chronic feelings of emptiness and boredom, identity disturbance, and difficulties in being alone, "frantic efforts to avoid real or imagined abandonment" (DSM-III-R, p. 347). The Affective cluster includes intense and inappropriate affects, unstable affects, and unstable interpersonal relationships. The third subgroup, the Impulse cluster, includes self-destructive and other impulsive behaviors, such as substance abuse, suicidal threats and gestures, and self-mutilation.

Although there are as yet no relevant studies, one can speculate about the treatment implications of these criterion clusters. For example, psychopharmacologic agents might be expected to be most useful for patients in the Affective and Impulse clusters, and least relevant for the Identity cluster. Patients with prominent identity difficulties, and less significant affective and impulsive symptomatology, might well include the minority of BPD patients most appropriately treated with exploratory psychotherapy. They are often the patients who are more introspective and more psychologically minded, positive indicators for that modality. In addition, if psychopharmacology is least relevant to this subgroup of patients, more ambitious psychotherapeutic approaches might well be appropriate. Conversely, the Impulse cluster patient may well require the structuring and limit setting of a more supportive treatment. They are likely to have difficulties in foregoing destructive and self-destructive behaviors, and in developing the introspective attitudes that are desirable for an exploratory psychotherapy.

The Impulse cluster describes patients who utilize acting out to handle internal dysphoria. They are the patients who are likely to present with severe substance abuse, eating disorders, or frequent crises involving self-mutilation and suicidality, all incompatible with the contemplative stance necessary for a successful exploratory treatment. In addition, the presence of substance abuse, serious eating disorders, or destructive attacks on the self require environmental structuring, sometimes hospitalization, plus a major treatment focus on the Axis I disorder or on the self-destructive and self-mutilating behaviors. All of these are extremely problematic in an exploratory psychotherapy and should incline the evaluator toward a primarily supportive approach, at least initially.

Associated Axis I Pathology. The nature of the Axis I pathology associated with BPD is frequently acute enough to demand the initial treatment focus. Major depressive disorder, with or without suicidality, usually requires treatment with an antidepressant drug. Severe eating disorders can rapidly become serious threats to health or survival, and force the initial treatment focus onto those symptoms. This initial treatment is supportive in nature and includes the generous use of psychopharmacology, firm environmental limits, frequent use of the hospital, and similar interventions.

Once the Axis I symptomatology is adequately treated, the therapist can turn his attention to the BPD pathology. Many patients will not be motivated to examine their disordered characters and insist that the treatment focus only on the Axis I symptomatology, for example, "just correct the chemical imbalance." (The increasingly common stance of managed-care companies that psychiatric treatment is acute care only, and that return to baseline function marks the end of the treatment, will probably cause more patients to insist on this "symptoms only" approach to treatment.)

Some patients, following subsidence of the presenting Axis I difficulties, are motivated, or can be motivated, to pursue the long-term issues of their BPD. In those cases, factors other than the Axis I disorder will generally determine the psychotherapeutic modality. One possible exception are patients who require maintenance medication, for example, maintenance antidepressants or lithium. Long-term psychopharmacologic treatment is more easily integrated with supportive than exploratory therapy, but this factor too is relative.

Concomitant Axis II Pathology. BPD is rarely found without one or more associated Axis II disorders, and the nature of the other Axis II pathology has a significant impact on the choice of psychotherapy for the borderline patient. For example, the BPD patient often meets criteria for Schizotypal Personality Disorder; this combination was present in over 50% of Soloff's (1986) inpatient borderline population. This combination will usually incline the evaluator toward a primarily supportive approach. The overlap of BPD with Paranoid Personality Disorder, Schizoid Personality Disorder, or Antisocial Personality Disorder (if the latter patients are treatable at all) also generally lead to a primarily supportive approach.

On the other hand, BPD overlap with some Narcissistic Personality Disorders, or with Dependent or Obsessional Personality Disorders, may include the minority of BPD patients appropriately treated with an exploratory approach. Similarly, higher level Histrionic and Avoidant Personality Disorder overlap often represents the healthier end of the BPD spectrum, with the expectable treatment implications.

The BPD Patient Who Frequently Lies and/or Withholds Information

These behaviors must be carefully evaluated. Their significance for treatment choice depends strongly upon the frequency, chronicity, and ego-syntonity of the behaviors. Many patients lie occasionally, often motivated by embarrassment; similarly it is not unusual for patients to withhold information, either from embarrassment or due to the acting out of transferences. These behaviors need not particularly influence the choice of psychotherapy.

However, chronic and severe ego-syntonic lying or information withholding represents a serious problem for any kind of psychotherapeutic attempt, and serious consideration should be given to the recommendation of no treatment at all. If the therapist does decide to attempt a psychotherapy in the face of these difficulties, a primarily supportive approach will likely be more effective. That is because the positive transferences are not undermined and analyzed, tending to make the patient more eager to please the therapist, assuming that the inevitable negative transferences are adequately handled. The wish to gain the therapist's love and approval may sometimes lead the patient to gradually become less accepting of chronic lying or withholding, and thus there is some possibility for positive change. However, the usual outcome of any type of therapeutic interventions with patients who chronically lie and withhold information, and who do so comfortably and without overt conflict, is limited and questionable.

The Severity of Acute Psychotic Regressions

Some BPD patients can usually function with some effectiveness, but have histories of *severe*, transient psychotic episodes under stress. Because some regression is unavoidable and, in fact, desirable in an exploratory psychotherapy, the therapist should hesitate to undertake such a treatment with these patients. In other words, the history of severe, however short lived, psychotic regressions that occur spontaneously, not precipitated by drugs, should incline the evaluator strongly toward a supportive approach.

On the other hand, there are other BPD patients who have transient psychotic regressions that are not only brief but also mild; for example, transient delusions of reference. Here the indication for supportive treatment is less clear, although such psychotic regressions are still a relative indication for that approach. Certainly, though, a history of transient psychoses with self-destructive behaviors, or the need for hospital treatment, should cause the evaluator to be wary of anything but a supportive treatment. Psychotic transference reactions during the exploratory therapies of BPD patients are not uncommon. Although they are usually manageable, the therapist should not be casual about such developments and should not begin a treatment that increases the chances of such regressions, particularly when the history suggests that they are likely to be malignant and/or accompanied by serious self-destructive behaviors.

SUMMARY

All of the issues discussed above, both the general factors and those specific to BPD, are relevant to the choice of the appropriate supportive/exploratory mix for the individual BPD patient. None is absolute, and the treatment is most usefully planned by evaluating all of the factors and integrating them into a positive and negative balance sheet for the specific patient. It is only this overview, taking into account all of the relevant elements, that furnishes the data necessary to plan the appropriate psychotherapy for the specific patient with BPD.

As noted above, my experience suggests that only a minority of BPD patients possess the balance of positive to negative qualities that would make an exploratory psychotherapy the appropriate treatment choice. In my view, at least 75% of patients who meet criteria for BPD should be treated, at least initially, with a primarily supportive treatment. A number of such patients may, after an extended period of supportive work, become appropriate candidates for a more exploratory treatment. However, it is not clear at present how often this sequential approach results in a successful outcome.

PART II

THE SUPPORTIVE THERAPY OF BORDERLINE PERSONALITY DISORDER

The next four chapters focus around the psychodynamically oriented supportive therapy (POST) of one borderlne (BPD) patient. Each chapter describes a stage of the treatment, summarizes the tasks of that stage, and illustrates each task with clinical material from the patient's treatment. Clinical material is presented in a two-column format, with patient/therapist dialogue in the left column and author commentary in the right.

Keeping simultaneously in mind the psychopathology of BPD and the basic strategies of POST, one can visualize the likely characteristics of such a treatment is broad strokes. Patient and therapist will meet once, sometimes twice per week, sitting up and facing each other. Acting out will be a major issue, and the therapist will have to constantly struggle to limit it, using the initial contract, limit setting, and praise, plus careful attention to the negative transferences and primitive defenses that drive it. Negative transferences will be common, and the therapist will rapidly intervene when they are manifest, but not try to uncover them when they are not. Positive transferences will be accepted and not commented upon, unless they become excessively idealized, constituting serious resistances to the treatment. The patient's resistances will be responded to based upon their adaptational values, and defenses supported or undermined based on the same criteria. There will be constant attempts by the therapist to maintain and to strengthen the therapeutic alliance.

Regression will be discouraged, logical thinking valued over free association, and dreams accorded a minor role in the treatment.

Finally, no matter how skilled and sensitive the therapist, there will be frequent upheavals, storms, and threats by the patient to quit. The therapist will struggle with difficult and painful countertransference feelings and against temptations to act out countertransference reactions. He will wonder what motivated him to undertake such a problematic, painful and often discouraging treatment, and he will struggle to do his best for the patient, knowing that these problems and feelings reflect the nature, and the challenge, of psychotherapy with the BPD patient.

CHAPTER 5

Diagnostic Evaluation and Treatment Planning

Psychiatric treatment, like all medical treatments, is preceded by and based upon a detailed diagnostic study of the patient. The treatment prescribed is carefully tailored to the pathology, strengths and deficits, goals, and motivations of the patient; the art of treatment planning consists of maximizing the closeness of fit between the results of the diagnostic evaluation and the modality(ies) of treatment administered. Thus the overall tasks of the first phase, summarized in the chapter title, are broken down into four separate, but interrelated, tasks. These are (1) clinical evaluation, (2) diagnostic formulation, (3) treatment planning, and (4) contract setting. Contract setting is particularly crucial to structuring the treatment of the borderline patient and therefore deserves its own focus, apart from overall treatment planning.

TASK 1: CLINICAL EVALUATION

The clinical evaluation consists of collecting historical data while observing the patient's thought processes, affects, behaviors, and early transference patterns; the last are observed directly, and also indirectly by noting the evaluator's countertransference (broad sense) responses to the patient. Thus, data gathering proceeds simultaneously on two levels. Level A, the patient's verbal account, is the History. Level B, the therapist's observations of patient "behaviors," is the Mental Status, the psychiatric equivalent of the Physical Exam.

Level B Mental Status data are frequently more significant and more useful than Level A data, particularly with sicker patients whose historical accounts are often spotty and inaccurate, distorted by the patient's current clinical state or by attempts to rationalize current difficulties or symptoms. By contrast, Level B data are "harder"; the therapist observes or experiences them in the interview, and therefore can be more confident of their validity.

Trainees have less difficulty with Level A data and require more clinical experience to sharpen Level B skills, to develop trust in their observations of patient behaviors and in their countertransference reactions. Honing these observational skills is analogous to becoming a skilled auscultator of the heart and is subject to the same limitations. Cross-sectional Mental Status or Physical Examination findings are most useful when integrated with the longitudinal history. Both historical and Mental Status are essential, and each becomes most convincing when it complements, and is complemented by, the other. Discrepancies are just as important and motivate the evaluator to further study in order to resolve contradictory data.

The variable reality testing, primitive defenses, and labile affective states of the Borderline Personality Disorder (BPD) patient, with the expectable effects on the validity of the history, make interviewer attention to Level B data especially crucial with borderline patients. Impulsive behavior may or may not be presented in the History, but it is convincingly demonstrated when the patient explodes in response to a relatively neutral interviewer comment. Identity diffusion may be reflected in the history of poor school and work performance, and chaotic interpersonal relations, but it is persuasively demonstrated when the patient presents contradictory views of herself and others, and demonstrates abrupt shifts in relationship to the interviewer, all with a complete lack of awareness. Similarly with projective identification; the interviewer may suspect its presence from the patient's accounts of difficult interpersonal relationships. But when the interviewer becomes aware that he is feeling subtly controlled and brutalized, while the patient simultaneously complains bitterly about the interviewer's hostility and brutality to him, the evidence is clear and convincing.

Having noted how important it is for the trainee to develop and sharpen his observational skills, both of the patient directly and of his own internal reactions to the patient, I want to again stress the absolute inseparability of mental status and historical data. Neither source, no matter how skillfully mined, is adequate by itself. Both are necessary, and they are most useful when they can be integrated into a total, cross-sectional and longitudinal, mental status and historical, view of the patient. When this is accomplished, the interviewer begins to feel that he really "knows" the patient.

Clinical Material

First Evaluative Interview

A 24-year-old, white, single female was referred for evaluation and possible treatment. Because the patient's interview behaviors (Level B data) were at least as informative as the historical material (Level A data), interview material is presented in detail.

The patient entered the office appearing slightly apprehensive.

EVALUATOR: As you know, Dr. A— referred you to me and suggested that we meet to see whether we could work effectively together. I would like you to tell me what you see as your main problem areas and what you would hope to get out of treatment.

It is very useful to open the interview with a standard probe because the patient's response is particularly informative and inclines the interviewer toward or away from various diagnostic possibilities (Kernberg, 1977). Adding a question about why the patient has come to see you at this point would be a useful addition to the probe presented here.

PATIENT: I am depressed all the time, and my parents are driving me crazy.

The patient's initial response is notable for its brevity, and for the fact that one of her two complaints externalizes the problem to other people. In addition, she responds to only one of the two issues raised in the probe.

There ensued about a 2-minute silence during which the patient alternately appeared bored and distracted, and looked apprehensively at the interviewer.

EVALUATOR: Yes?

PATIENT: What else do you want to know?

The patients behavior during the 2-minute silence suggests

EVALUATOR: Well, I asked two questions and I believe you responded partially to one of them.

PATIENT: I'm sorry, I don't remember the questions, except that you asked me what was bothering me.

EVALUATOR: Do you often have trouble remembering things?

PATIENT: No. But I felt very nervous when I came in here, and I'm not sure I was really listening to you.

EVALUATOR: What I asked you was, What are your main areas of difficulty and what would you hope to get out of treatment?

PATIENT: I live in a crazy house and there's fighting going on all the time between my parents, between myself and my parents. I told you that I feel depressed, and sometimes I feel depressed and sometimes I feel so badly that I think about committing suicide.

EVALUATOR: Tell me some more about your depression.

PATIENT: That's it. I told you. There's nothing else.

EVALUATOR: You've mentioned two main problems, that you feel depressed and that you fight a lot with your parents. I would like to learn more about your experience of being depressed. What else can you tell me about it?

PATIENT: There's nothing else to say. Most of the time I feel depressed, and sometimes I feel very depressed.

EVALUATOR: What are the symptoms of your depression?

PATIENT: (*Obvious irritation*) I sleep OK, except sometimes I spend all day

passivity, negativism, and withholding; simultaneously she appears concerned with trying to please the interviewer.

When the interviewer points out that the patient ignored one question entirely, her response raises questions about her memory.

The interviewer asks about her memory and the patient responds with a reasonable explanation, which reassures the therapist. Had an explanation not been forthcoming, it would be necessary to actively pursue the memory difficulty, while the interviewer's differential diagnosis would include the question of an organic deficit.

Instead, the interviewer decides to simply repeat the initial questions, and his willingness to do so elicits further details from the patient. However, she rapidly returns to her minimal communication, and withholding, negativistic stance, and still does not respond to the question about treatment.

By this point in the interview, the interviewer appear to be feeling frustrated and probably somewhat irritated by the patient's minimal responses. He seems to be trying harder

in bed because I feel so lousy. I used to have an eating disorder, bulimia I think, and I still tend to overeat somewhat when I'm down. Sometimes I feel heavy and I feel like my thinking slows down, but most of the time there's no problems like that.

EVALUATOR: I'm curious about something here. You seem to be giving quite skimpy answers to my questions, and I also have the feeling that you're getting increasingly irritated as we go along. Can you tell me why you're responding like this?

PATIENT: (*Explodes*) You're damn right! I've already seen three other psychiatrists, and I thought you would get all this history from them. I don't see why I have to keep repeating the same crap over and over again.

EVALUATOR: Frankly, I didn't know that you had been in three previous treatments. But even if I had, my practice is to do my own evaluation first and then to obtain information from others later if it's appropriate to do so. So you should know that I'm starting from square one with you because that is my customary way of evaluating a patient. What are your thoughts about that?

PATIENT: (*With moderate irritation*) I still don't see why I have to keep telling the same story over and over again.

EVALUATOR: Well, I've explained exactly where I am with you at the mo-

to get the patient to talk, and her responses become briefer and less revealing the more he tries.

The patient now shows obvious irritation. The interviewer, integrating the patients overt irritation with his own inner feelings of frustration and irritation, decides to confront her behavior. This is totally appropriate, because although the interviewer is learning something from what the patient is saying, the more striking phenomena are going on in the interaction. In other words, at this point Level B observational data are much more impressive than the patient's verbal productions. To ignore these transference-countertransference phenomena might well lead to a stalemated interview.

The appropriateness of this confrontation is shown by the patient's next response. She explodes and reveals that she expected a very different kind of interaction than is occurring. In the process, she sheds light on her withholding and negativistic behavior, her irritation, and her final explosion.

The therapist's response is reality oriented. He explains how he views the evaluative interview, and what his working procedure is. The patient's behavior and affective explosion is multiply determined

ment. I feel strongly that it's important that I form my own impressions before I receive any information from other doctors.

PATIENT: (*Now appears quite contrite*) Oh, I didn't know that. But now that I think about it, I'm really kind of relieved that you want to make your own judgements about me and my situation without information from my previous doctors. Because those treatments really went very badly, and part of my fear in coming here was that you wouldn't like me from the beginning because of my past treatment experiences. I'm really very relieved, and I appreciate your being straight with me.

and could be approached on any number of levels. However, it is totally appropriate, particularly early in this initial evaluative interview, that the first priority is to clarify the reality.

It is also important to educate the patient about the therapist's style of collecting data. Not all therapists operate as does this one. Many collect data from previous therapists before they see the patient. This particular interviewer's style is totally acceptable, but when it leads to misunderstandings, as occurs here, it is important to spell out the realistic facts of the interaction.

The wisdom of confronting the patient's behavior and explaining the realities of the interview situation becomes clear. The patient has changed from a relatively uncooperative and negativistic stance to an open, cooperative, and grateful one. She reveals that her initial irritation about the interviewer not knowing more about her covered a deeper fear that he would know too much and have a negative impression of her from the previous therapists. She ends up expressing relief and gratitude, and in the process begins to talk more freely. This continues for the remainder of the session.

The patient continued to speak more freely, describing the chaos in the parental home where she lives, the frequent arguments filled with bitter recriminations, particularly between herself and her mother, and further details about her mild to moderate depressive symptoms. During this discussion, carried out primarily by the patient, the interviewer became aware that she had a soft disorder of thought form characterized by circumstantiality, tangentiality, and occasional odd word usage; infrequently a word was slightly off the intended meaning and mildly jarring to the interviewer.

She described some of her early life, growing up as the youngest of three children in an upper middle-class family. She had been a successful student with a wide circle of friends, but her life became problematic beginning at about 13. In junior high school academic performance dropped off markedly, she began to socialize with the "out group" and started moderate to severe illegal drug ingestion, primarily alcohol and marijuana, occasionally hallucinogens. She graduated from high school with a B minus average and attended a college about 200 miles from her home.

At college she was markedly homesick, increased her marijuana and alcohol abuse and developed bulimia, characterized by 8–10 times per week bingeing and purging. Her academic performance deteriorated, she began staying away from classes, received failing grades, and was expelled from college in the middle of her second year (age 19½) to return to live with her parents.

At home, her functioning continued to deteriorate. During the 4½ years prior to this evaluation, the patient worked occasionally but could never hold a job for more than 2 months. She dated sporadically, usually socially inappropriate men, and was sexually promiscuous. Relationships with men were characterized by desperate clinging, alternating with bitter fighting, leading to a rapid breakup of the relationship. At the same time, acrimonious fighting with her parents increased, particularly with mother, and especially when the mother attempted to push her into more traditional activities, that is, returning to school, dating appropriate men, getting a good job, etc. These always ended in screaming fights. The patient began an intermittent pattern of banging her head against the wall and scratching her arms with nails or other sharp objects, particularly after fights with mother.

She had been treated by three competent psychoanalytic or psychodynamic therapists during the prior 4½ years, but no treatment had lasted more than 4 months. She left two of the treatments impulsively, enraged because the therapists were "silent, withdrawn, and disinterested." The third treatment ended when the therapist began to confront her about her increasingly frequent telephone calls to his home and refusals to leave his waiting room. On one occasion, she arrived at his home extremely distraught and intoxicated at 4:00 A.M. When she was confronted, the patient became furious and abruptly quit treatment.

One of the therapists had suggested a psychopharmacology consultation. The patient was treated with low-dose thiothixene for a brief time, developed mild akathisia, became furious at the pharmacologist, and refused to return to him or to consider any other pharmacologic interventions.

Psychotic symptomatology was denied, as was any recent ingestion of street drugs. The soft-thought disorder described above was intermittently present during the interview. Neurotic symptomatology was denied. The patient appeared to be of above-average intelligence, although her fund of knowledge was less than anticipated. She did not appear either depressed or hypomanic. She was a slightly heavy, moderately attractive woman, looking about her stated age, and dressed appropriately, in a slightly "Bohemian" attire. With about 3 minutes remaining in the first session—

EVALUATOR: We have just a few minutes left. I'm not clear what you want to change in your life. What is it that you find particularly distressing in your current life situation?

PATIENT: (*Explodes again*) That's a stupid question! What do you think I want to change? What would you want to change if you were in my situation?

EVALUATOR: I can't help but be impressed by the sudden change in the way you're relating to me. What happened?

PATIENT: Nothing happened. You just asked a really stupid question!

The patient's attitude suddenly changes again at the end of the session. The change is notable for its abruptness, lack of obvious etiology, and the appearance of projective trends. It reveals her emotional lability, as well as the instability of her views of the interviewer. He has suddenly changed from a helpful professional to a stupid and insensitive person.

EVALUATOR: Perhaps. But it seemed to me that your whole attitude toward me changed when I said we'd have to stop in a few minutes.

The interviewer attempts to tie the change to the ending of the session. But what is so striking is the patient's behavior, particularly its explosive

In any event, I'll see you on Friday at—P.M. You might give some thought to your sudden attitude change in the meantime.

PATIENT: Yeah, yeah, yeah!

quality. This degree of affective explosiveness and dramatically changed view of the other person might raise a question in the interviewer's mind about subtle neurological impairment, such as Minimal Brain Dysfunction (MBD) or temporal lobe pathology.

Second Evaluative Interview

The patient arrived for the second session 10 minutes late, in a good mood, and explained "I couldn't find my car keys." This was not challenged. When the therapist asked for her thoughts about their first meeting, the patient replied, "I was really feeling good after I left. I really liked your explaining to me how you operate and why you were asking me about my problems. You seemed down to earth and I liked the fact that you talked a lot." She continued spontaneously talking about her previous therapists, painting them in totally negative terms. They were "idiots, withholding, exploitative of me, seeing me only for the money." In addition, the third therapist was a "wimp, weak, and indecisive, who let me totally control him." When asked if she had always felt so negatively about the previous therapists, she replied that she had liked all of them at the beginning, but that the treatments had rapidly soured. When asked what she had learned from her previous treatment experiences, she replied, "Absolutely nothing." In response to the interviewer's skeptical look, she reiterated, "Nothing they ever said was worth anything." When the therapist pressed, asking whether she couldn't recall *anything* positive about *any* of the previous therapists, she responded that she guessed they had tried hard and had meant well, but they just weren't able to be helpful to her because of their "severe personality problems."

The patient's father was 53 years old, an extremely successful lawyer, totally wrapped up in his profession, at which he worked 14–16 hours a day. She respected his accomplishments, thought he was very intelligent, but felt that she had received very little from him; in addition, he was an intermittent heavy drinker. Her mother was 54 years old, had never worked, and was a "slave" to the father, an angry, complaining, sour, and depressed woman. The patient had little respect for her mother, who had had episodes of postpartum depression after each of the first two children, both of which resolved with psychotherapy alone. The marriage was "awful," with little closeness and continual bickering, interrupted by explosive outbursts by both parents. The patient's siblings were both quite successful. Her sister, 6 years older, was a physiotherapist, married to a lawyer, and had two children. Her brother, 4 years older, was doing a residency in internal medicine. He was in his third year of psychoanalytic treatment, but the patient denied any significant psychopathology in either sibling.

The evaluator asked again about her treatment goals. She complained of the quality of her life, her inability to hold a job or to sustain a heterosexual relationship, her excessive possessiveness and then rejection of male partners, all of whom she felt were inferior to her, and her promiscuity. She wanted a more normal life with either a gratifying job, or a marriage and family. She felt confused about herself, not knowing either who she really was, or what she really wanted out of life. She rapidly returned to the subject of her parents, angrily denouncing them for their lack of acceptance of her and wishing that they would not be so demanding of her. The interviewer noted that she did not seem to consider living with her parents a problem.

The second history-gathering session ended on an up note; the patient seemed quite pleased with herself and stated she was looking forward to the next session. The soft-thought disorder noted above was again present. The patient mentioned several positive aspects of the interview, contrasting the evaluator with her previous therapists. The interviewer, however, found himself vaguely, but definitely, uncomfortable; the evaluation thus far had the quality of a transient "honeymoon"; when would it end?

That weekend, the evaluator received an emergency telephone call from the patient's mother. The patient was drunk, hysterical, and inflicting superficial cuts on both of her arms with a razor blade. The evaluator felt perplexed about how to respond; he did not have a treatment contract with the patient. He asked to speak to the patient, who was very drunk, alternately yelling and crying, and unable to communicate clearly.

The mother returned to the phone and the evaluator explained that there was no treatment contract in place; they were still in an evaluation phase. He suggested that the parents take her to the local emergency room for examination and appropriate treatment. The mother kept insisting that *she* needed to come in to talk to the doctor about the patient's problems, communicating her severe distress. The evaluator replied that he would discuss a family meeting with the patient at their next session, but that such a meeting had to include both parents as well as the patient. This decreased the mother's agitation somewhat, and she agreed to take the patient to the emergency room. She ended the phone call stating she would ask her husband to attend, but "I know he won't come."

Third Evaluative Interview

The patient arrived for the third session on time and enraged. The doctor "owed it" to her to see her when she was so distraught, and had shown a total lack of caring and responsibility by suggesting evaluation in an emergency room. She was "entitled" to be seen by the evaluator because "you're my doctor and you're responsible for me." The interviewer clarified that they were still in an evaluative phase and had not yet decided whether or not to work together. In addition, her intoxication had made any useful talk on the phone impossible. Most important, he could not imagine being "responsible" for her in the sense she implied, namely, that she was not responsible for her behavior. The patient calmed down slightly but remained angry and argumentative. When the interviewer inquired about the precipitants of the drinking and self-mutilation, she exploded again. Had the therapist seen her at the time of the crisis, he wouldn't have to ask these stupid questions now. Again the therapist clarified the realities of their relationship.

In a loud, angry, and disjointed fashion, the patient described how her mother had again begun arguing with her about dating a particular man and about getting a job. The patient had begun to feel increasingly depressed and hopeless, started to drink heavily, and did not have a clear memory of the ensuing events. She had a vague memory of cutting herself, said she really would rather have cut her mother's throat, and that she "couldn't take it at home any more." Her father had retired into his den and had also begun drinking.

The interviewer raised the issue of the mother's wish to come to a session and of his insistence that it include both parents. How did the patient feel about that? She again became angry but eventually agreed that it might be useful for the therapist "to see what I'm up against." She hoped the interviewer could "talk some sense into my mother and get her off my back." The patient also warned that her father would not attend and the therapist reiterated that her father had to be included.

The patient, suddenly and unexpectedly, looked guilty and embarrassed. In response to the interviewer's inquiry, she replied that she had lied about her early school history. She had had significant learning difficulties, had always felt stupid, and specifically had been diagnosed as dyslexic in the third grade and had received special tutoring. The patient seemed genuinely distressed about the lying, the learning difficulties, or both. She had wondered whether there was something wrong with her brain, particularly when in later years she found herself reversing numbers and letters while reading. After further elaboration of this history, the therapist praised her candor and commented that lack of truthfulness represented a serious problem to any psychotherapy. Patient and therapist together decided that psychological testing would be useful and an appropriate referral was made.

The final issue addressed in the third interview was the patient's intoxication and self-mutilation. The patient kept insisting that it had all been precipitated by the fight with mother, her rage at mother, and "anyhow, it wasn't really my fault because I was drunk." The interviewer wondered whether the behavior could possibly have had any connection to their previous meetings, or specifically to the previous session. The patient insisted that this was a ludicrous idea; the evaluator was looking for complicated explanations for simple events. The interviewer continued, speculating about a possible connection between the self-mutilation and the patient's extremely positive feelings toward him in the previous session. Was it possible that she had to try to destroy any treatment before it began? Or did she have to reassure herself that the therapist would accept that degree of upset, and upsetting, behavior? The patient responded that these were ridiculous ideas, that the drinking and cutting were totally irrelevant to the evaluation and the evaluator, and had been caused only by her being upset with her mother.

The mother called the next day, confirming that she would attend the family meeting. When the evaluator asked about the father, she insisted that he would not come. When asked whether father had been invited, she repeated that it would be a total waste of time; it was clear he had not been asked. The evaluator reiterated that the father must attend and that there would be no meeting without him.

Fourth Interview—Family Meeting

Father, mother, and patient appeared on time. The patient and her mother started arguing almost immediately, while the father looked distant and uncomfortable. When this behavior was confronted, the mother and patient stated that the father didn't want to be involved, while the father complained that he was systematically excluded by the patient and mother. He continued, complaining about the distant marital relationship and the mother's lack of availability to him; then the parents began a series of bitter counteraccusations. The patient appeared distant and saddened, and an occasional smile flitted across her face. When asked about this, she disparaged both parents; they were acting like "idiots and children." She denied smiling.

Both parents expressed their distress about the marital situation and about the patient. The mother began crying, the father yelling, and the session became increasingly disorganized. The interviewer intervened, and stated that (1) there were obviously major marital difficulties, and (2) it appeared that the patient and mother were actively collaborating to help both feel better, keeping the patient dependent, while the father withdrew into work and alcohol. Each was suffering in his or her own way. Why had the parents not sought help previously for their dysfunctional marriage?

Over the succeeding 15 minutes the interviewer repeated these points several times while both parents kept insisting that if only the patient would behave and be successful everything would be fine. The interviewer pointed out that in the session the patient was not overtly participating much, and yet major difficulties were obvious between the parents. He also stated that any alleviation of the distant parental relationship, any increase in their turning towards each other, would be helpful both for them and for the patient. She might feel freer to begin to pursue her own life, which they claimed was all they wanted. This last point, made repeatedly, apparently got across and the session ended with their agreeing to a referral to a dynamically trained marital therapist. Somewhat to the surprise of the interviewer, the marital treatment continued on a weekly basis over 18 months and appeared to lead to significant positive changes.

Psychological Testing

Psychological testing revealed that the patient had a full-scale IQ of 128, 130 verbal/125 performance. There was marked subtest variability on the WAIS, with poorest functioning on tasks affected by anxiety and depression. Thinking tended to be literal and concrete, with some cognitive slippage, but without evidence of MBD, Attention Deficit Disorder (ADD), or schizophrenia. There was some mixed laterality, but "this does not appear to be the primary source of the present difficulties, which appear secondary to personality issues."

Personality functioning was on a low borderline level, with considerable affective dyscontrol, identity diffusion, and primitive defensive operations. Splitting was prominent, with a predominance of devaluation. Self–other boundaries were weak and part–object representations common. Dependency needs were marked. A preoccupation with sex seemed to meet primarily oral dependent needs. The patient seemed to entertain magical expectations about psychotherapy, together with a need to spoil it and to make it come out badly. Sufficient affective dyscontrol was present to warrant possible consideration of medication.

The psychologist concluded, "the symptomatology that raised questions of ADD or dyslexia appears to be secondary to nonspecific ego weakness, further compromised by marked anxiety and depression. Following traditional assumptions, a generally supportive type of psychotherapy is indicated."

TASK 2: DIAGNOSTIC FORMULATION

The five axis DSM-III-R diagnosis is neither an academic exercise nor relevant only to research protocols. It is a central part of the diagnostic process and is extremely relevant to treatment planning. However, it is only the first step in that process, and requires extensive supplementation to achieve the full diagnostic formulation required for skillful treatment planning (Perry, Cooper, & Michels, 1987; Schlesinger, 1969).

The first two axes of DSM-III-R encompass all currently diagnosable psychiatric disorders. The focus of Axis I is specific syndromes or symptoms, for example, Schizophrenia or Panic Disorder, while that of Axis II is the personality disorders (and developmental disorders in children), for example, Borderline or Antisocial Personality disorders. Patients with an Axis II disorder, for example, Borderline Personality Disorder, frequently also meet criteria for an Axis I disorder, for example an Affective Disorder, or Eating or Substance Abuse Disorders. Axis III allows the clinician to identify relevant physical disorders. They may be contributory to the psychiatric symptomatology, for example, Seizure Disorder in a BPD patient, or important in the psychiatric management of the patient, for example, Diabetes Mellitus in a BPD patient. Axis IV rates the severity of psychosocial stressors on a one to six (six is most severe) scale. Axis V is an opportunity to rate the patient's overall functioning on the 90-point Global Assessment of Functioning (GAF) Scale. The evaluator rates both the current level of function and the patient's highest level over at least several months during the preceding year.

Focusing specifically on the patient with BPD, concurrent Axis I pathology often demands the primary treatment focus. For example, somatic treatment of the severely depressed BPD patient takes precedence over treatment of the character pathology. The same applies to the severely anorectic patient with BPD, who should approach normal body weight before a major therapeutic focus on the personality disorder is appropriate. On the other hand, minor affective disorders in BPD patients require complex judgments about treatment. The therapist might choose an initial psychotherapeutic focus on the personality disorder, a primarily pharmacologic approach to the Dysthymia or Cyclothymia, or a combined treatment approach, concomitantly or sequentially.

Other Axis II personality disorders or traits affect the treatment choice for the BPD patient. Concurrent Antisocial Personality Disorder makes any outpatient psychotherapy difficult to impossible, while marked paranoid or schizotypal features would likely incline the therapist toward a more supportive psychotherapy, with or without adjunctive low-dose neuroleptics. Concomitant Narcissistic Personality Disorder or traits lead the therapist to anticipate transferences and resistances centered around splitting, omnipotence, idealization, and devaluation, while a marked Dependent Personality Disorder could raise the fear of whether an intensive, long-term psychotherapy can be successfully terminated.

The relationship of Axis III physical disorders to treatment planning is illustrated above. The quantification of psychosocial stressors is more relevant to acute Axis I syndromes than to personality disorders, but attention to these stressors may help to identify areas for possible environmental intervention in the future. The Axis V quantification of overall function is highly relevant to the choice of supportive versus exploratory psychotherapy, as well as to the determination of treatment goals, potential for change, ability to sustain the treatment relationship, and so forth.

Having completed the five axis DSM-III-R diagnosis, the second step in the full diagnostic formulation involves a detailed consideration of the patient's assets and liabilities, such as level of intelligence, "likability," capacity for introspection and thinking in psychological terms, motivations, talents and successes, social supports, and so on. These factors are all relevant to treatment choice and generally correlate positively with Axis V ratings of overall function. The patient's vulnerability to psychotic regressions is relevant, as is the quality of object relations. A complete lack of close relationships, currently and in the past, should make the evaluator leery about undertaking an intensive, exploratory psychotherapy.

The third step is a brief formulation of the patient's core psychodynamic issues, particularly the evaluation of ego functions and of genetic factors. The former describes the patient's main areas of conflict and preferred defensive and coping styles. The balance of fixation versus regression, and the predominance of higher level versus lower level defenses, are highly relevant to treatment choice. Significant genetic (gene-related and psychogenetic) issues include a history of physical or sexual abuse during childhood; a history of ADD, MBD, or Dyslexia; a strong family history of Affective Disorder or substance abuse; and so forth.

Relevant, but not identical, to the dynamic formulation is the determination of the patient's level of personality organization (Kernberg, 1984). Almost all patients who meet DSM-III-R criteria for BPD have BPO; the reverse is not true. However, there are occasional patients who meet criteria for BPD, who on careful interviewing turn out to have a Psychotic Personality Organization, with definite, usually subtle, loss of reality testing. These patients are often high-level schizoaffective patients with significant Axis II pathology, rather than suffering only from a personality disorder.

Personality organization, as defined by Kernberg, consists of three discrete categories: Neurotic, Borderline, and Psychotic Personality Or-

TABLE 5.1. Personality Organizations

	Identity	Defenses	Reality testing
Neurotic	Integration	Higher level	Intact
Borderline	Diffusion	Lower level	Intact
Psychotic	Diffusion	Lower level	Lost

ganizations. The three levels of personality organization are determined, in turn, by three major "structural" variables: identity integration versus diffusion, predominantly higher level (centered around repression) versus lower level (centered around splitting) "primitive" defenses, and maintenance versus loss of reality testing (see Table 5.1). Thus Neurotic Organization is distinguished from Borderline Organization by the two variables of identity and defenses, while Borderline Organization is differentiated from Psychotic Organization by the variable of reality testing.

In summary, a complete diagnostic assessment starts with a five-axis DSM-III-R diagnosis and is supplemented by at least the additional factors listed above. No single factor will determine the treatment by itself. An appropriate treatment plan can only result from the careful integration of all of the relevant diagnostic elements.

Clinical Material

The patient clearly met criteria for DSM-III-R BPD. Her functioning over time was characterized by intense and unstable interpersonal relationships; impulsivity in the areas of sex, substance abuse, and eating; affective instability and inappropriate intense anger; self-mutilating behavior; severe identity disturbance, manifested by a vague and chaotic lifestyle; and frantic efforts to avoid abandonment. She did not complain of feelings of emptiness or boredom, even when queried. Thus she met seven of the eight DSM-III-R BPD criteria. In addition, narcissistic traits were present, illustrated by the entitlement in the evaluative interviews, plus marked tendencies to project and to externalize difficulties. On Axis I she met criteria for the diagnosis of Dysthymia. The five Axis DSM-III-R diagnosis was

Axis I: Dysthymia
           Rule out current substance abuse
Axis II: BPD, with narcissistic and paranoid traits
Axis III: 0
Axis IV: 2 (mild)
Axis V: Present GAF = 45
           Highest GAF during past year = 45

Assets and Liabilities

On the positive side, the patient was intelligent, seemed genuinely concerned about her aimless, chaotic life, and seemed to want to improve at least aspects of it. The therapist found her likable, while anticipating a very difficult treatment. She appeared to have some moderate capacity for thinking in psychological terms, and there was no evidence of psychotic regressions.

On the negative side, there were limitations in her capacity for introspection, a lack of specific talents or successes in her life, and questionable social supports. There were no close peer relationships, either male or female. Her three failed exploratory treatments, and the abrupt unilateral terminations, were negative factors.

The evaluator was surprised by his positive feelings about treating her and wondered how much was a response to the patient and how much might be due to other factors, such as succeeding where others had failed or accepting the challenge of a very difficult case.

Formulation

The evaluator viewed the patient as struggling primarily with issues of symbiosis versus autonomy, with little evidence of regression from oedipal conflicts. There was marked use of primitive defenses, with splitting and devaluation notable and some beginning idealization present in the transference, with little evidence of higher level defenses. The evaluator viewed the patient's tendency to project as a potentially serious problem and felt that this should be a major focus of the early work. The patient's apparent comfort in living with her parents, her suggesting that they owed this to her, her focus on "They're driving me crazy," and the attribution of all past treatment difficulties to the therapists illustrate her dependency, entitlement, and marked tendencies to externalize and project. The parents' marital conflict was viewed as contributory to the patient's difficulties with autonomy, while their willingness to undertake a treatment for themselves was a positive prognostic sign. There were no other striking genetic issues; the evaluator's concern about MBD or Dyslexia was allayed by the psychological testing.

Personality Organization

The patient's personality organization was borderline, as demonstrated by severe identity diffusion and predominant use of lower level primitive defenses, both in the context of relatively intact reality testing.

TASK 3: TREATMENT PLANNING

In discussing the planning of appropriate treatment for the patient with BPD, two general principles deserve emphasis:

1. There is no "correct" treatment of the patient with BPD, and this applies equally to psychopharmacology and to psychotherapy. The patients who meet DSM-III-R BPD criteria are too heterogeneous a group to be appropriately treated by any one treatment modality. Concomitant Axis I diagnoses, associated Axis II diagnoses or traits, level of function (GAF score), and severity of BPD pathology (five of eight versus eight of eight criteria), as well as the other factors noted above, such as intelligence, motivation, likability, honesty, capacity for introspection, and so forth, all influence the choice of treatment best suited for the specific patient with BPD.

2. The art of treatment selection consists of achieving the closest possible fit between the treatment selected and the full evaluative and diagnostic assessment (Schlesinger, 1969). Controlled studies of specific treatment interventions for specific subtypes of BPD (Hurt & Clarkin, 1990) are lacking, and until such a scientific base is available treatment selection remains, by necessity, an art.

In addition, I believe that the majority of BPD patients are most effectively treated by supportive, rather than exploratory, treatments. Although a generally supportive model (Linehan, 1987a, 1987b) is receiving increasing attention in the literature, it is anchored in cognitive/behavioral, rather than psychodynamic, principles. The psychodynamic clinician interested in treating borderline patients has available a number of modified psychoanalytic approaches (Adler, 1985; Kernberg et al., 1989; Masterson, 1981), but no supportive treatment based on psychodynamic principles.

Frances, Clarkin, and Perry (1984) list several parameters to be considered in choosing an appropriate treatment for any patient:

1. The setting—inpatient versus day hospital versus outpatient
2. The format—individual versus marital versus family versus group
3. The orientation—exploratory versus directive (behavioral) versus experiential
4. The duration and frequency—time-limited versus time-unlimited

In addition, they discuss combined treatments, either concomitantly or sequentially, and give serious attention to the recommendation of "no treatment." Their schema is a useful outline for thinking about the process of treatment selection, and the reader is referred to that book for further details. More specific to the borderline patient, Figure 5.1 can be useful in focusing on the sequential decisions to be made in planning treatment for these patients.

The first decision that the evaluator of the borderline patient must make is whether any treatment is indicated. Psychotherapy is clearly effective (Smith, Glass, & Miller, 1980), but any effective treatment can also produce negative results; only a totally ineffectual treatment is with-

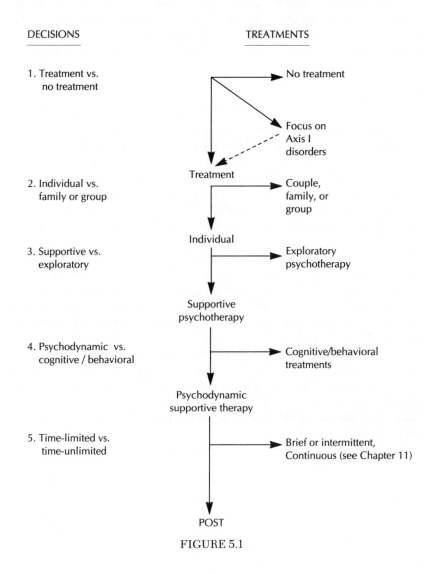

FIGURE 5.1

out risk. Thus the decision to begin any psychiatric intervention should include a careful weighing of the risks and benefits of applying those interventions to the specific patient at the particular time. On the other hand, the patient with BPD has serious difficulties, usually disruptive of crucial areas of her life. What would lead the evaluator to decide not to treat such serious psychopathology?

One group of patients who should not be treated are those who refuse to meet even minimal requirements for treatment. The actively substance-abusing borderline patient who refuses to stop abusing, or the eating-disordered patient who refuses even minimal requirements for safety built into the treatment (but is not ill enough to require involuntary hospitalization), are examples of such patients. A third such patient is described below.

Case Example

This 22-year-old single female met criteria for both Borderline and Narcissistic Personality Disorders. She insisted at the end of the evaluation that the evaluator/potential psychotherapist had to tell her as much about his private life and inner thoughts as he now knew about hers. To do otherwise would be to begin the treatment relationship on an unequal footing, which the patient experienced as unbearably humiliating. In spite of this unusual request, there was no evidence of a major defect in reality testing—the patient was not psychotic.

All attempts on the part of the evaluator to explain the unreasonableness of her request, to educate the patient about the rationales for the usual psychotherapeutic arrangements, and to investigate as fully as possible the patient's sensitivity to humiliation were unsuccessful. The patient recognized that her request was very unusual but repeatedly stated, "That's how I feel and I feel it very strongly." Eventually the evaluator pointed out that the patient was making treatment impossible, to which the patient replied that she preferred not being treated to relinquishing her demands. The evaluator's final comment was that the patient's intransigence made treatment impossible at this time, but she should feel free to reconsult him should she feel that she could accept the more usual arrangements.

The patient left, but reconsulted the same therapist several months later willing to begin treatment under standard conditions. Her explanation for her previous demands was, "I knew it was unreasonable, but I had to prove to myself that you would not give in to my crazy demands. When you didn't, and you maintained your position and didn't call me, I felt I could safely begin treatment with you." Needless to say, the same issues arose repetitively during the treatment.

Another group of patients probably better not treated are those who have repetitively experienced severe negative therapeutic reactions in past treatments, becoming worse than they were prior to treatment. Negative therapeutic reactions must be differentiated from inappropriate and inadequate treatments, but with patients who clearly were worse after adequate treatments, the evaluator should very carefully consider any recommendation of further treatment. A different modality of treatment might be offered, but often the patients are better off untreated or treated with the most minimal interventions.

In patients with a serious, even life-threatening, Axis I diagnosis, that disorder must become the initial focus of treatment, with the BPD receding into the background for the moment. Examples are major affective disorders with serious endogenous features and/or active suicidality, and eating-disordered patients with potentially life-threatening symptoms. Some of these patients, after treatment of the Axis I disorder, will wish to seek further treatment for their personality disorder, but many will not. The evaluator or therapist should not hesitate to make his opinion clear and stress the inter-relatedness of the Axis I and Axis II disorders; nor should he be reticent about exploring the patient's fears about further treatment and educating the patient about the reasons for such treatment. Nevertheless, a significant number of such patients will still choose to limit their treatment to the Axis I disorder, and this wish is respected.

Once it is decided that treatment is indicated, the second decision relates to the size of the patient group. Is the patient best treated individually, in a marital couple, a family treatment, or a group treatment? A very pathological marital relationship between two partners of Borderline Organization may be more effectively treated in a couple therapy, where the constant projection and projective identification can be easily diagnosed and confronted; this is particularly so when financial limitations make two individual treatments impractical.

Family therapy can be preferable for an unmotivated borderline adolescent from a very pathological family, who comes for evaluation only under extreme pressure from his parents, and who will strenuously resist individual treatment for himself. Such a patient may be more accepting of a treatment that focuses on the family pathology, taking the exclusive attention off his individual problems. An initial family approach may sometimes allow the adolescent to undertake an individual treatment for himself later on.

Borderline patients who tend to get into intense and interminable individual treatments, those whose less attractive personality attributes can be more successfully confronted by other patients than by a therapist, or those for whom a group offers more opportunity for examination of the extreme transferences that result from marked splitting operations—these and other kinds of BPD patients may be better treated in a group than individually.

Assuming the choice of an individual treatment, the next major variable is whether the treatment should be primarily exploratory or primarily supportive. As described elsewhere (p. 54), all dynamic psychotherapies are actually varying mixtures of exploratory and supportive interventions, and are most reasonably conceptualized on a supportive/exploratory continuum. Such factors as the severity of the borderline symptomatology; the patient's motivation, psychological mindedness, intelligence, goals, and likability; combined into an integrated view of the patient, will allow the evaluator to plan a treatment appropriately located on the supportive/exploratory continuum. The specifics of this decision are discussed in a previous chapter (Chapter 4).

If the decision is for a primarily supportive psychotherapy, the next choice is whether it will be psychodynamically oriented or follow a cognitive/behavioral model. Many of the factors mentioned above are also relevant to this decision. Borderline patients who tend to be concrete in their thinking, who see their disorders as due to a biological abnormality, who tend to act out on the environment or on their own bodies rather than to think about and experience feelings, may do better in a cognitive/behavioral treatment. The opposite attributes would suggest a psychodynamic treatment. The presenting symptomatology also plays a role. The patient whose difficulties center around impulsivity, or food and substance abuse, might better be treated with a cognitive/behavioral modality, while the patient whose complaints are of inner confusion, identity problems and interpersonal difficulties might more effectively be treated with a dynamic approach. These are the most general of guidelines, and it is only the whole picture of the patient that emerges from the diagnostic assessment that will adequately determine the appropriate treatment modality.

The final issue is that of duration. In Chapter 11, Perry describes "Intermittent Continuous Therapy," a series of brief crisis focused interventions in the context of a lifelong commitment to the borderline patient. The dynamically oriented supportive therapy described in this book can be done in a time-limited fashion, but is usually fairly prolonged and in some cases without a definitive termination. Acute crises in the life of the BPD patient can be handled with a brief supportive treatment, but longer term treatments are usually required for any effective approach to the personality disorder itself.

Clinical Material

There was no Axis I disorder in the patient that demanded immediate attention. Therefore the first decision to be made was whether or not the patient should be treated. Her rapid, premature, and unilateral terminations of her three previous treatments made this a legitimate question. However, there was no clear evidence of negative therapeutic reactions, nor were there other definite contraindications to treatment. Therefore the therapist decided that another attempt at psychotherapy was indicated, but that a different modality was preferable. Although there were major family difficulties, the parents had already accepted a marital treatment of their own. In addition, the patient was 24 years old and her stated treatment goals would not ideally be addressed in a family treatment. The decision was made that the patient would be best treated in an individual treatment format.

Because of the evaluator's strong feelings that the treatment should be of a different modality from the three previous failed attempts, it was easy to make the decision for a primarily supportive treatment (the previous treatments had all been primarily exploratory). Clinical indicators also suggested a primarily supportive treatment. Although the patient had a strong tendency to action, including attacking her own body, there was no major psychosomatic illness, nor was the symptomatology primarily related to acting out on the environment. Rather she complained of inner confusion and of disturbed interpersonal relations, and demonstrated severe identity diffusion in her chaotic and dysfunctional lifestyle. Therefore, the evaluator decided on a psychodynamically oriented supportive therapy, rather than a cognitive/behavioral treatment.

The final decision regarding the duration of treatment was made on the basis of the lack of acute crisis, the patient's goals of significant changes in her lifestyle, and the positive indicators of motivation to change, high intelligence, and likability. For these reasons, the evaluator decided on a time-unlimited psychotherapy.

Other factors that influenced the choice of a time-unlimited, dynamically oriented, supportive psychotherapy included the patient's severe borderline pathology, as manifested by seven out of eight BPD criteria, a GAF score of 45 (present and past year), and the patient's narcissistic entitlement and marked tendencies to externalization. Because the evaluator considered it possible that the treatment might eventually move into a more exploratory mode, he decided on a twice per week frequency, rather than the more usual once weekly schedule of supportive therapy.

The therapist was somewhat surprised at his wish to treat this patient and viewed his countertransference (broad sense) response to the patient as indicating something positive about her that was difficult to define. He also noted that his decision to treat the patient did not minimize the anticipation of an extremely tumultuous and problematic treatment, and occurred when the therapist was not actively seeking additional treatment hours. It seemed to have to do specifically with the patient, although the therapist speculated about possible competitive feelings toward the colleagues who had failed with the patient. However, he recalled that he had also treated a number of borderline patients who terminated abruptly and prematurely. He also believed that some patients had to run through a number of therapists and that the outcome partially depended on the "fit" between therapist and patient. He did not feel that countertransference (narrow sense) factors were playing a major role in his decision to treat the patient; instead, it indicated something positive, but vague and hard to characterize, about the patient.

TASK 4: CONTRACT SETTING

Contract setting is the final part of the treatment planning process. It occurs in all psychotherapies, at least around issues of duration, frequency, fees, missed sessions, etc., but it is particularly crucial in the treatment of borderline patients because of the marked potential for acting out that characterizes these patients. Acting out, in turn, results from the widespread use of primitive defenses and the impulsivity that shape the expressions of the inevitable negative transferences. The purpose of the contract setting is to structure and thereby safeguard the treatment by attempting to predict patient behaviors that will threaten the viability of the treatment. These anticipated behaviors are identified, discussed with the patient, and decisions are made about how they will be handled. The contract sets up a realistic backdrop, a set of agreements that can be referred to and used when major resistances and acting out threaten to sabotage the treatment.

The terms of the contract are determined not only by the patient's potential acting out, but also by the therapist's tolerance for specific patient behaviors. The therapist should not make contractual arrangements that gratify patient's needs when he is likely to resent them later on. This will inevitably lead to growing irritation and anger toward the patient as the therapist feels increasingly exploited. He should also always keep in mind that excessive gratifications of the patient often represent countertransference (narrow sense) acting out of the therapist. In short, we all have our deficiencies and strengths, and we need to be realistic about our tolerances and accepting of our limitations. If a particular patient really needs more than the therapist can comfortably deliver, it is far better to refer the patient on than to begin a treatment that, from the start, at best contains the likelihood of severe countertransference difficulties and at worst the seeds of its own destruction.

Consider, as an example of a common problem, the likelihood that the patient will make between-session phone calls to the therapist with some frequency. Authors vary in their responses to this behavior. Selzer et al. (1987) and Kernberg et al. (1989) appear to view any phone calls, except in an absolute emergency, as an acting out and therefore a resistance to treatment. On the other hand, Adler (1985), based more in a Kohutian frame, emphasizes the borderline patient's inability to maintain positive internal images of the therapist without such contacts, and he is accepting, even encouraging, of them.

In deciding how to structure the contract to effectively deal with this behavior so that it does not become onerous to the therapist or excessively gratifying to the patient, the following factors are relevant:

1. The therapist's estimate of the patient's clinical need for between-session contacts.
2. The therapist's availability, time constraints, and tolerance for extra contacts between sessions.
3. The supportive/exploratory mix of the psychotherapy.
4. The therapist's estimation of exploitative and entitled qualities in the patient and in the specific behavior. Gratification of entitled exploitativeness can lead to subsequent guilt and self-punishment in the patient; in addition, marked entitlement is maladaptive and should not be supported.
5. The therapist's awareness of his countertransferential tendencies to be either excessively gratifying or excessively restrictive.

Kernberg et al. (1989) suggest that the therapist, having ascertained the likely patterns of patient acting out from the history, interview behaviors, and accounts of past treatments, sets down the guidelines for dealing with those behaviors in the initial contract. As an example, a fall of body weight below a certain level in an anorectic patient means immediate hospitalization.

In my view, this structure building and limit setting is appropriate, but too one sided. In supportive psychotherapy, and probably in all psychotherapies, this can be better accomplished by identifying the potential problems and then setting response guidelines in joint collaborative discussions with the patient. For example, "When your weight falls below X pounds, you are in serious medical danger. Can you see any alternatives to going into the hospital at that point? What else might be appropriate?"

The behavioral limits are similar in both cases because options for appropriate responses are limited in such situations. The process, however, is different—more collaborative, more respectful of the patient, and, I believe, reaches the same end point with less conflict, fewer hurt feelings in the patient, and an early collaborative experience. However, the therapist must always retain final control of the contract arrangements so that he doesn't allow guidelines that he cannot tolerate with reasonable comfort.

Returning to our patient:

Clinical Material

EVALUATOR: I've been thinking about your difficulties, our talks together thus far, and the psychological testing, and I feel that we have a reasonable chance of being able to work effectively together. . . .

PATIENT: Good, let's start.

EVALUATOR: I suggest that we meet twice a week, at ___ and at ___, and my fee per session is ___. I will present a bill at the end of each month, and would like it paid within 10 days. I expect you to make every effort to keep your appointments. If a problem arises I expect at least 48 hours notice, and it must be absolutely clear that you cannot keep the appointment. There may be some sessions which you feel are not possible for you to make where you will be charged. We can discuss those situations together, but the final decision is mine. I am away at times, either on business or vacation, and I will give you as much advance notice as I can of those absences. Is all of this acceptable to you?

PATIENT: I don't like the idea of having to pay for sessions that I miss, even though it's not really my money; but I do accept. It's like before, sort of.

EVALUATOR: If and when you begin to work and earn money, I would expect

The modal frequency of dynamic supportive therapy is one session per week. However, this is not fixed, and the actual frequency can vary from one session per month to two sessions per week. I would not be comfortable with a supportive psychotherapy that met more than twice a week, except in acute crisis situations where this may be clinically necessary. Thus, although the twice a week schedule here is unusual, it is certainly acceptable.

The therapist, in setting up arrangements for missed appointments, is deviating from the psychoanalytic rule that the patient is always responsible for them. On the other hand, some supportive therapists would be more lenient than this therapist about excusing missed sessions. This is a clinical judgment and a matter of

that you would take responsibility for the fee or for an appropriate part of it.

PATIENT: That's fair if I can afford it.

EVALUATOR: Now let's talk about some possible problems that might arise in the treatment, and decide together how to handle them.

style, and the arrangements presented here are reasonable, but certainly not the only acceptable ones. Wisely, the therapist states that the final decision about charging for missed sessions remains in his hands. The alternative is to open a channel for serious acting out around missed sessions and the likelihood of bitter arguments about who is right, what is allowed, and who makes the decision.

PATIENT: I don't know what you're talking about.

EVALUATOR: Well, for example, most recently the mutilation of your body. And the alcohol that played a role in your hurting yourself. How can we most sensibly deal with those problems if or when they should arise again?

PATIENT: I'm not doing drugs these days, and that amount of drinking was strictly a flake (sic). I don't see the problem.

EVALUATOR: Using drugs or alcohol to change the way you feel or to avoid uncomfortable feelings can become a serious problem. I would ask that you continue to not take street drugs at all, and that you limit yourself to a small amount of social drinking. Should either drugs or alcohol become a significant problem, I am going to insist that you join AA or NA and attend on a regular basis. If it becomes too severe, it can destroy the treatment.

Up until this point the issues dealt with in the contract setting have been issues common to all psychotherapies, although the arrangements differ from those of the usual psychoanalysis or exploratory psychotherapy. Here, however, the therapist begins to attend to the specifics of contract setting as applied to borderline patients. These patients are extremely prone to acting out and the acting out frequently destroys the treatment. Therefore, it is in the best interest of the patient, and of the therapy, that behaviors likely to be destructive to the treatment are identified beforehand and structures are set up to deal with them. Failure to do so leaves the patient and the treatment at the

PATIENT: I think you're overdoing the whole thing, but yes, it's OK, if it becomes a problem. I don't want it to get control of my life either. Yes, I will go to AA if things get out of control.

EVALUATOR: In terms of the mutilation, it's not something I can effectively deal with over the telephone. If you can allow yourself to experience the feelings that lead to cutting rather than immediately cutting yourself, I hope that we will be able to understand eventually what kinds of feelings lead to that behavior. In the meantime, since I can't do much about it, I would like us to consider your hurting your body as your problem, to be talked about fully in the following sessions should it occur. If necessary, you'll need to get evaluated and treated in your local emergency room.

PATIENT: I don't expect that to happen much either, and I will accept the responsibility and go to an emergency room if I need to.

EVALUATOR: Good. Now, more serious problems have to do with your quitting three previous treatments unilaterally and prematurely. And in one case it sounds like you were really intruding into the therapist's personal life. How can we prevent those kinds of problems?

PATIENT: I don't think that will happen either because I feel very differently with you.

EVALUATOR: You may feel differently right now, but I think it is quite likely mercy at the patient's self-destructiveness and destructiveness to others.

Note particularly that because the therapist has decided on a supportive treatment, he is presenting the problems as joint difficulties for both therapist and patient. Thus, "How can we most sensibly deal with those problems . . . ?" He also begins with the behaviors that have occurred most recently, and thus are freshest in the patient's mind. Referring to the problem of substance abuse, the therapist takes a strong position and does so unilaterally; the patient is minimizing and denying the problems. In borderline patients with substance-abuse problems, these can rapidly lead to a meaningless "pseudo-treatment," wasting the time of both participants.

My personal preference would have been to discuss this in somewhat greater detail with the patient, attempt some undermining of the denial, and to set up the same limits but in a more collaborative fashion. Perhaps in response to his unilateral presentation, the patient continues to minimize the problems, but she also wants to please the therapist, and to begin the treatment. Thus she agrees to conditions she has not actively participated in establishing.

that you will feel at times the same rejection, anger, and wish to quit that you felt before. I think we should both be aware of that and concerned about it, so that if it happens again we can remember this discussion. But the important thing is that you honestly face the fact that you will probably feel all those things again, and try to talk about the feelings instead of impulsively stopping.

PATIENT: OK, OK, I'll try, I'll do my best, lay off already!

EVALUATOR: I have the general feeling that you're minimizing this potential problem . . . and all the problems for that matter . . . as though you've decided that you want to start treatment with me and you'll agree to anything. What do you think?

PATIENT: I do want to start treatment with you, but I'm certainly not lying. And I don't think I'm bullshitting you either. If I say I'll do my best, I'll do my best.

EVALUATOR: You also need to be aware that I have been more active and talkative in these initial sessions in order to learn as much as I can about you. It is likely that I will talk less during the treatment, and, again, it is not at all unlikely that you will feel toward me some of the same feelings you had towards the other doctors. I think you

The therapist presents guidelines for dealing with self-mutilation, also in a unilateral fashion and without adequate discussion with the patient. Again, I feel it would have been preferable to engage her in further discussions of the self-mutilating behavior and its motivations, leading to a bilateral agreement about responses to the behaviors. The therapist is going on about rules at great length, while the patient continues to minimize the difficulties; this is not an ideally collaborative process. The patient appears to be willing to agree to almost anything in order to get started in treatment.

The therapist begins to undermine the patient's minimalization and denial, and the patient responds with annoyance. Finally, the therapist confronts her denial and the patient responds with a reassuring, but not very convincing, answer.

Once again, I feel that this contract-setting process is too one sided, and the therapist too long winded. I have no conviction from the material that the patient really understands the issues and is really experiencing affectively what she is agreeing to.

should assume that some or all of that will happen again, that you will be angry and tempted to again leave treatment prematurely. Hopefully you won't act on it impulsively, but allow time for the feelings to be experienced and hopefully to be understood, so that you don't need to act on them as automatically as you did before.

This brings us to the issues of my privacy and phone calls. If I understand correctly, you began calling one of the previous therapists almost nightly, and that when he questioned this, you immediately quit. That's not good for you because you lost your therapist, and the treatment that you need so much.

PATIENT: But I don't get it. What am I supposed to do when I'm upset and I need somebody to talk to and I can't talk to my parents? Call Dial a Prayer?

EVALUATOR: You certainly are entitled to call me in an emergency. However, you must understand that I have other activities and responsibilities, and I cannot accept frequent phone calls from patients.

PATIENT: Well then what am I supposed to do when I'm upset?

EVALUATOR: First of all, it is possible to just sit when you're upset and experience the upsetness, and come and talk about it in the next session; you don't need to immediately do anything. Second, I hope that in time you will find people to talk with other than myself or your parents. The important thing for you to realize is that although I will not refuse your phone calls if you are in an emergency situation, this also has a serious potential danger— that excessive needs to call me may

The contract pseudoalliance finally breaks down over the issue of phone calls, but I believe the groundwork for it has been laid since the beginning of the contract setting. Perhaps it is the nature of the issue involved, the patient's access to the therapist between sessions, that finally arouses her from her seeming agreeableness but relative nonparticipation. Finally, one has the impression of two people intensely involved with each other, trying to settle a conflictual issue. But again, the therapist appears to be arguing with the patient and unilaterally setting restrictions, rather than promoting discussion and negotiation.

conflict with my other responsibilities and needs. I think that to some extent we can "play it by ear" and see what happens. But you must understand that I don't want you to call me except in an emergency situation, and that it is likely, if the calls become excessive, that I will have to help you control them by setting strict limits.

PATIENT: I don't like that at all. I don't understand this. You mean when I'm really upset I can't call you? . . . when I'm *really* upset?

EVALUATOR: That is both correct and incorrect. If you are terribly upset, and the calls aren't excessive and don't take up too much time, that's OK. But if I feel that you are abusing the privilege, calling me every time you're upset, or really upset but consuming too much of my time, I will limit the calls from you. You have to realize that.

PATIENT: This totally pisses me off. What am I paying you for? I have every right to call you if I'm upset and I have no one to talk to.

EVALUATOR: This is clearly a problem and I'm glad it's out in the open. You do not have the right to call me any time you feel upset. We have decided to meet on a twice a week basis; that is the treatment. In addition, I am telling you that in an emergency situation we can talk on the phone. But I am feeling now that by your insistence that you can call me any time you want to, that you feel entitled to do so knowing that it will interfere with my other commitments, and that I will end up resenting it, that we are right up against a problem that could very well sink the treat-

The patient is intensely involved now. She expresses the feeling that she is entitled to call the therapist any time she is upset, and the therapist responds that she does not have the right. The therapist is entirely correct in setting limits on the phone calls, but he could have done it more skillfully by promoting further discussion and patient participation in the rules setting. This would take more time. Sometimes contract setting can take three or four sessions, which is time well spent. Instead, one gets the feeling here that both partici-

ment before it starts. That doesn't seem in your best interest. What are your thoughts?

pants are rushing to get the structures set and move on to the treatment. However, contract setting is a crucial part of the treatment process with these patients; in addition, the negotiation of structures is easily integrated with simultaneous attention to the patient's psychological problems.

PATIENT: I already told you I don't like it at all. But I want to start treatment with you. I could lie to you and tell you I won't call you at all and then start calling you once we get started, but I chose not to do that and you should respect my honesty. On the other hand, I realize that you do have other things in your life, I don't want to destroy my treatment this time, I really don't, and I will make every effort to keep any phone calls infrequent and reasonable.

When the therapist raises the threat of the argument destroying the treatment before it starts, the patient backs down and responds in a conciliatory fashion. But she also reveals her real motivations, "But I want to start treatment with you," and "I don't want to destroy my treatment this time, I really don't."

EVALUATOR: I appreciate that, and I appreciate your honesty. Talking straight about your feelings here is extremely important; lying will only sabotage your own treatment. I think we're starting treatment with a potential time bomb in the phone calls issue, but it also feels tolerable to me. I guess we'll both have to have some trust, keep in mind that the phone issue could become a major problem . . . we can agree about that, get started, and see how it actually goes.

The therapist acknowledges his awareness of problems in the contract setting but nevertheless is willing to begin the treatment. The patient responds by parroting what she knows the therapist wants to hear, another sign of a less than ideally successful contract setting.

PATIENT: That makes a lot of sense to me.

EVALUATOR: What about other feelings that led to your leaving your previous treatments?

This dialogue illustrates the problems that can result from too one sided a contract setting. The patient must be truly involved in the process, and hopefully even suggest ways of handling the problems that are likely to come

PATIENT: I've already told you that I don't think it will be the same here, but apparently you don't believe me. If what you want me to say is that I am aware that I will feel rejected and frustrated if you don't talk as much as I'd like, then I'm aware of it, and I will make every effort not to run out of treatment when I feel rejected or angry. Look, that's the best I can do. What do you want? I can't give you an iron-clad guarantee.

EVALUATOR: I'm not asking for an iron-clad guarantee. We are two separate individuals working together on a common task, and as long as each of us does the best he can, that's all that can be reasonably asked. One last thought—in view of the fact that your mother called last week, we should talk about how further contacts with your family should be handled.

PATIENT: What do you usually do?

EVALUATOR: I would rather not have any further telephone conversations with your parents. It may be necessary in an emergency, and in fact, if there is a major emergency and I'm worried about your safety I may have to contact your parents. Otherwise, I hope that the marital treatment they're starting will contain their anxieties. Should one of your parents call, I will insist that they tell you about the call, and I won't talk further with them until you and I have a chance to discuss it fully. In a serious emergency, though, that will need to take precedence over everything else.

PATIENT: That's more than fair, and I appreciate your saying that.

up. This is particularly important in setting a contract for a supportive treatment, because of the strong and verbalized emphasis in that treatment on collaboration and joint responsibilities for the outcome. The problem here is that the patient does not appear to have been really involved in the process, except around the phone-call issue, and is likely to not have registered most of what was discussed. It is much preferable that the contract setting be done slowly, over a number of sessions, that the patient's appearance of pseudo-agreement be confronted and questioned, rather than accepted as though the patient is really agreeing to the arrangements.

In short, a treatment that is structured to be egalitarian and collaborative should begin with a contract-setting process in which those same qualities are stressed over and over again, while the patient's difficulties with an appropriate amount of involvement are questioned and undermined repetitively. Otherwise therapist and patient finish with very different senses of what was agreed upon, and the contract represents an unrealistic comfort to the therapist, while the patient feels primarily divorced from

EVALUATOR: Are there any other questions?

PATIENT: No.

EVALUATOR: Then I will see you next week at the agreed upon time and we will begin our work together.

PATIENT: I'm feeling good about most of this. And the rest of it, I think I can live with. So long.

it, and often controlled and exploited.

FINAL THOUGHTS

Although the twin foci of this chapter, careful and detailed evaluation and well-thought-out treatment planning, may appear to be self-evident, they are often honored in the breach. I have had the opportunity to consult on a number of cases in which severe treatment difficulties seemed due primarily to therapist misperceptions of the severity of patient psychopathology, motivation, psychological talents, and so on. These errors were usually secondary to inadequate evaluations (in some cases, almost no evaluation) or to unrealistic, poorly conceptualized treatment planning. For example, I have seen several schizophrenic patients in remission and very low-level borderlines treated psychoanalytically, without any therapist appreciation of the severity of psychopathology until the patient suddenly became psychotic on the couch.

The main point is clear. If our treatments are effective, they can also produce negative effects; they are not benign. Therefore, they are not applied without prior careful study of the patient, thoughtful consideration of the plusses and minuses of various treatment choices, and a judicious choice of a treatment carefully tailored to the patient's strengths and weaknesses.

CHAPTER 6

The Early Phase of Treatment

T he tasks of the Early Phase of treatment are fourfold: (1) educating the patient about the treatment, (2) setting goals for the treatment, (3) structuring and strengthening the therapeutic alliance, and (4) identifying the main maladaptive behaviors and defenses to be undermined, and the strengths and adaptive defenses that will be supported and strengthened. Each task is discussed in turn and then illustrated with clinical material.

TASK 1: EDUCATING THE PATIENT ABOUT THE PSYCHOTHERAPY

Both the education of the patient and the goal setting are carried out at the beginning of the Early Phase, as opposed to the other two tasks, which continue throughout the Early Phase and beyond. In educating the patient about the treatment, the therapist should not assume that the patient knows anything, even if she has previously been in psychotherapy. The patient may have been in a different form of treatment or may have been treated by a therapist with a very different style.

Some education about the treatment should occur in all psychotherapies, but this is particularly important in supportive therapy because of its contribution to the emphasis on joint collaboration. In addition, patients treated with this modality tend to be more disturbed, and can become confused and paranoid about the structuring of the treatment; explaining it fully decreases that possibility. For the same reasons, repetition of early educative efforts may be desirable later in the treatment. Presenting a clear description of the treatment tends to strengthen intellectualizing defenses, while simultaneously demystifying the treatment process.

Education about the treatment covers a number of areas:

1. A general description of why the psychotherapy is structured as it is. Why it is desirable that the patient talk as openly as possible, why the therapist sometimes does not answer questions, the importance of the continuity of sessions, and the reasons for various structures and restrictions. A general discussion of psychological conflict and of unconscious processes may also be helpful.

2. The respective roles of the two participants and the rationale for those roles. This should include an acknowledgment that the patient may find the treatment frustrating at times, that this is understandable, and that the patient should talk freely about such feelings.

3. A description of how the therapist views the patient's difficulties, including basic conflicts, preferred maladaptive and adaptive defenses, and liabilities and strengths, all presented with a minimum of psychiatric jargon. Projection is more usefully described as "focusing on troubles in the other person that you don't want to see in yourself" and denial as "sweeping everything under the rug because you don't want to have to deal with it."

General comments about Borderline Personality Disorder (BPD) psychopathology should be included, for example, the tendency for symptomatic improvement with increasing age. The interrelationships between idealization, devaluation, rage, and acting out, or the frequency of inner confusion and/or emptiness, are other examples of useful information to share with the patient.

4. Tying together the main themes of the patient's psychopathology with the goals that will be determined and discussing how the pathology, the processes of psychotherapy, and the goals are interrelated.

5. Simplified, jargon-free descriptions of basic concepts, such as transference, resistance, therapeutic alliance, and so forth, is useful. The attitude toward dreams in supportive therapy can be described, together with an explanation of why dreams are of less significance in that treatment than the patient might expect.

6. Finally, the therapist should ask about questions and confusions in the patient's mind and respond to them in detail, unless they are inappropriately personal or intrusive.

In the educative process, the therapist's attitude is that he hopes the patient will understand as clearly as possible what they will be doing together and the reasons that the treatment is structured as it is. This is consistent with the basic supportive therapy stance of not encouraging transferences; the more reality is emphasized, the less stimulation of transferences. (Of course, powerful transferences will invade the treatment no matter how diligent the educative efforts.)

Clinical Material

The Early Phase of treatment with this patient lasted about 6 months and was characterized by a very positive to mildly idealizing transference, punctuated by acute flare-ups of rage and upset. The therapist utilized the positive transference to suggest that the patient move from her parental home to a halfway house, and this was accomplished near the end of the Early Phase. Following the move, this phase of the treatment ended with increasing depressive symptomatology, the missing of several sessions, and a change in the transference from very positive to increasingly negative.

First Treatment Session (Fifth Overall Session)

THERAPIST: Well we've talked about a lot of things so far, and we'll be talking about some more in this hour. But first, do you have any questions from last time?

PATIENT: No, I'm still feeling good about the treatment, and I sure hope that it will go better than the other ones.

THERAPIST: Well, I hope so too. I would like to talk some now about the treatment that we'll be doing together, and spell out what I think are some of its important aspects.

First of all I feel that it's essential that you view this treatment as collaborative work, in which successful treatment will only be possible if both of us put our best effort into it. Your responsibilities are primarily to speak

Although all psychotherapies are collaborative, some emphasize the collaboration more than others. For example, in behavior and cognitive therapies, the therapist plans and

about what's on your mind, what you're feeling, what you're experiencing, what problems you feel up against, as openly and as honestly as you can. This is different from the usual social conversation, and you will probably find it slightly difficult in the beginning, and easier as you go along. You might also make an effort to maintain an attitude of some curiosity about what you are saying, thinking, feeling, and experiencing, so that you and I can work together in understanding how you function, and help you develop healthier patterns of acting. Some people find, after a period of time, that they are able to express their feelings and simultaneously examine what they're saying and feeling, but this varies from person to person.

My responsibilities are to listen to what comes to your mind, to do my best to understand it, and to respond when I feel I have something useful to say. I may not always talk when you would like me to, and there may be times when you ask me questions and I will not directly answer them. I'm mentioning this because some people are bothered by that, and I want to explain the reason for it. Although I am not hesitant to share personal feelings or values, or shy about giving advice when I feel that it is appropriate, my advice and suggestions will, I hope, be sparse. Changes in you, in your feelings, or in your behaviors will tend to be more solid when you come to decisions by yourself, instead of someone else suggesting what to do. I will not answer questions sometimes because I feel I have nothing useful to say, or I feel that the question is not a useful

organizes the treatment and suggests various behaviors to the patient, or acts as a teacher and gives homework assignments. By contrast, in dynamic supportive psychotherapy, collaborative efforts and joint responsibilities are constantly stressed. Therefore it is wholly appropriate that the therapist begin by stressing the collaborative nature of the work. This attitude can be reinforced by stating that each of the two participants deserves 50% of the credit for successful outcomes and 50% of the responsibility for less than successful outcomes, as the therapist states below.

The therapist is assuming that the patient knows nothing about psychotherapy and spells out in great detail the relative roles of each participant. He introduces the concept of an observing ego (the patient's contribution to the therapeutic alliance in the psychoanalytic sense), while reassuring the patient that this is a difficult attainment. He anticipates the patient's negative reactions to his not answering some questions and explains the rationale for this behavior.

one, or it is something that you can answer for yourself. I feel it's important that you understand the reasons for this and that I'm not doing it simply to frustrate you. On the other hand, if it bothers you a lot, I would expect you to talk about that and then we'll see if we can understand why it disturbs you.

I don't know the details of your previous treatments, but it may be that I will talk more and be less frustrating than your previous therapists. In suggesting a primarily supportive treatment for you, I'm implying a more active role for the therapist. But in fact, therapists vary a lot in how they work, and so I really don't know how our work together will compare with your previous treatment.

But I want to restress the main point here and that is that this kind of work requires the best efforts of both of us. If either of us wants this treatment to fail, we can probably see that that happens. So I see this as a treatment in which, if it works out well, at least 50% of the credit is yours; and likewise if it goes badly you need to assume 50% of the responsibility for that too. It's going to take both of us performing our work here as well as we can to make this treatment come out well. Do you have questions about any of that?

PATIENT: What did you say about answering my questions? Did you say you wouldn't answer any of my questions? That really upsets me. Why wouldn't you answer my questions? That scares me. That's like what went wrong in the previous treatments, and

I'm feeling afraid that the same thing will happen here. But I'm also angry if what you're saying is that you won't answer any of my questions. What are you saying?

THERAPIST: I can see that this is really a frightening issue for you. First let me be clear that I did not say I would not answer any of your questions. I did say that there might be some questions that I would not answer, and I tried to explain why. I didn't say that I would not answer any of your questions, and that misperception is striking, as well as how terribly upset you've gotten all of a sudden. Can we look at the confusion and upset right now?

PATIENT: You seem awfully stupid sometimes. Don't you understand that I'm terrified that this treatment will go like the others and that I'll run away from it? Don't you understand how scared I am of that? Sometimes I think that you're really insensitive or just stupid. But I'm not so upset any more. I thought you said that you wouldn't answer any questions. The way you put it now will probably upset me when it happens but I don't find it as scary as before.

THERAPIST: I wonder if your hearing my not answering *some* questions as my not answering *any* questions represents a general difficulty with seeing shades of gray, rather than seeing everything as all black or all white. However, I'm glad that you're somewhat less upset, and I certainly can understand your fear that this treatment would go badly. I was struck, however, by the suddenness of the reaction you had, the intensity with which

The patient misperceives the therapist's statement about answering questions and rapidly becomes upset. The therapist responds by repeating and clarifying what he said, after an initial empathic comment. This is consistent with the supportive treatment focus on reality rather than on transferences. The therapist could have responded to the patient's upset on many levels, for example, the meaning of her misperception, but chose, wisely I think, to state again as clearly as possible what he actually had said.

He calls attention to the repetitiveness and acuteness of the patient's reaction, and continues with the crucial issue of the patient's propensity for seeing things in black or white terms, a derivative of splitting. He appropriately interrupts the educative process to focus on the pathological phenomena that are interfering with the educational efforts.

I would have preferred that the therapist spend more time

it came up, and now the fact that it's rapidly dying down again.

PATIENT: Well, you're right about that. I still don't like the idea of your not answering some of my questions, but I must say I'm feeling pretty calm about the whole thing now. I feel good about you, but I also think that you can be unbelievably stupid sometimes, and I don't like that, but neither do I feel like quitting over it.

THERAPIST: Good. Let me also explain why we've set up a certain structure of visits, fees, and billing, and why it's important that we stick to this structure. Let me repeat the rules on missing sessions. . . .

focusing on the splitting and its effects on the interaction and communication, but he chooses to reassure the patient and focuses on the intensity of her reaction. He also chooses to ignore the patient's calling him insensitive and stupid; I believe it was because this occurs in the context of a generally positive transference.

This excerpt illustrates the process of educating the patient about the process of psychotherapy, the structure of the treatment, and the rationales for the structuring. It also demonstrates the interruption of the educative process to deal with pathological reactions that are interfering with the main task.

TASK 2: SETTING TREATMENT GOALS

The general goals of POST are the reestablishment of intrapsychic equilibrium in the patient in acute crisis and the strengthening of ego functions and consequent improved adaptations to inner and outer worlds in the patient with significant ego defects. Specific ego functions can be strengthened either directly or indirectly, the latter by decreasing stressful demands on the ego from the other three psychic agencies (see Chapter 3).

While the ultimate goals of all dynamic psychotherapies are increased ego strength and flexibility, with subsequent improved adaptation to inner and outer realities, the proximal goals of exploratory therapy are usually described in terms of increased insight into unconscious processes and/or structural change. By contrast, the proximal goals of dynamic supportive treatment are more specific, are generally expressed in concrete behaviorial terms, and are identical to the ultimate goals.

Common goals of the dynamic supportive treatment of the BPD patient are a decrease in self-mutilating or other self-destructive behaviors;

increased consistency of life plans reflecting improved identity integration; more stable interpersonal relations with decreased evidence of splitting, idealization, and devaluation; less impulsivity; diminished affective lability; and increased tolerance for being alone. The goals jointly decided upon should be realistic, and the patient may need some help in setting realistic goals. For example, the goal of a borderline patient with severe character pathology and a low normal IQ of going to law school is unrealistic and requires attention to reality testing and realistic guidance. Therapist and patient should be able to reach general agreement about the goals of the treatment, but not necessarily total agreement, particularly in the relative emphases placed on goals. For example, the patient may focus on the goal of increased self-esteem, while the therapist emphasizes the integration of split self and object images. These goals are not identical, but they certainly are related to each other.

Clinical Material

First Treatment Session (Fifth Overall Session)

Later in the same session quoted above ("Educating the Patient"), the therapist brings up the issue of treatment goals.

THERAPIST: It is useful to agree beforehand on what are our goals for this treatment. There ought to be at least some similarity between what you want to get out of treatment and what are appropriate goals. They don't need to be identical, but at the very least we should understand each other's goals. In addition, the goals we set are our best approximations at this time; some of them may be too high, some too low, while others may miss the main point. So, although I think that this discussion and joint setting of goals is important, we should both understand that they can be changed in the future if that is warranted.

So what do you think would be appropriate goals for this treatment, as you see them?

PATIENT: Let me tell you what I was thinking as you were talking. I thought, "What is with this guy? You're the doctor, you know what's wrong, you know what should be fixed. You set the goals and you tell me what they are." I'm telling you that because I thought it, though now I don't find your question quite as idiotic as I did before.

OK. Let me give it a try. I would like to feel less depressed, and I'd like my moods to be more stable instead of jumping all over the place like they do now. I'd like to get my life figured out better, I'd like to start dating appropriate guys, and frankly, even though my mother is an idiot, I wouldn't mind marrying a doctor like she keeps pushing me to look for.

THERAPIST: I think your goals of improved self-esteem, of less mood instability, and of clearer notions about yourself and your future make sense. But I'm curious about two other things. You seem strangely comfortable about continuing to live in your parents' home. Secondly, I don't hear very much about the kind of job or profession that would be of interest to you and that you might want to work toward. Is choice of work an important issue in your own thinking?

PATIENT: Look, in terms of my parents, they owe it to me because they really fucked me up, and frankly I live there because then I don't have to support myself. I don't know whether they would pay my rent if I didn't live at home. I don't want to live there, I'm just giving them a chance to make up for all their fucking me over.

About a job, I have to agree with

The therapist's request that the patient think about her goals for the treatment elicits an initial retreat from the collaborative work. The patient expresses the wish to be passive and nonparticipant in the process; the doctor should set the goals unilaterally. However, she spontaneously recovers and is then able to describe very appropriate goals.

The therapist praises the patient's reasonable goals, but then introduces two other issues that are likely to make the patient feel uncomfortable. She responds by becoming somewhat regressed and very entitled. I believe this mini-regression is a response to the anxiety she experiences when the therapist introduces possible goals that frighten her.

you; I never think too much about that.
I do think about getting married, and
having a home, and maybe a kid, but I
don't think much about working. I don't
know whether I'm scared, or I'm lazy,
or I'm afraid I never could do a job
well or I feel that any job I could get
would not be up to what I deserve. I'm
really unsure about it but you're right. I
think very little about the kind of work
that I would like to do. It just doesn't
really seem to be an issue for me.

THERAPIST: In terms of your feelings
about working and jobs, I think that's
something we're going to have to understand a great deal better before we
can say anything useful about it. I do
have to tell you that I wonder whether
you're best off in your parents' home,
whether it works against your wishes
to have more of a life with peers and
to meet more appropriate guys, and I
even wonder whether your attitude
that they owe it to you might also be
covering up the feeling that you're
scared to move out and afraid to be on
your own. In other words, that the
"they owe it to me for fucking me
over" statement is in good part a rationalization. Any thoughts about that?

PATIENT: I don't think that's a crazy
thought. I've had some of those
thoughts myself. When I think to myself about what I feel my parents owe
me, sometimes I feel like a real bitch.
At other times I feel that it really is my
due, they really do owe it to me. So
you can see that I'm all screwed up
about that, and I probably am all
screwed up about living at home or
not living at home, and it's just another
thing that's all confused in my mind.

Here the therapist reintro-
duces the issue of the patient
not living at home but in a
different context. He puts it
in terms of whether it's in the
patient's best interest to remain in her parents' home,
a context that is more supportive and less threatening
to the patient. He continues
by questioning the defen-
sive aspects of her entitlement, again in a very accepting and supportive manner.
The patient is able to respond
nondefensively, admits that
she has had similar thoughts,
and ends by expressing her
confusion, rather than by attacking the therapist or being
otherwise defensive.

THERAPIST: Then maybe we could add to our goals your attempting to understand more clearly what's keeping you at home and whether it really is the best place for you to be.

I think we have some consensus on goals having to do with your self-esteem, with your views of yourself and others, with your confusions about your life, with your difficulties in relating to peers and appropriate guys, and your confusions about working and jobs. Although our views aren't identical, they do overlap considerably. How do you feel about that, and do you have any other questions?

The therapist concludes by stating that their views of the goals of the treatment are not identical, but that they are roughly equivalent, and that is alright. He communicates a general feeling of acceptance of the patient's goals for the treatment and of the patient.

PATIENT: I'm comfortable with the way you spelled it out. I don't have any other questions but I am feeling nervous about something. There's something else I really want to talk about, and I want to get on to it. I went out with this guy last week and he turned out to be a real druggy character. . . .

TASK 3: STRUCTURING AND STRENGTHENING THE THERAPEUTIC ALLIANCE

The term "therapeutic alliance" is used today in two different ways. It has a long history as a psychoanalytic construct (Sterba, 1934) referring to the collaboration between the analyst's working ego and the patient's observing ego. More recently the same term has been applied by psychotherapy researchers to a measure, usually made early in the treatment, of the working climate of the therapeutic relationship. In the latter sense, measures of therapeutic alliance tend to correlate highly with the outcomes of at least brief psychotherapies (Gomes-Schwartz, 1978; Horowitz et al., 1984; Maziali, Marmar, & Krupnick, 1981). In addition, it appears that patient contributions to the therapeutic alliance are more powerful predictors of outcome than are therapist variables (Gomes-Schwartz, 1978).

Therapeutic alliance, in the psychoanalytic sense, is an unstable and unreliable phenomenon in the psychotherapy of borderline patients. Although there may be phenomena that appear to represent an alliance, they tend to rapidly disappear in the face of negative transferences. Adler (1981, 1985) believes that borderline patients can only sustain a therapeutic alliance late in the treatment and that when they are capable of a sustained alliance, they are no longer borderline.

As used here, the term "therapeutic alliance" partakes of both the psychoanalytic and the psychotherapy research meanings, and refers to anything that contributes to both participants working effectively together to help the patient. In this sense, many of the interactions described above are helpful to the structuring and strengthening of the alliance. The joint discussions in the contract-setting process about the handling of anticipated resistances and other behaviors that would threaten the treatment is an example. Similarly, collaborative discussions of treatment goals and the therapist's educative efforts both contain the message that treatment is a joint endeavor in which both participants have important roles to play. Although the therapeutic alliance is an important aspect in all psychotherapies, it receives more active attention in supportive treatment, because it is very likely a more powerful therapeutic element in that treatment. In addition, the emphasis on the reality of the alliance tends to diminish the intensity of transferences, particularly the negative transferences that can so easily destroy the treatment.

All of these interventions and implied attitudes help to strengthen the therapeutic alliance by reinforcing the collaborative nature of the work and the joint therapist–patient responsibility for the treatment. They create a therapeutic relationship that is relatively reality oriented and egalitarian, that discourages regression and transferences, and that constantly emphasizes the patient's full share of responsibility for each session and for the whole treatment. This is a very different atmosphere from that of the usual exploratory treatment, and this distinction deserves reemphasis.

In addition, certain interventions directed to strengthening the therapeutic alliance are most marked during the Early Phase but continue throughout the psychotherapy. The alliance is strengthened each time that the therapist uses the term "we" or implies it by his language. Questions such as "How can we understand this?" or "How are we going to deal with that disruptive problem?" imply a different therapeutic climate from the usual exploratory treatment.

No matter how much the supportive psychotherapist emphasizes and supports the therapeutic alliance, negative transferences in the treatment of borderline patients are inevitable. The therapeutic alliance, beginning with the treatment contract, sets up agreed-upon structures and procedures, serving as a reality backdrop to be used to highlight, and hopefully to diminish, negative transferences. On the other hand, the negative transferences must be diagnosed, confronted, clarified, and undermined as rapidly as possible; they can destroy the treatment very quickly because of the patient's impulsivity. Thus, negative transferences, primitive and unmodulated quantities of rage shaped by the extensive use of primitive defenses, plus the patient's tendency to impulsivity and acting out, represent the major threat to the maintenance of the therapeutic alliance and the entire treatment.

Case Example

A borderline patient, in an increasingly intense struggle over wishes for the therapist's approval, and rage and devaluation of him when she feels that the approval is not adequately forthcoming, begins to give increasing clues that she has resumed cocaine abuse.

THERAPIST: As your feelings about me have become more complicated, you are giving me increasing reason to believe that you are abusing cocaine to a significant degree. Let me remind you that when we started this treatment, we agreed that significant drug abuse would render the treatment difficult, if not impossible. Therefore, I must insist at this time that you do your best to refrain from further cocaine use and also that you begin to attend NA meetings on a regular basis. I say this because your using cocaine to relieve painful feelings in yourself, whether generated by our work together or by other problems, is bad for you and bad for the treatment.

PATIENT: I'm not using drugs.

THERAPIST: Perhaps, but on the other hand, you have been dropping hints to me for about 4 weeks on a regular basis that, in fact, you are using cocaine.

PATIENT: It's none of your business what I do outside of here.

THERAPIST: I would be remiss if I did not take very seriously this drug problem, which is destructive to you and destructive to the treatment. Therefore, again I must insist on regular NA attendance.

PATIENT: And what if I don't?

THERAPIST: We will continue to work together for a short period of time to try to understand why you are using cocaine at this point and refusing to take reasonable steps to stop it. However, if our best efforts to understand this lead only to continued cocaine abuse, it will be necessary to terminate the treatment.

Here the therapist reminds the patient of the terms of the contract and the therapeutic alliance, and suggests remedial steps consistent with them. When the patient's responses raise serious questions about an adequate observing ego, reveal negativistic transferences and outright defiance of the contract/alliance, and result in an apparent lack of concern about her behavior, the therapist makes it clear that he takes the contract/alliance seriously and will terminate the treatment if it is ignored. In subsequent sessions he will also appeal to the patient's observing ego and attempt to establish some collaborative struggle against the self-destructive behavior. However, if none of this is successful, the alliance and the treatment are seriously compromised and he is prepared to terminate.

Clinical Material

Eighteenth Session

The following exchange occurred during the ninth week of treatment. This was the first time since the evaluation that the patient did not arrive on time; she was 20 minutes late and presented a flimsy excuse involving her automobile. The verbal material early in the abbreviated session was of a trivial nature. The therapist commented upon this and wondered about the significance of the patient's lateness and trivialization of the material. The patient responded that that was ridiculous and then began to talk with moderate affect about the three previous therapists, all described in wholly negative terms. The therapist called attention to this material, wondering about its significance; this also met with a negative response from the patient. As we pick up the clinical material, the therapist is making a summarizing statement prior to ending the session.

THERAPIST: Well, I don't know. The combination of your coming late, then talking about fairly unimportant stuff when there's so much going on in your life, and then criticizing your previous therapists, all of which you seem to feel is unrelated to this treatment, makes me feel somewhat confused. I very much doubt that what I've just described is simply random noise. However, we need to stop now; perhaps we can make some more sense out of this at our next meeting.

PATIENT: Stop now? We've only been meeting for 25 minutes.

THERAPIST: That's correct but that is because you arrived 20 minutes late, and as I explained when we first set up this treatment, when you are late I generally will not run over with you.

PATIENT: You never told me any such thing. Besides which, doctors A and B would always run over with me when I was late, and I expect you to do the same thing; you never told me anything different.

THERAPIST: I am quite sure that I did make clear that if I were late, of course, I would make up the time; but if the lateness resulted from your behavior, you would need to take responsibility for that and that we would end at the regular time. It's always possible that I forgot to mention it, but that would be unusual and I'm pretty sure I did. In any event, we seem to have a difference in our memories.

First of all, please hear clearly what I'm saying now because it will apply in the future. Secondly, however, we seem to have some honest difference of opinion here, and I think we should talk briefly about how to resolve it.

PATIENT: (*Yelling loudly*) There's no resolving anything! We are supposed to meet for 45 minutes, you never told me anything different, and you have to give me the full time here.

THERAPIST: You act as though you either totally get your way and win, or you totally lose. Let me remind you that this is serious work together, and not a contest about who gets his way. Can

The therapist uses the initial treatment contract, a critical forerunner of the therapeutic alliance, to remind the patient of their rules for working together. However, the patient claims that this was never part of their agreement. This may be fall out from what I felt was an excessively unilateral setting of the contract. In any event, the therapist is in a difficult position; he and the patient don't agree on the details of the contract. It is possible that he omitted that issue in their initial discussions. He doesn't wish to allow himself to be exploited by the patient, but neither does he want to be perceived as controlling, heavy-handed, and unfair. There does appear to be an "honest difference of opinion."

The patient makes the situation more difficult by yelling and screaming, and initially refusing to negotiate anything. The therapist sidesteps the conflict for the moment and points out another derivative of splitting in the payou see any way of negotiating a compromise?

PATIENT: (*Screaming more loudly*) There's no compromise, there's no negotiation. . . . Wait a minute. I'm acting crazy. Why don't we split the time? Is that possible for you?

THERAPIST: That's what I had in mind, but I'm glad you were able to come to that by yourself.

tient, "Either you totally win or you totally lose." The patient quickly calms down, suggests that they divide the difference, and this is accepted by the therapist.

Again, the therapist first reiterates the reality of the issue, admits that his memory is fallible and that there is an "honest difference of opinion." But, most effectively, he intervenes on a less reality-bound level and points out the primitive defense involved in the patient's response. I believe that it is this intervention that allows the patient to recover and to suggest a sensible compromise to the conflict.

The comment regarding splitting is clearly useful and stimulates the patient to associate to other "all-or-none" experiences. Thus, what could have been an intense, bitter argument was turned to good therapeutic use by skillfully undermining the splitting tendencies.

The patient was very upset by her intense affective display and her initial inability to deviate from a "black-or-white" position or to consider compromise or negotiation. She spent the remainder of the session describing situations that she had handled in a similar "all-or-none" fashion. At the end of the 10-minute overtime, the patient spontaneously got up after checking her watch, thanked the therapist, and left.

In the 23rd session (12th week), about midway through the Early Phase of treatment, the patient opened the session by describing in great detail yet another of the interminable fights that occurred between herself and her mother. The therapist had the impression that the parents' marital treatment was helping. The mother seemed less intensely involved with the patient and made some comments that sounded like she wanted the patient to make her own decisions. On the other hand, the patient seemed more intense and desperate than ever to keep the fights with her mother going.

The following dialogue began at about the 15th minute:

THERAPIST: Each time you describe one of these terrible fights that never seem to get resolved, I find myself wondering why you don't think more about leaving your parents' home. You've talked about feeling that they owe it to you to support you, and I have mentioned the possibility that you're more afraid than you'd like to think about moving out. Yet, the thought of leaving never seems to arise spontaneously in you. I'm curious about that.

PATIENT: (*Rapidly gets extremely agitated*) You have a fixation about my moving out of that house! You're worse than my parents. I can see where they'd want to get rid of me because I'm such a pain in the ass, but what's your motivation? I think you feel it's all my fault, and I am ruining my parents' middle age and preventing them from enjoying their leisure time and money, and you must think it's all my fault. Or maybe you feel you owe it to my parents because they're paying the bills here. I think you are absolutely nuts on this subject, and I don't understand your bringing it up. But one thing I'm sure about— it's not in my best interest!—and you're either out to get me, or you're doing it for my parents, or you think it's all my fault, and I'm furious at you.

THERAPIST: Again I'm struck by how quickly your upset can escalate and

I find the end of the therapist comment somewhat hypocritical and insensitive. He knows that reintroducing this topic will get the patient upset, yet it is presented with "pseudo-objectivity," including his final "I'm curious about that." The patient's initial response is an exaggeration of a basic kernel of truth. The therapist does appear to have an agenda that includes the patient moving from her parents' home. However, as she becomes increasingly agitated, she begins to lose reality testing. She projects her guilt into the therapist and ends up accusing the therapist of being loyal to the bill-paying parents. This is the kind of transient, nonpsychotic regression in the reality-testing function that is seen so often

how easily you can begin to attribute all kinds of malignant motivations to the other person, in this case me. I think this is already clear to you, but if not, let me repeat it. My obligations here are only to you and to myself; I have no obligations to your parents. I do feel that your continuing to live at home is probably not in your best interest, and that it is difficult to reconcile with another of your wishes, to meet more men and women of your own age and to become more comfortable with them. I can only assume from the intensity of your reaction that this remains a very upsetting issue for you.

PATIENT: (*As suddenly as the anger started it stops and is replaced by bitter crying, which appears genuine*) I hate it in my house. I would love to leave, but I'm terrified. People won't like me, they'll think I'm stupid or uneducated. They'll find me boring, and I have no talents that other people would be interested in. I'm miserable at home, but I'm even more scared to leave.

Also, I want to please you, and I feel that you think that this is in my best interest. At least most of the time I think you're right and I trust you. But don't you understand how frightened I am? I'm terrified. Other people might not even care enough to argue with me; at least my parents do that.

THERAPIST: I'm impressed by how upsetting the issue is to you and how rapidly your anger escalated. But I'm also impressed by how quickly it decreased again, and how you were able to talk in a much more open and hon-

in borderline patients. Her accusations are qualified by "I think" and "maybe you feel," and it certainly appears that she is not psychotic (although her final "three possibilities" statement might be viewed as leaving the reality-testing issue unclear).

The therapist responds by clarifying the reality. Again, he couches the issues of moving in terms of the "patient's best interest." She responds to his support of her reality-testing function and to the therapist's expressed interest and concern for her, by reestablishing adequate reality testing. She drops her projective attempts and becomes depressed. The badness, which a few seconds before was all in the therapist, is now back in the patient.

The therapist responds to these changes with praise and stimulation of hopefulness. It seems to me that he does not adequately respond to the paest way about your anxieties, your wish to please me, and your fears of moving. I feel optimistic about that. I also think you and I together have to understand a lot more about why it's so frightening for you to think about not living at home.

PATIENT: I've always felt anxious away from my house. That's what happened up in college; that's what happened when I tried new jobs. I'm terrified to be on my own. I feel that I can't make it, and I feel that nobody will pay any attention to me, let alone like me. I only stay home because it seems like the least of the evils. . . .

tient's expressions of her wish to please him and her trust in him. However, the patient responds with further associations about the anxieties of separation and autonomy, and once again one has the feeling that the therapist has intervened skillfully.

The patient continues talking about experiences of separation and aloneness, and feelings of emptiness and incompetence.

The above are examples of threats to the therapeutic alliance due to acute upsurges of negative transference. The therapist's ability to maintain stability, to remind the patient of the alliance and of their work together, to allow the patient to suggest a compromise in the first instance, and correcting the patient's transient loss of reality testing in the second, allowed the reestablishment of the therapeutic alliance as the negative transferences abated.

TASK 4: IDENTIFYING MAJOR MALADAPTIVE AND ADAPTIVE BEHAVIORS AND DEFENSES

This is the last, and probably the most important, of the tasks of the Early Phase. It is a continuation and deepening of efforts begun during the evaluative process, allowing the therapist to study the phenomena in greater detail. In short, during the Early Phase of treatment, the therapist continues the process of identifying the maladaptive behaviors and defenses to be undermined, and the adaptive defenses and behaviors to be supported and strengthened.

The maladaptive behaviors to be undermined in the patient with BPD generally result from projection, denial, splitting, and other primitive defenses; from deficient ego functions, such as a soft-thought disorder; and from the marked tendency to acting out. Nonpsychotic distortions of reality testing resulting from excessive use of primitive defenses, exploitative and immature object relations, and difficulties delaying gratification, leading to impulsive, self-destructive acts, are behaviors frequently undermined or otherwise discouraged. Common strengths in borderline patients to be supported and strengthened are (1) behaviors, thoughts, and affects shaped by higher level defenses (clustered around repression rather than splitting); (2) specific talents and abilities in the arts, in athletics, or in intellectual pursuits; and (3) nonspecific ego strengths, such as high intelligence, likability, or the ability to think clearly.

The undermining of externalization and projection is illustrated in the following vignette (Rockland, 1989, p. 224).

Case Example

PATIENT: My wife has been especially cold and withdrawn this week. She's all over the children, but treats me as though I am an outcast. How am I supposed to feel good when my wife is treating me like this?

THERAPIST: Your wife has her own difficulties, and she is in treatment for that. But you seem to have a terrible time looking at yourself and your problems, and considering how your difficulties might be contributing to the trouble in the marriage. Rather, you seem totally engrossed in what she is doing to you. I am reminded of the couple session we had and how impossible it was to get either of you to do anything but blame everything on the other. As long as you continue to talk only about what your wife is doing to you, you are continuing the pattern that has led three previous marital therapists to throw up their hands in despair.

PATIENT: Yes, I understand what you are saying, but how can I think about myself when my wife is being so unfair to me? Let me tell you what she did the other day. She began to criticize me the moment I came home . . .

THERAPIST: I think that you are focused on your wife's difficulties in order to stay away from any examination or serious consideration of yourself and what you are contributing. It's a cop out. I would imagine that if your wife were here now, she would say that she became angry at you for this or that behavior of yours. But, in any event, until you can begin to examine yourself, your qualities, positive and negative, you are on the same merry-go-round that you have been on for several years. Let's try an experiment. Try to say three sentences consecutively without mentioning your wife.

PATIENT: I'll give it a try, but my wife said . . .

THERAPIST: Unh-unh!

PATIENT: I felt so badly and so rejected the other night. My wife . . . Oh shit! . . . I got so sad, and it lasted all the next day while I was in my office. I felt that I would never be happy again.

THERAPIST: So you see it is possible to talk without immediately bringing in your wife.

The marked use of splitting operations with unintegrated grandiose and devalued self and object images is illustrated in the following example (Rockland, 1989, pp. 226-7).

Case Example

PATIENT: I don't know why I don't have a more successful practice. I know a guy who has four different offices and is probably making a quarter million a year. I'm much smarter than he is, so why can't I do the same thing? Sometimes I sit in my office with a patient and I feel totally stupid. If only I were a real doctor, I wouldn't feel this way. I think I'm a fairly good podiatrist, but I feel totally inadequate.

THERAPIST: Within a 1-minute period of time, you have told me both that you feel totally inadequate and that you should make more money than any other podiatrist around. These are very discrepant views of yourself—that you're worthless and that you ought to be the greatest. Can you see where these two views of yourself are totally inconsistent with each other? Yet they seem to exist comfortably side by side.

PATIENT: I don't know whether I feel basically worthless and therefore I have to imagine that I am the greatest, or whether I feel like I have to be the greatest and therefore anything I actually do is worthless. The whole business confuses me, and I'm all mixed up.

THERAPIST: That's an excellent question. I don't know the answer, but I do know that it is something we need to keep talking a lot about.

To illustrate the process of identifying specific strengths, talents, and interests to be supported, note the following (Rockland, 1989, p. 227):

> The patient also had several strengths that could be supported. He was an excellent athlete and got great pleasure out of athletic activities. The therapist advised him to indulge in his athletic activities more often, explaining that he had to be less totally dependent on his wife, that active exercise would directly make him feel better, and that he would also feel better about himself by doing something at which he was so successful. In addition, he had several good male friends. The therapist advised him to see more of them, again with the rationale that having additional important figures in his life would make him less dependent

on his wife and less sensitive to her rejections; thus he would probably get gradually more positive responses from her. The patient accepted both suggestions and carried them out with success. In addition, when the patient discussed the possibility of taking a postgraduate course to improve his professional skills in a particular specialized area, the therapist was supportive and encouraging, suggesting that he would probably feel better about himself, more confident, and so on.

Each patient presents his own individual pattern of maladaptive and adaptive behaviors and defenses, strengths and abilities; the above are common examples. The essence of this Early-Phase task is to individualize the treatment to the specific strengths and deficits of the patient. The outcome of the task is the detailed construction of a set of adaptive and maladaptive behaviors that will be the focus of the remainder of the treatment.

The dividing line between the end of the Early Phase and the beginning of the Middle Phase is often vague. Sometimes, as in our case, it is marked by a significant movement in the treatment or a change in the patient's behavior. At other times, it is signaled only by the therapist's feeling that he finally has a good grasp and understanding of the core issues that will constitute the remainder of the treatment.

By the end of the Early Phase, there should be (1) an understanding in the patient of how the psychotherapy operates and why it is structured as it is, although these understandings will often melt in the heat of powerful negative transferences; (2) reasonable agreement on the desired goals of the treatment; (3) a rudimentary therapeutic alliance, which can be expected to intermittently disappear under the onslaught of powerful negative transferences; and (4) some conviction in the mind of the therapist about the core adaptive and maladaptive behavioral foci of the treatment, their relative importance, and the order in which they are likely to be addressed in the treatment. In addition, from the initial phase, a treatment contract should be in place, a set of understandings about how behaviors disruptive to the treatment will be handled. In total, this constitutes a fragile arrangement for working together, but hopefully one that is strong enough to weather the onslaughts of negative transference, acting out, primitive defenses, etc., which, in all probability, will characterize the Middle Phase of the supportive psychotherapy of the borderline patient.

Clinical Material

Following the initial evaluation and diagnostic assessment, the therapist was most impressed by the patient's externalization and projection, her sense of entitlement, her marked tendencies to splitting, manifested by poor object relations and a chaotic, directionless lifestyle, and her acceptance of dependence on the parents and seeming total lack of concern about leaving the parental home. Those were the major maladaptive behaviors and defenses noted. There was not a great deal on the positive side; her intelligence and likability, plus her consciously stated wish to change were the main plusses. There was little use of higher level defenses in the initial evaluative sessions, and outstanding talents and other strengths were lacking.

The Early Phase of treatment was characterized by a highly positive transference, punctuated by acute outbursts of rage and devaluation in situations of frustration and disappointment with the therapist. However, the predominance of the highly positive, even mildly idealized, transference made the Early Phase of the treatment relatively smooth.

Positive transferences are generally left untouched in dynamically oriented supportive therapy. However, in this case, the transference sometimes took on overidealizing qualities. The therapist's handling of this issue is illustrated below.

16th Session. The patient is talking at length about her anger at her parents and at the three previous psychotherapists. This is occurring in the general transferential context of viewing the therapist as the opposite of the depreciated others; he is understanding, sensitive, always knows what's best for her, etc. At about the eighth minute, the therapist intervenes

THERAPIST: I am, of course, glad that you find working with me a positive experience. On the other hand, however, I sometimes wonder if you are not seeing me in overly positive terms, in total contrast to your previous therapists and your parents. I say this for a number of reasons. First of all, there are times when I don't really understand what you are trying to say. Furthermore, let me remind you that there have been a number of brief periods in which you have expressed quite opposite feelings toward me, feelings very similar to how you are now describing your previous psychotherapists. Is it possible that you are seeing me in overly positive terms?

The therapist begins by accepting the patient's positive feelings, but rapidly begins to undermine the idealization and its origin in splitting operations. He points out several realities that are inconsistent with the patient's idealization, and ends by directly questioning it.

The patient's angry response, including the projection of negative aspects into the ther-

PATIENT: (*Explodes*) You're just like all the other psychiatrists! Always trying to make something different out of what's going on than what's really happening. What's your problem? Are you uncomfortable because I like you and I feel that this treatment is going well? What the hell is the matter with you anyhow?

apist, tends to support the validity of the therapist's intervention. It appears that the idealization defends against rage and devaluation.

The theoretical formulations of Kernberg (1984) and Kohut (1977) would lead one to perceive this interaction differently. Kernberg would see it as supporting his view that idealization defends against primitive rage, devaluation, and envy, and I believe he would be comfortable with the intervention. Kohut, or Gerald Adler (1985), whose views tend to be more consistent with Kohut's formulations, would probably not approve of the intervention. They would consider the idealization to be necessary for the patient at the time, and the therapist's undermining and questioning of it as an unempathic response. From their standpoint, the patient's rage is appropriate and reactive to the unempathic therapist response. They might even agree with the patient's attributing "a problem" to the therapist. His problem, in their view, would be that he cannot comfortably accept the patient's idealization and this is a countertransference problem.

THERAPIST: I think that you're hurt by what I said, as though I didn't appreciate your positive feelings for me. That isn't so. I do appreciate your pos-

This therapist intervention is partially consistent with the Kohut/Adler viewpoint, in that the therapist states his

itive feelings, and I do agree that the treatment is going well. However, I do feel that you tend to paint the important figures in your life in overly black or white terms, and at the moment you are describing the previous therapists and your parents as one kind of extreme and myself as the opposite extreme. I'm calling your attention to this not because I have a problem with your feelings toward me, but rather because I wonder if this isn't indicative of a problem of yours, tending to see others in totally positive or totally negative ways.

PATIENT: (*Totally calm again*) Well, it's funny you should say that. When I think about it, the feelings I have toward you are the same feelings that I had toward the other doctors at the beginning of treatment. Then something happened with each of them to

awareness of the patient's being hurt by what seemed like his lack of appreciation of her positive feelings. On the other hand, positive feelings are not equivalent to idealization, and in that sense Kohut/Adler would probably not be totally comfortable with this interaction. In any event, the therapist returns to the splitting issue and generalizes it to the patient's relationships with other people.

If splitting is a defense, then its undermining should increase the patient's level of anxiety. In fact, as shown in the following material, the patient becomes calm again. Furthermore, her next associations relate to other experiences involving splitting. This suggests that the undermining of the idealization was appropriate, but does not support the view that splitting is a defense. The patient continues to insist that the therapist has a problem, which can be viewed as a projection or as supporting the Kohutian view of a problematic response to the patient's idealization.

This patient material supports the theoretical formulation that idealization protects the patient's positive internal image of the therapist from being overwhelmed by nega-

make the relationship sour. I am terrified that the same will happen here and the treatment will be ruined. That's the way I feel, but I also feel that you have a problem accepting my positive feelings.

THERAPIST: As you just pointed out, the danger in seeing the other person in overly positive terms is that the relationship is fragile and in danger of being turned into its opposite. I understand your anxieties about that here, but I still wonder whether a relationship really has to be totally positive or negative. That omits all intermediate shades of grey, and I do feel that this tendency causes you problems with other people; for example, the kinds of difficulties that you had in your relationships with boyfriends.

PATIENT: I hear you, and I think maybe there is some truth to it, but I really do experience this relationship as different and positive, and it bothers me a lot that you have a problem with that.

THERAPIST: I am comfortable with your view of this at the moment, but it is also true that rage and quitting treat-

tive, hateful feelings. The patient says that only by keeping her view of the therapist idealized can she control her terror that her internalized image of him will become suffused with primitive rage, and she will have to leave this treatment as she did the others. She is frightened that this will happen, doesn't want it to happen again, and therefore must maintain an idealized view of the therapist. The idealization seems clearly defensive against the devaluation and destruction of the good-therapist image, which is more consistent with Kernberg's formulations.

ment are not the only alternatives to the highly positive way in which you see me at this time. I also think that this issue will continue to be a focus in our future work.

Externalization and entitlement tended to occur together in this patient, according to the formula "you (they) did 'X' to me and therefore you (they) owe me 'Y'." The vast majority of this material in the Early Phase involved the patient and her parents. Descriptions of fights between the patient and her mother and attempts by the patient to get her father involved in the arguments were frequent. The dialogue below from the 26th session illustrates the therapist's attempts to deal with the externalization, projection, and entitlement.

PATIENT: You must be getting bored of hearing these stories over and over again. My mother and I spent most of yesterday arguing about the same things we have always argued about. Boys, jobs, doing more chores around the house, the same old issues. She was outrageous! She kept screaming at me that I had to start dating, look for a job . . .

THERAPIST: How did this fight get started?

PATIENT: I can't remember . . . Oh yeah, she mentioned that their marriage counselor had asked why I was still living at home and why my parents aren't more active in helping me to move out. What the hell is it her business? She shouldn't intrude in my life like that. They caused my problems, and now they owe it to me to take care of me.

THERAPIST: How did they cause your problems?

This question appears to be an attempt at clarification; but it also begins the process of undermining the externalization by implicitly questioning the patient's attribution of all of her problems to her parents.

PATIENT: They were never supportive, always critical. When I left college they got very upset with me. My mother keeps intruding into my life and telling me how to live. They are not going to tell me when to move out. And I wish that other damned therapist would mind her own damn business. And they've always had this crazy marriage. My father hides out in his library and gets drunk, and my mother looks miserable all the time and picks fights with me. The hell with them if they think they are going to tell me what to do. And the other therapist too . . . and that goes for you too, Doc! I am absolutely entitled to stay in my parents house, and that's it!

THERAPIST: I would agree that you are entitled, but I think that you are entitled to your own life, and a family of your own, and some real gratifications in your life. Of course your parents have contributed to your difficulties; but it's also true that you're now 24 years old, and you would treat yourself much better if you began to take more responsibility for your own life. It seems to me a kind of cop-out to attribute what you feel, think, and do to your parents. I think you have more control over yourself than that, and it seems to me that you are hurting yourself terribly in order to punish them. Is that really in your best interest?

The therapist continues the process of undermining the patient's infantile entitlement, using the same "entitled" to apply to more age-appropriate gratifications. As he continues he undermines the patient's projections and rationalizations, in the context of supporting more mature ego functions—"you have more control over yourself"—and ends by questioning the self-destructive aspects of the patient's exploitative and controlling behaviors toward her parents.

PATIENT: (*Explodes again*) I told you that you are not going to tell me what to do, and I don't like you taking my parents' side either. I was afraid this would happen; now you think that they're right and I'm wrong. That really pisses me off. Who the hell are you to make such judgments? You're not there. You don't know what happened. God damn it all, it's not my fault (*patient begins to cry*).

THERAPIST: Here again, you seem to alternate between arguing that it's all their fault or attributing to me the belief that it's all your fault. That kind of all-or-none thinking really gets you in trouble. I don't think it's your fault or their fault. What happened happened, and it can't be undone. But you have the power to decide at this point what's in your best interest, and you seem willing to sacrifice your own life to prove to them that they have treated you badly. Again, is this really in your best interest?

PATIENT: (*Crying uncontrollably*) It's not all my fault . . . It's not all my fault, it can't be all my fault.

THERAPIST: I agree. We don't understand all of the factors that contributed to your having the difficulties that you do. But my focus is on what's best for you now. I am not on your parents' side, I am on your side. But I don't think that reinforcing your feelings that it's all their fault is the way that I can be most helpful to you. I am asking you to consider what is in *your* best interest right now.

PATIENT: (*Keeps crying uncontrollably*) It's not my fault . . . it's their fault. You won't make me move out, I won't let you. The whole bunch of you can go to hell! (*As she continues to cry, the patient becomes less belligerent and*

Not surprisingly, because the patient is terrified of moving out, she again blows up. After the therapist again calls attention to the patient's black-or-white style of thinking, a manifestation of splitting, the patient reveals the fear that underlies the entitlement and externalization. She is afraid that she is totally to blame for the whole situation, and she expresses this by protesting that it isn't so. Another way to view this is that the undermining of the patient's projections led to a reintrojection of all the bad feelings, and the patient is now in a depressive/masochistic assault upon herself, protesting all the

much more pathetic) . . . I can't move out, I'm terrified, who would take care of me? People wouldn't like me and I'll fail, and I'll be humiliated. You don't know what you're asking. Don't you know I am doing the very best I can? Stop it, please, I can't stand any more of this. What are you asking me to do?

THERAPIST: I am asking you only two things. First, to think very carefully about what is in your best interest at this point in your life. Second, I am suggesting to you that you have more power and control over your life than you feel you do, and that you are capable of making decisions about what's best for you. I am not surprised at all that the thought of leaving your parents' home terrifies you. But I would also remind you that you would not be all alone were you to do that and that we would continue to work together whatever you decide is in your best interest.

while that she shouldn't have to feel that way.

The therapist continues to emphasize his commitment to the patient, continues to undermine splitting operations, and focuses on the adaptational question of what is best for the patient. The patient's belligerent crying becomes pathetic crying, and she begins to talk about basic anxieties of not being able to get along by herself. In addition, she makes it clear that the therapist's opinion is extremely important to her and that pleasing him is one of her primary motivations. The therapist continues to stress the adaptational issues, reminds the patient of their alliance and of his commitment to her, and that she would not be totally alone were she to move out of her parents' home.

The patient's entitlement as it appeared in the transference is illustrated in the following excerpt from the 35th session:

PATIENT: How can you understand me? Have you ever had these kinds of troubles? . . . Well have you? I am asking you a question—why won't you answer me? Answer me. . . . Answer me, God damn it, you owe me an answer. I asked you a question and you are not answering me. (*Her voice and attitude are rapidly escalating into a temper tantrum*) What are you doing? Why won't you answer my question? You owe it to me, you owe me an answer. I asked you a question and you owe me an answer. Answer me. . . . Answer me, damn it!

THERAPIST: What I owe you is to try to understand what you are experiencing and to try to be helpful to you in whatever way seems best. You seem to be suggesting that unless I have had the same experiences and feelings that you have, I can't be helpful to you.

When we originally set up this treatment, I explained to you that I would not always answer questions and why I operated that way. I do not owe it to you to answer all your questions. What I do owe you is to try to understand why you are getting so upset here, and it seems to have at least two components. One is your fear that unless I have experienced the very same thing that you have, I won't be able to understand you. The second is that you are entitled to answers to any questions that you ask. You are not entitled to that. Are you able to experience the frustration and still feel that I am doing my best to work with you in a helpful manner?

The therapist uses the educational efforts and contract setting of the Early Phase to explain to the patient why he is not responding to her question. This illustrates the usefulness of early educative and contract-setting efforts in dealing with the patient's regressive tendencies. Simultaneously, he attempts to undermine the patient's entitlement as it appears in the transference.

The patient's negative feelings are confronted with the reality of the therapeutic relationship. Simultaneously, the therapist tries to help the patient understand why she is feeling so upset. His manner seems perhaps somewhat harsh and preachy, though he ends up reassuring her that he is "doing my best to work with you in a helpful manner."

PATIENT: (*Cries inconsolably for 5 minutes*) I feel like if you don't do what I want, you are not really interested in me. I feel very sad now. I know you wouldn't do that on purpose just to hurt me, so you must have some reason for what you are doing. But I feel very sad. Why wouldn't you give me what I want? I was furious before, and then I felt totally destroyed, but now I feel mostly sad. I would like to yell

This is another example of the patient's all-or-none thinking, but she apparently feels that the therapist is empathically with her. She is able to contain her feelings rather than projecting them and accusing the therapist, and she maintains a generally positive image of the therapist. The result is a feeling of

and scream, and tell you that you really don't care at all about me, but I don't believe that. I believe that you can help me, whether or not you have experienced the same things I have. But why do I feel so damn sad? (*Begins to cry again, but this time softly and not out of control*) I feel so sad. I feel better when I yell and scream, and blame everybody else, but now I just feel sad. I wish you had answered my question but I don't feel destroyed. I don't feel like running out of here and quitting. I feel sad but there is something good about it. It's crazy, I never felt like this before, I don't understand it.

loss and sadness, which the patient can perceive as a positive experience and a step forward.

THERAPIST: I think that what you are experiencing here is that you can survive without getting everything you want; and there is a loss involved in that realization. You don't have to terrorize me to feel that I am working with you. And you don't have to feel in absolute control of the situation to avoid feeling totally destroyed. I'm curious, you said there was something in the sadness that felt postive?

The therapist helps the patient to understand what she is experiencing, and this intervention has a genuinely supportive and accepting ring to it.

PATIENT: (*Still crying softly*) You could say that. . . . I feel a stability, it's a kind of solidity, it's a strange feeling for me. But I do think there is something positive in the sadness I feel.

THERAPIST: I think this is very important experience for you, and you might remember it as an example of the usefulness of my not answering every question. But in any event, perhaps what you are beginning to consider is that you don't have to brutalize those around you, either to feel that they are interested in you or because you feel you can only survive by being in total control of the situation. I think this was a very important thing that happened here, and I think the issue will come up again and again. But I think you should be pleased with yourself that you were able to get through this difficult experience without feeling totally destroyed. I think you should feel really good about yourself about this experience. What it means to me is that not only do you wish to change, but I think that you have just accomplished the first beginnings of actual change, and I think we should both feel good about that.

The therapist utilizes praise and support for the patient's ability to tolerate the painful experience. The praise expands into an attitude of hopefulness, and he ends by expressing his pleasure in her accomplishment and by suggesting that she should feel gratified by her handling of her feelings.

The session was over at that point; the patient left still crying softly and looking very sad.

The patient's marked splitting tendencies were dealt with repeatedly in the Early Phase, some of it illustrated above. Whenever she portrayed either her parents or the previous therapists in totally negative terms while presenting a very positive view of the therapist, these images were commented upon. The following dialogue illustrates splitting in the transference (30th session):

PATIENT: I was talking to my parents about how well the treatment is going, and how much I like you, and how much better you are than the other therapists, and they just didn't know what I was talking about. My mother particularly kept saying she doesn't see any changes in me and things started to escalate into another bitter fight. My parents are absolutely unable to understand me. I tried to explain to them that you were different from the other therapists, but they kept saying, "Watch out, you will do the same thing you did before." They don't seem to understand. Those other therapists were crazy, they didn't understand anything, they had severe personal problems themselves. Can't my parents act more like you do? Can't they try to understand me, why do they have to be so shitty?

THERAPIST: I have commented on this many times before, but I am struck by it again. You present both your parents and the previous therapists in wholly negative terms, while simultaneously painting me in totally positive terms. Do you see your tendency to see everybody in extreme, black-or-white, all-or-none, kinds of ways?

PATIENT: (*Screaming*) Why are you criticizing me? You're as bad as they are. I was wrong, you're all a bunch of shits. You're as crazy as the other doctors. Here I am saying positive and loving things to you, and you are coming back and criticizing me. You are being vicious to me, disgusting. You don't understand me at all. I am saying positive things to you, and I would think that you would say positive things back to me. But instead all you do is point out how it's all my fault, and criticize me, and make me feel terrible. Fuck you, you're the same as the rest of them. You're a critical, sick, disgusting person!

Here the therapist is specifically focused on the patient's splitting operations, with its consequent idealization and devaluation. Predictably, the patient again responds with an outpouring of negative feelings toward the therapist. Projective mechanisms are marked. In addition, the patient reveals another motivation for her idealization of the therapist. She would like the therapist to reciprocate her idealization. This is an example of mirroring aspects in the transference, as described by Kohut (1971, 1977). As noted above, Kohut and Adler would probably criticize the attention to splitting and the undermining of the idealization, viewing them as unempathic responses from the therapist, and seeing the patient's responses as an expectable reaction to an unempathic therapist.

In this case, however, the therapist continues to focus on the patient's splitting operations, with some eventual success. However, the patient continues her projective trends, which are not addressed here.

THERAPIST: Once again, I think you are feeling hurt by what I said. But I am trying to make what I believe is an extremely important point, one that is very relevant to your difficulties with yourself and with others. And notice how your view of me immediately switched from one extreme to the other, from an all-good and understanding person to an all-bad, frustrating, not understanding, unempathic, totally bad person. Can you take a step back and see how in the space of 2 minutes you have presented me in totally contradictory and discrepant terms? Can you see that? Are you as impressed by it as I am?

PATIENT: There you go blaming it on me again. It's not you who responds to praise with criticism and blaming, it's all my problem. I was saying something loving to you and you end up shitting all over me (*starts crying*). . . .

THERAPIST: I understand that you are very hurt because you wanted your positive feelings to be responded to by similar feelings from me. But this is a crucial point. Please try to understand it. Look at how your view of me changed from one extreme to the other, based on what you perceived as one negative stimulus from me. Are you as impressed by that as I am?

PATIENT: (*Beginning to regain composure*) Look I can see how my view of you changed, but it's not my problem, it's yours. You said a critical and disgusting thing to me. I told you you were good, and you told me I was bad.

THERAPIST: I think the sad fact is that no one can be as good as you would like to see me. But by the same token, no one is totally bad. And these comments apply to you as well as to the people that you are talking about. Your own views of yourself can flip-flop in 1 minute from thinking that you're all good and powerful and the world owes you everything, to a totally negative, bad, and worthless, deserving-of-nothing view of yourself. I am pointing out how your views of me went through the same flip-flop. And again I want to emphasize that I keep pointing this out because I feel that it is such a crucial issue.

PATIENT: You're certainly right about my views of myself, and I am struck by how fast I changed you from good to bad. That is pretty crazy when you think about it. But you hurt my feelings, God damn you, and that's why I attacked you. You started it.

THERAPIST: I know that your feelings were hurt, but that doesn't make either you or me into an all-bad, worthless person. I want you to remember how quickly your view of me flipped from one extreme to another, how your views of yourself can flip from moment to moment based on the same mechanism, and how crucial to your difficulties, both with other people and with yourself, is this tendency to see yourself and others in extreme, no grey middle area, just black or white, all good or all bad. Tuck this experience away in your mind because it is central to many of your difficulties.

The therapist acknowledges the patient's hurt feelings but keeps the focus on the splitting operations. He ends the interaction by focusing once again on the importance of this issue and suggests that the patient keep it in her mind because it is so centrally important.

In the 37th session, the issue of the patient's living arrangements came up directly. This was based in all of the previous Early-Phase work, the positive transference, and increasing signals from the patient's parents that they would prefer that she not live at home much longer, which was evidence of progress in their own treatment.

PATIENT: My parents finally asked me when I was going to move. I must say their treatment seems to be helping. Hah, hah, you like that! My father is much more involved with my mother, and my mother seems less depressed. And I hate to admit it, but I think I am starting most of the fights with her now. She seems much less interested in getting into battles with me. She tries to stop them and keeps telling me it's my life and I should make my own decisions. This time I think they are really serious about my moving out.

THERAPIST: How do you feel about that?

PATIENT: I don't know where to go. I can't support myself, and I am terrified that I will be awful lonely. I really don't have any good friends, at least anybody I could move in with. I'm afraid I'll spend the whole day in bed, getting more and more depressed. Well, you ought to be happy about this Doc, I think you're finally going to get your way. They are really serious.

THERAPIST: I agree with you that I think it would be asking too much to move directly from your parent's home into your own apartment. What would you think of the idea of moving into a halfway house? You will be more separated from your parents, but you will be with a group of people with more or less similar difficulties, and there is a lot of support built into those situations. It's positive that you will be with people of your own age, rather than your parents, and we will be able to

The therapist makes an environmental intervention in the patient's life. He begins by suggesting a possible move to a halfway house, but ends by offering direct advice that the patient make the move. This technical intervention is wholly appropriate in a supportive psychotherapy.

begin examining the difficulties that you have with your peers. You are not asking for my opinion, but I'll offer it anyhow. My advice is that if you are going to move out of your home, you think in terms of moving into a half-way house at this point.

PATIENT: That's a relief, but it also terrifies me. Nobody will like me there. It scares the hell out of me.

THERAPIST: I can understand that, but there are also some definite positives to it. Let's continue to talk about it next time we meet.

The move into a halfway house became the focus of the work over the next four sessions. The patient repeatedly expressed her fears about "not making it," of everybody hating her, that no one would put up with her nonsense like her parents would, etc. In the 41st session, the patient decided to move into a halfway house, and this was accomplished over the succeeding 2 weeks. The therapist praised the patient's decision, always together with an awareness of her severe anxieties about the move. Material dealing with her difficulties at college came up again. She was terrified of being exposed to drugs and of getting into the drug scene again in the halfway house.

The move was accomplished without incident. The patient reported that both parents were pleased and very supportive of the move.

In the sessions, the patient became mildly and then moderately depressed, and this was accompanied by occasional missed sessions. The therapist commented that the patient was probably angry at him for suggesting and then supporting the move, and this was confirmed by the patient's material. Simultaneously, however, the patient said that the move had really been necessary, that her parents had become increasingly intolerant of her living at home. In addition, she felt some sense of excitement and adventure, as well as sad and frightened.

The Early Phase ended with the patient in a halfway house, feeling angry both at the therapist and at her parents, sad and then depressed, and acting out by her occasional missing of sessions with flimsy rationalizations. The therapist felt pleased with the move and also that the "honeymoon was over." The patient had made a significant step forward, but she would not accept it easily.

FINAL THOUGHTS

The four tasks of the Early Phase are essential in a supportive psychotherapy, but they are not irrelevant to exploratory psychotherapy. Educating the patient is often ignored in exploratory therapy and in psychoanalysis, to the detriment, I believe, of the patient and the treatment. Similarly, goal setting should probably receive at least some attention in the nonsupportive treatments, though not necessarily verbalized.

The therapeutic alliance, although derived from psychoanalysis, is controversial among current theorists. Some writers stress it (Greenson, 1967), while others criticize the concept as being a variety of transference (Brenner, 1979). Nevertheless, without at least some rudimentary version of an alliance, the patient will not appear for the next session. Therefore, whatever steps are needed to ensure a minimal alliance must be attended to in any treatment.

The fourth task, identifying the adaptive and maladaptive behaviors and defenses, is the supportive therapy version of identifying the core conflicts and primary defensive maneuvers in an exploratory therapy. Thus, the four tasks of the Early Phase in POST all have their analogues in all psychotherapies, to differing degrees and with different emphases.

CHAPTER 7

The Middle Phase
of Treatment

The main task of the Middle Phase is the working through of the major issues identified in the Early Phase, plus identifying and working through new issues as they arise. In some patients, as in the patient presented here, the Middle Phase is characterized by dramatic new developments, which by necessity become the focus of the treatment. In other cases this is not so, and the Middle Phase consists of the repetitive working through of the maladaptive behaviors and defenses identified in the Early Phase, from every relevant viewpoint, both in the transference and extratransferentially. Simultaneously, adaptive behaviors and defenses are repetitively supported and strengthened, and progress is responded to with praise and as an indication that further change is possible.

Otherwise, few guidelines usefully characterize the work of the Middle Phase; it is extremely variable, as in any extended psychotherapy. The strategies and techniques of psychodynamically oriented supportive therapy (POST) determine the overall tone of the treatment. Transferences are not stimulated. Negative, overidealized, and erotized transferences are responded to rapidly. They are confronted, clarified, and undermined; contrasted with the realities of the treatment relationship; and directed out of the treatment by stressing parallels in relationships with other key figures. Resistances are evaluated according to their adaptive/maladaptive values, and supported or undermined accordingly. Regression is discouraged but nevertheless occurs frequently; associating to dreams, free associations, and therapist anonymity are discouraged in order to limit the potential for regression. The goals set at the beginning of the Early Phase are kept constantly in focus, but may also require modifications as the patient's clinical state changes, and the therapist becomes increasingly knowledgeable about the patient's strengths and deficits. Praise and encouragement are utilized to respond to positive changes, while limit setting and prohibitions are used to respond to acting out. The therapeutic alliance requires constant attention, as it functions as a reality backdrop against which regressive transference developments are compared; also it is constantly protected from the onslaughts of negative transferences, primitive defenses, and acting out. These points are illustrated in the clinical material below.

CLINICAL MATERIAL

The ending of the Early Phase and the beginning of the Middle Phase in the patient's treatment was marked by the move from her parent's home to a halfway house. This was accompanied by increasing depressive affects, the beginning of some acting out, and a change in the transference from primarily positive to primarily negative. There were occasional missed sessions and escalating threats to stop the treatment; the depression became increasingly severe, requiring treatment with a tricyclic antidepressant. The patient began to make frequent telephone calls to the therapist between sessions, requiring strict limit setting. Acting out in other areas,—street drugs, head banging, and self-mutilation—required an inpatient stay.

After 3 weeks in the hospital, the patient returned to outpatient psychotherapy and was able to secure her first successful employment in several years. She started an affair with her male employer, became pregnant, and had an abortion. As the issues underlying these behaviors were examined and confronted, with consistent undermining of the most maladaptive defenses and behaviors, the patient began a slow uphill course near the end of the second year of treatment. Her improving function was demonstrated by keeping higher level jobs and beginning to date a young man seriously. Simultaneously she began evening college courses with the goal of completing an undergraduate degree.

The overall description, above, of the Middle Phase is illustrated by excerpts from sessions 50 through 225 (6 months through 30 months.) Throughout, the patient intermittently threatened to unilaterally terminate the treatment. However, this did not occur, perhaps because of the stability furnished by the very positive transference of the first 6 months, the structure provided by the contract, and the constant focus on therapeutic alliance and primitive defenses.

The patient's clinical state early in the Middle Phase is illustrated by the following material from the 58th session. The patient arrived 20 minutes late.

PATIENT: I feel terrible. Everything is going bad. No matter how hard I try, nobody at the halfway house likes me. I am feeling depressed all the time, and I guess I act nasty and irritable. I'm sleeping badly and I feel tired all the time. I don't know if I can make it in the halfway house. . . . I have nothing else to say. . . . You say something. . . . Say something, I have nothing else to say.

THERAPIST: I am wondering about two things. First of all I am curious as to why you would miss almost half of the sessions when you are feeling so badly. Secondly, I wonder whether you have any ideas at all about why you are feeling so badly.

The patient is both depressed and angry. The anger is being acted out in missed sessions and latenesses. The therapist addresses the verbally covert, but acted out, negative transference.

PATIENT: I have no idea why I'm feeling so terrible—that's your job. I don't feel like I have any brains left. Why are you asking me that question? You're the doctor, I'm the patient, you tell me.

THERAPIST: What about your coming late when you are feeling so poorly?

PATIENT: What's the difference? You don't help me anyhow. I came late because I was talking to somebody, and it just didn't seem very important to get here on time because I feel so lousy and nothing helps.

THERAPIST: Tell me more about how you are feeling.

PATIENT: I just feel all alone, I feel totally empty inside, and I feel like nobody likes me at all. When I went home last weekend I got my old Raggedy Ann doll, and now I sleep with it all the time just like when I was a little girl. It's like that doll is the only

This is an example of the use of transitional objects by borderline patients, particularly

thing I have in the world, and the only thing that comforts me. I can't ever remember feeling like this before, I feel like there's a great big empty hole inside of me, and no one will ever fill it. It's hopeless. Only Raggedy Ann gives me any comfort at all.

THERAPIST: I am sorry that you're feeling badly. It also sounds like you are feeling disappointed and angry with me. The sessions are not as important, you didn't care about getting here on time, and you feel that nothing here is of any use to you. Any thoughts about that?

PATIENT: (*Explodes*) You don't do anything for me, you jerk! You just keep giving me the same psychiatric bullshit. You don't comfort me, you don't make me feel any better, and as far as I am concerned you don't have anything to offer me; you're useless!

THERAPIST: What I am struck by is how your whole psychological state has changed since you moved out of your parent's house and into the halfway house. You are increasingly depressed, feel hopeless about getting any help from me, and you're feeling angry with me, but I am not sure I know why.

PATIENT: You made me move into the halfway house, you pressured me, you and my parents. I knew this was a mistake. You should have protected me from it. Instead you pushed me, you twisted my arm, you made me do it, and now look at me! And here I am, feeling absolutely horrible, and you have nothing to offer me except more bullshit.

in situations of object loss and resultant depression (Modell, 1963).

In addition, the patient now dramatically describes feelings of inner emptiness, the one BPD criteria that was missing in the initial evaluative process. The transitional object is being used to try to fill this inner emptiness, but it is not sufficient.

The therapist expresses his regrets that the patient is feeling so badly, but goes on to try to elucidate the negative transference that is being acted out. In response to a fairly benign intervention by the therapist, the rageful transference floods out of the patient.

THERAPIST: While I did feel that this move was desirable and I supported it, I don't agree that I forced you or twisted your arm. But in any event, how can we understand why this move is so terribly distressing to you?

PATIENT: (*Begins to sob*) I moved because I wanted to please you. I wanted you to be proud of me. You were everything to me, and I wanted to please you ... so maybe ... maybe, I hoped that I would be everything to you. I thought that if I made the move you would really care for me. But the treatment goes on just like before, nothing special from you, and I am devastated ... and I hate your guts. ... I wanted to be everything to you and now I am nothing ... I have lost my parents ... (*huge sobs*) ... I have nothing, I am nothing, ... I did it for you and you gave me nothing. ...

THERAPIST: What's "everything to me"?

PATIENT: (*Continued sobbing*) I don't know ... I don't know, God damn you ... that I'd be as important to you as you were to me ... and I am not important to you, and now you are not important to me ... and you can go to Hell, along with everybody else. I hate your guts! (*continued violent sobbing*).

THERAPIST: I think I understand something about what you are saying. You had made me into a wholly positive, unreal figure, and you hoped that by moving, and pleasing me, that you would attain unending love and admiration from this idealized person. But the reality is that I never was that person, and now you feel fooled, taken advantage of, let down, and furious

The therapist addresses the rageful transference, and it is replaced by the hurt, frustration, and depression that underlie it. The patient reveals that her move to the halfway house was powerfully motivated by the wish that the therapist return her idealized and loving feelings toward him. But those wishes are frustrated and the treatment goes on as before. The patient is struggling with intense feelings of hurt, depression, and rage, focused in the frustration of her wish to be loved and adored by the therapist, to have her loving feelings reciprocated by him. This is illustrated below, "I hate your guts!" combined with continued violent sobbing. The therapist responds by continuing to address the issues of idealization, mirroring, and the reactions to its disappointment. "I never was what you thought I was."

with me. I never was what you thought I was, and you are correct that our work here is to continue the psychotherapy and to help you, at the moment, to live with the fact that unending love from an idealized person was never a reality and never can be. That is a great hurt and disappointment and loss. But I also feel that with our working together this is something that you can tolerate and survive.

PATIENT: I have half a mind to quit. You suckered me in, you promised me that you would be everything I wanted. I would have done anything for you and I did, and now you are leaving me high and dry. Go to hell, I really should quit . . . if I had any self-respect I'd quit.

THERAPIST: I am sure that quitting is a temptation for you because you are so hurt, disappointed, and let down. But also notice how I have changed from an all-positive figure for whom you would do anything into someone that you see at the moment as worthless to you. Just as I never was that positive figure, neither am I worthless to you now, even though you are feeling disappointed and let down. I would feel badly should you end this treatment prematurely, but I would survive, and you would once again be hurting yourself in order to punish someone else. That is clearly not in your best interest, and I very much hope that you continue the work. Furthermore, I have confidence that we'll both survive this difficult time, that you will eventually come out of this, and that this suffering will have its positive aspects for you in the future.

The therapist is empathic with the patient's painful inner experiences. He stresses the therapeutic alliance and attempts to instill some hopefulness in the patient, placing her present experiences in a larger framework so that it has meaning and a context. The latter is an example of reframing.

The patient's response, "I have half a mind to quit" is a real step forward. She is obviously tempted to quit but simultaneously feels very tied to the therapist and the treatment. She expresses her ambivalence, neither idealizing the therapist nor impulsively quitting the treatment. Her ambivalence is expressed in the phrase "half a mind."

The therapist is empathic, addresses the rapid switch from idealization to devaluation, and responds in a useful way to the patient's threats to quit. He hopes that she won't, but reassures her that he would survive and focuses again on the adaptational issues for the patient. He provides hopefulness, reframing, and the suggestion that the patient's suffering has its positive aspects.

In spite of repeated reworking of the themes of disappointment of the wished-for responses to the early idealization and the resulting frustration and rage, the patient's depression escalated. She gradually developed signs and symptoms of a major depressive disorder: early waking, appetite loss, feelings of hopelessness and helplessness, difficulty concentrating, and increasing suicidal preoccupation. In response to the worsening clinical picture, the therapist decided to introduce a tricyclic antidepressant.

THERAPIST: It seems to me that your depression is becoming sufficiently severe that it is both causing you enormous suffering and also working against the treatment rather than for it. Therefore I am suggesting that we begin you on some antidepressant medication. What do you think?

PATIENT: I hate medications and they scare me. Are you getting discouraged with me? Do you think I'm sicker than you thought originally? I feel terrible and I will do anything that would help, but I am not sure about medications. What medication would you try?

THERAPIST: In no way does your depression change my views of you or of your difficulties, and I am not discouraged. I am not even totally surprised, because I know how difficult it was for you to separate from your parents and begin your own life. But your sleep and appetite are disturbed, you seem to feel quite hopeless, and I am becoming increasingly concerned about your suicidal thoughts. In addition, there are these long silences during the sessions as though you are too preoccupied with what's going on inside of you to be able to use the treatment maximally. For all these reasons, I am suggesting that we use some medication.

This illustrates the use of medications in supportive treatment. The therapist remains very reality oriented and medical, beginning by presenting his reasons for suggesting the medication. He reassures the patient about her fear that she is sicker than the therapist originally thought. He educates the patient about the pharmacologic agent to be used, the lag time involved in antidepressant response, and anticipated common side effects.

Note that there is no addressing of unconscious symbolic meanings of the medication. The therapist may well be thinking of the oral gratification to the patient of taking the drug he prescribes and suggests this later in his recommendation of a three times per day schedule for the drug.

The medication I am suggesting is called nortriptyline, and because the dosage is determined by its blood levels, some blood drawing will be necessary to check the levels. It is very important that you understand that with all of these medications there is a lag time between the time that you begin taking them and the time that they become effective. That lag time is between 2 and 3 weeks, and I really don't want this depression to get any worse for you. Nortriptyline is a fairly safe medication, although there may be some mild side effects, like dry mouth or constipation or a tendency to become dizzy if you stand up too quickly. I would also like you to see your family doctor as soon as possible and ask him to do an electrocardiogram. That will be useful as a baseline, although in a young person like yourself heart problems are uncommon with this drug. With your permission, I would also like to call your doctor and explain to him what I am doing and why I want the examination. What do you think?

PATIENT: You mean this drug can give me a heart attack? That terrifies me. I am already having pains in my heart sometimes. I feel like my heart is breaking. Will it give me a heart attack?

THERAPIST: In some patients, particularly older people, there may be some changes in the electrical conduction system of the heart. This does not have to do with having a heart attack, and in a young healthy person like yourself I don't anticipate any difficulty at all. No, it will not give you a heart attack, I want a baseline cardiogram because that is the safe way to use this medication.

PATIENT: What is nortriptyline? Why nortriptyline? I keep hearing all these wonderful things about Prozac.

THERAPIST: Nortriptyline is one of a class of drugs that are called tricyclic antidepressants. I am choosing nortriptyline because it is usually effective with minimal side effects. I am choosing nortriptyline over Prozac because I think that with the type of depression that you are experiencing, it is more likely to be effective.

PATIENT: What if it doesn't work? What if I get worse? I can't stand much more of this.

THERAPIST: The likelihood is that it will be effective, assuming the usual blood levels and sufficient time. That's why I told you about the lag time, because I don't want you to become prematurely discouraged if you don't feel better right away. The lag time is unfortunate but it is characteristic of all these drugs, and no one really understands exactly why it is so. But as I said before, because there will be a couple of weeks before you feel some relief, I don't want to wait any longer before starting the medication. So I would like you to see your family doctor as soon as possible, and as soon as you do, please call me and we will start the medication.

The therapist utilizes reassurance in his optimism about the effectiveness of the drug. He might have added that if the drug chosen is not effective, there are many other agents to try, thus guarding against total disillusionment in the patient if she does not respond to the nortriptyline.

PATIENT: How do I take it?

THERAPIST: We will start it gradually and build up the dosage to a level that will give us the desired blood levels.

Although this medication can be taken on an once per day basis, I would prefer that you take it on a several times a day basis. I will go over the details of that when we start it. Again let me assure you that this is a relatively safe drug, that the side effects in most patients are not onerous, and that I anticipate it will be effective. If it is not, there are other drugs that we can try, but I expect that it probably will be effective.

PATIENT: How does it work? How will it help me?

THERAPIST: The exact mechanisms of action are not known. However, it does have the effect of raising levels of certain neurotransmitters in the brain that tend to drop when you are depressed. That may be connected to why it takes some time to be effective. I can't exactly answer your question, except that it raises neurotransmitter levels that are usually decreased when one is significantly depressed.

PATIENT: I am terrified. A girl in the halfway house is on some medication like this and she keeps having trouble peeing. Will I have trouble peeing? One night she couldn't pee at all, and they had to take her to the emergency room. This scares the hell out of me.

The therapist chooses to prescribe the antidepressant on a several times per day basis. Antidepressants and neuroleptics, in contrast to benzodiazopines or lithium, are usually prescribed once per day. In many cases this is preferable, so that the patient doesn't "forget" doses.

In this case the therapist prescribes it in divided does to take advantage of the symbolic meanings of the medication. The patient will recall the therapist several times each day as she takes the pharmacologic agent, and this can be experienced as a symbolic feeding, as a symbolic contact with the caring prescriber. In addition, it represents a compulsive symptom built into her day, and this too may have some depression-relieving effects. It is an example of the prescribing of medication taking into account the psychological and symbolic meanings of the drugs, as well as its pharmacological properties.

The therapist educates the patient about the neuropharmacologic effects of the drug, hoping that the patient will feel less helpless and more in control. Were this explanation given earlier and emphasized more, it would be an example of pseudobiologization. This refers to a strong emphasis on "chemical imbalances," "stimulus barrier difficulties," or other biological factors, in an attempt to make the patient feel less responsible, more that she is suffering from a medical illness, and therefore less concerned with psychological issues.

THERAPIST: I have chosen nortriptyline because it is the least likely of these drugs to cause a lot of difficulty with urination, constipation, or dry mouth. You may have some of that, but there again, if it becomes problematic there are ways to help you with that too. I understand your anxiety, but I feel that it's necessary to start the drug now, and I really feel that you are overworrying the side effects. Most people experience only annoying side effects on this drug, not seriously problematic ones.

PATIENT: (*Begins to cry*) I feel caught in the middle. I am scared of this medication but I am feeling terrible. . . . I guess I will give it a try, I don't feel like I have much choice. . . . Okay I'll go to my family doctor this afternoon or tomorrow morning, and I will call you as soon as I have seen him. Of course, you have my permission to call him.

THERAPIST: Let me reassure you that increased depression such as you are experiencing now is not unusual in treatments that are producing real change. I know that you are totally discouraged now and that everything looks black—past, present, and future—but let me reassure you that, in all likeli-

The therapist utilizes reassurance, stimulates hopefulness, and offers reframing, helping the patient to feel less despairing and hopeless. In addition, he praises the patient's willingness to try the medication that frightens her, which

hood, the world will soon look different to you, and so will your view of yourself. I am impressed that you are increasingly willing to try things that simultaneously terrify you. I think you will feel in a couple of weeks that we have made the right decision. So call me as soon as you have seen your doctor and we will start the medication.

probably reflects her increasing trust in the therapist. It may also partake of her ongoing wishes to please him and to be loved by him, the same issues that were involved in her move to the halfway house.

The patient responded to the nortriptyline and the worst of the depression was over by 3 weeks. Her vegetative symptoms responded, suicidal thoughts stopped, and feelings of helplessness and hopelessness abated. However, with the patient on 75 mg per day of nortriptyline (blood level 112 ng/ml), she began an escalating pattern of acting out, which eventually required a short hospitalization.

The acting out began as increasing numbers of between session telephone calls to the therapist, while intermittently missing or coming late to sessions. The sessions consisted of long silences intermixed with vitriolic attacks on the therapist, as illustrated below.

The patient arrived for this session 25 minutes late. During the prior week she had called the therapist on three occasions, complaining of unbearable feelings of loneliness. No one in the halfway house liked her, everybody ignored and avoided her. When the therapist set limits on the phone calls, the patient became furious.

THERAPIST: It's difficult for me to understand what you're doing. You arrived here 25 minutes late and now you have sat for the first 5 minutes of our short session totally silent. At the same time, you are calling me between sessions complaining about painful feelings of emptiness and other problems; but it's very difficult for us to deal with your problems when you are not here or not talking. How can we understand this strange combination?

PATIENT: (*Silence, 3 minutes*)

THERAPIST: Again, you are attempting to spend increasing amounts of time on the phone with me while simul-

This is an example of a confrontation. The therapist points out the contradictory nature of the patient's behavior. On the one hand, she arrives after the session is more than half over and then sits silently. On the other, she is calling him frantically between sessions on the telephone, complaining of very painful feelings. These behaviors are incompatible, and the therapist addresses this in his question at the end of the intervention.

taneously avoiding the sessions or shortening them significantly. This is totally confusing to me. What's going on?

PATIENT: Don't complain to me about the damned sessions. My parents are paying for them, and it's none of your fucking business whether I am here or not. I call you when I feel upset and you give me a hard time; but you want to see me during the daytime when I'm not feeling so bad. Why aren't you there for me when I need you? What do you mean I can't call you at night? You said I could call you if I was upset.

THERAPIST: My memory is that we agreed that you could call me in an emergency. However, the feeling I have now is that you are trying to change our face-to-face sessions into telephone sessions. Why would you want to do that?

PATIENT: I can call you any time I want, and I don't have to come here if I don't want to. What's so great about coming here anyhow? All it's gotten me so far is more depressed than I have ever been in my life. With friends like you who needs enemies! You'd better shut up; I have half a mind to quit right now.

THERAPIST: You cannot call me any time you want, and I will not allow this treatment to become a treatment on the phone rather than in this office. You are trying to tell me something about your feelings by your behavior, and you certainly seem angry at me, but you cannot use these phone calls as you have been. You are not calling me in emergency situations, and you are

The therapist sets limits on the phone calls. The patient, in this contradictory behavior, appears to be expressing a number of conflictual feelings. For example, "I need you, you're not helping me, I will punish you with phone calls, I will force you to give me what I want, I will punish

combining the phone calls with missing significant amounts of session time. That is not acceptable; what's going on?

PATIENT: (*Screaming*) Fuck you and your "acceptable." I am going to do exactly what I want, and I'm warning you again—shut up or I am going to quit!

THERAPIST: I cannot stop you from leaving the treatment, although I trust it is absolutely clear to you that I would consider that a serious error. But I can stop you from calling me as you have been, and I am going to do that. You may call me in the future only in a true emergency. If it appears to me after the first minute that it is not an emergency situation, I am going to ask you to hang up, and if you do not, I am going to hang up on you. I am not doing this to punish you, but rather because the treatment must take place in this room. The telephone calls are disruptive to me, and I cannot continue to receive them as I have been. I hope you will not quit but neither may you continue the phone calls.

myself by putting the treatment in jeopardy," among others.

In no way is it helpful to allow the patient to act out her feelings instead of talking about them. In order to get the patient to talk about them, strict limits must be placed on the acting out, and the therapist is doing this. The phone calls are inconvenient and annoying. From the standpoint of the patient, he is interdicting the acting out and saying, "You must put it into words so we can talk about what you are struggling with."

The patient continued with a loud display of cursing and crying, threatening to quit and screaming at the therapist, mixed with racking sobs. The therapist's response was to end the session at the regular time;

the patient looked mildly confused, but got up and left. There were no further phone calls over the succeeding weeks, except for two appropriate emergency calls, and the patient did not terminate.

Attendance at sessions continued to be spotty, however, with latenesses as well as missed sessions. In the sessions, the patient was either angrily silent or negativistically contradictory, attacking and devaluing everything the therapist said. The therapist also noted the return of the soft-thinking disorder that had been observed in the initial evaluation, but had disappeared entirely during the Early Phase of treatment. This was characterized by moderate circumstantiality and tangentiality, as well as responses to therapist comments that seemed irrelevant or missed the point. The therapist's attempts to point this out and to investigate the associated inner experiences of the patient were met with denial, derision, and disinterest. The patient seemed primarily motivated by wishes to totally denigrate the therapist and the treatment. Through all of this, she continued to attend sessions erratically.

When not attacking the therapist, the patient talked about unbearable feelings of loneliness and emptiness. She felt unacceptable to herself and to the other patients in the halfway house. She described the empty feeling in physical terms.

PATIENT: You don't understand me, you never will understand me. I am all alone. No one is really interested in me. I have the feeling of a big empty space inside of my chest. It's like there is a big hole in there or it's filled with gas. Nothing can fill it, either eating or talking to people, or going to the movies, or anything. There is a big empty space right in the middle of my chest and it feels terrible. It's unbearable and I can't do anything about it. And neither can you, because you are worthless to me. Your understanding and a token will get me into the subway. I don't know why I even come here anymore, this is meaningless. You are worthless, I am worthless and everybody knows I am worthless. You and I are wasting each other's time here and nothing is happening. I don't know how you can make your living doing this shit. You interfere in other people's lives, get them depressed, and then offer them "understanding" when what they need is real help. You're a charlatan, a phoney, and a total jerk. The only bigger jerk than you is me because I bother to come here. We're a couple of morons sitting together, wasting time, and going nowhere.

Can't you do something about this terrible emptiness in me? Can't you fill it up in some way, can't you give me a different medicine? I feel terrible and you're totally useless. I despise you!

THERAPIST: It is true that I have nothing magical to offer you that will fill the empty space in your chest. But I think I can help you understand what you're feeling, if we can work together. Do you have any ideas about it?

PATIENT: More psychiatric bullshit! You're going to help me understand this and then you ask me what I think it's about? You're unbelievable!

THERAPIST: I don't really understand it totally, but I think it has something to do with your growing up, with your trying to go off and make it on your own, and with what you feel you want from others, probably primarily me, that would make you feel filled up. But I view this as a part of a growing-up process in you, and if I'm right, the pain is unavoidable. And although you are undoubtedly suffering a lot with these feelings, the fact is that you're surviving and that you're no longer so depressed. And in spite of your feeling that no one at the halfway house wants to have anything to do with you, it is

In response to the patient's continued devaluation of him, the therapist first emphasizes the reality of their work together, including the fact that he cannot "cure" her painful feelings and physical sensations. He then attempts to place the patient's suffering in an intellectual context, to give the patient a cognitive grasp of the meaning of her pain. He offers her encouragement—"the fact is that you're surviving"—and points out the discrepancies be-my understanding from a recent conversation with the social worker that you were proposed for president of the halfway house. That is not consistent with the ways you are describing your relationships with the other people there.

PATIENT: Come off it! President of the halfway house; that's like king of the garbage can. You're a real idiot if you think that's anything to be proud of.

THERAPIST: You seem so fixed on your anger at me, and on punishing me for the hurts, disappointments, and frustration that you experience with me, that you won't agree with anything I say. I think you should take some realistic pride in being proposed as president of the halfway house. In fact, I sense as we're talking that you are pleased about it; but you won't give me the satisfaction of agreeing with anything I say. And I also have to notice that while you are being so angry and negativistic with me, you continue to attend these sessions, and you haven't quit. I think that's something you should feel pleased about; I certainly do. I'm sorry that you're suffering with this emptiness. I don't think it will last forever, but neither do I think that your present life is devoid of positive accomplishments, although you seem to want to present it that way here.

PATIENT: (After 5 minutes of silence) I bought a bird. I bought a bird because I thought maybe it would help a little bit, because my Raggedy Anne Doll is useless to me now. I really wanted a dog, I love dogs but they weren't allowed there . . . so I bought a bird. I

tween her views of her functioning and those of the outside world.

He praises her accomplishments at the halfway house in the context of clarifying her anger and negativism. He praises her continuing to attend sessions, although she is again tempted to quit. Finally, he is empathic to her suffering and offers her hope that it is not a permanent state.

This illustrates the borderline patient's use of transitional objects to deal with depression and object loss. It represents an attempt to deal with her disapointment and frustration in the relationship with

have a parakeet, and I think it knows me, and it jumps around when I come into the room. I don't know. ... I think it's crazy. How could I love that pinheaded bird? But I do, I have a real relationship with him, and he makes me feel better, a little bit, when I feel so empty and alone. Congratulations Doc, 2 years of treatment, and your patient bought a fucking bird!

THERAPIST: What made you decide to do that?

PATIENT: I don't know. I saw it in the pet shop, and I just seemed to connect with him, and I felt better for a moment and I thought that maybe I'd feel better if I took the bird home. So I bought it and now he lives in my room and I feed him. He's a good guy.

the therapist and has adaptive value in furnishing a substitute object.

We probably do not adequately appreciate the role of pets as transitional objects for borderline patients. In my experience, several patients have signalled their beginning reinvestment in the world of objects by becoming involved with pets. The patient's comments about the bird, including her final "he's a good guy," suggests the investment of her internal loving object representation in the pet that won't reject her as she feels the therapist has.

During this period, the 18th month of treatment, the therapist began to receive alarming telephone calls from the staff of the halfway house. The patient was spending long periods of time alone in her room, was beginning to bang her head against the wall, and had told other residents that she was driving 90 miles an hour at night up local highways. There was also a question in the minds of the staff whether the patient was again abusing street drugs. The patient continued to have therapeutic blood levels of nortriptyline. The therapist requested that staff make sure that the patient knew that this information had been shared and prepared to confront the patient about it in the next session (Session 138).

THERAPIST: As you know, the staff at the halfway house called me and told me of their concerns about you. Can you tell me what's going on?

PATIENT: Nothing is going on. They're lying about me.

THERAPIST: Why would they do something like that?

PATIENT: How should I know why they lie? They're lying about me.

THERAPIST: I honestly can't imagine why they would lie about you, or why you would think that they would. They are seriously concerned, feel that your behavior is self-destructive, even life threatening, and are concerned that you're taking drugs again.

PATIENT: They're lying. None of that is true.

THERAPIST: I can't help noticing that you have a marked discoloration on your right temple. The halfway house staff is saying that you're banging your head against the wall. You deny it, and yet you have this marked discoloration. What's going on here?

PATIENT: I don't have any discoloration, and you're lying too.

THERAPIST: The discoloration on your temple is very marked and you must be aware of that, and you must also be aware that I would see it and that it would cause me concern about your behavior. Again, how can we understand what's going on here?

PATIENT: It's none of your business what I do outside of here, and I wish those nosey people at the halfway house would mind their business too. I don't want to talk with you about this, and I won't.

THERAPIST: Of course I can't force you to. But I'm concerned about you, and I'm very concerned about what's going on, and I don't really understand it. I don't understand how you can come in here with your temple discolored and simultaneously deny that you're banging your head on the wall.

Lying represents a serious problem in any psychotherapy. Here, however, the patient's lying is so transparent that it appears to be more of a temper tantrum.

Her depression has responded to the nortriptyline, but now the conflicts are being expressed in self-destructive acting out. In other words, I believe that the same issues that resulted in the depression are now manifesting themselves in her behavior. The therapist's limit setting on her phone calls is probably also contributing to the acting out.

PATIENT: I don't care what you don't understand. Mind your own fucking business. I don't feel like talking to you about anything, and I won't.

THERAPIST: (*After 5 minutes of silence*) It seems clear to me that you're feeling badly and also furious with me, that you see me as being of no use to you and are communicating your distress to me nonverbally while simultaneously denying that you're in any distress. But I'm very concerned about the possibility of drugs, and I am even more concerned about the fast driving, which could end up with you dead or seriously injured. I feel in a bind; I'm seriously concerned about your safety on one hand, and on the other, confused about why you're doing what you're doing and why you're refusing to discuss this with me.

PATIENT: (*Silence*)

The remainder of the hour was spent with the therapist expressing confusion and frustration, and the patient totally silent.

That evening the therapist received an emergency phone call from the halfway house. The patient had been stopped by a state trooper for driving 90 miles per hour and escorted back to the halfway house. Afterwards, she went out and smoked several marijuana cigarettes. Returning to the halfway house, she went to her room, slashed both arms multiple times with a razor blade, and with blood dripping from both arms ran through the living room and began climbing out of the sixth-story window. She was stopped by other residents of the halfway house, who notified staff. Staff requested an emergency evaluation and the therapist agreed.

The early part of the unscheduled appointment involved therapist, patient, and two staff members from the halfway house. They reported in detail the events described above, emphasized their great concern about the patient's safety, and their worries about whether the patient could remain in the halfway house. The therapist then asked them to leave the office and the following dialogue ensued:

THERAPIST: I can no longer permit you to keep from me what's going on because at this point your safety and your life are clearly at stake. So please tell me how this all came about.

PATIENT: (*Still slightly intoxicated*) I've been doing pot for the last several weeks. I don't even know why all of this is going on. I don't honestly feel all that terrible. I mostly feel furious and it's mostly at you. You're not helping me anymore, you can't do anything for my loneliness and emptiness, and I just don't care about living anymore. I'm not so depressed, I just don't see anything to live for. Life is a huge empty bore to me and nothing is meaningful. I would have done anything for you if only you had loved me like I wanted you to. But you wouldn't, you kept your goddamn distance and your shrink role, and I'm left high and dry, alone, deserted, with nothing to live for. I was driving like that just inviting God to kill me. I didn't want to do it myself, I really didn't feel suicidal, but neither did I care much about living. And it's all because you don't really care about me. You don't care what happens to me at all. You suckered me in, you seemed like a nice guy, you seemed to really care, but when the chips were down you're a big nothing. (*Starts crying softly*)

And I'll tell you something else. I'm not gonna stop this stuff, because I really don't care whether I'm dead or alive. I really don't think that you care whether I'm dead or alive either. So I'm gonna go back, and I'm gonna get high on pot, and I'm gonna keep invit-

When the acting out takes forms that endanger the patient's safety, and even her life, the therapist interdicts her silence and angry noncommunicativeness, and insists that she must tell him what's going on.

The patient describes her multiple forms of acting out, which seem more related to feelings of emptiness and rage than to depression. She clearly identifies the transference frustrations and rage that lead to the depression and now to the self-destructive acting out.

I find the patient's descriptions of her feelings for the therapist and her frustration over his lack of reciprocal response extremely moving. As I read the material I felt that her ability to express her feelings so honestly and so meaningfully augered well for her future, even though she's so distressed and regressed at the moment.

ing death to come and get me, because I don't give a shit. You don't give
a shit, I don't give a shit, I'm not even
sure whether the damn bird gives a
shit.

THERAPIST: I take very seriously your
lack of concern about whether you're
dead or alive, and it concerns me a lot.
I hear you telling me that for your own
safety you ought to be in hospital at
this point . . .

PATIENT: (*Screaming*) Hospital, hospital, I belong in a hospital? I belong in a
fucking cemetery! Let me out of here,
let me go. I'm going to get in my car
and drive even faster than I did before, and if I get scared I'll just smoke
more weed until I'm not scared anymore. Let me out of here, I'm going.

THERAPIST: You cannot leave in this
state. At this point the halfway house
staff is very frightened of having you
back, and I must say that I agree. I
know that you're slightly tipsy from
the marijuana at the moment, but your
judgment is terrible, and I'm very concerned about your safety. I feel that
you need to be in a hospital tonight,
probably for not too long a time, but
definitely you need to be hospitalized
tonight. Furthermore, I feel strongly
enough about this that if you are not
willing to go into the hospital voluntarily, I will arrange to have you certified as an involuntary patient.

PATIENT: You bastard! I'm not gonna be
committed to a hospital. If that's what
you're gonna do, I'll go myself, I'll go
in voluntarily.

THERAPIST: That's it. I'm glad you're
going in voluntarily.

A statement from the therapist, at this point, about the
distinction between appropriate therapist "caring" and
her transference wishes might
have been helpful to the patient. The therapist could also
have included the fact that his
decision to hospitalize her for
her own safety is also an expression of "caring."

Although the patient is still
mildly intoxicated, her statements that she plans to continue the behaviors and
doesn't care whether she is
dead or alive appropriately
lead the therapist to make this
environmental intervention.
He suggests that a hospitalization is appropriate at this
point in order to ensure the
patient's safety. He indicates
how strongly he feels about
this by telling the patient that
if she will not go into the hospital voluntarily, he will take
the responsibility and have
her certified against her will.

The patient spent 2½ weeks on an acute inpatient unit. Her in-hospital course was very stormy for the first week and a half. She ranted and raved, acted out, and cursed out the therapist and the staff. This behavior alternated with pitiful crying, sobbing, and feeling sorry for herself. She was extremely seductive with her resident therapist and asked him to treat her after discharge because he obviously cared much more for her than her outpatient therapist.

The therapist stayed in touch with the unit staff, encouraged them to hear out the patient's rage and complaints about him, and to raise questions about her very negative and devalued current view of him. The resident therapist raised the question of augmenting the nortriptyline with lithium carbonate, hoping to also decrease the patient's impulsivity and emotional lability. This was agreed upon, and the patient was begun on lithium carbonate 300 mg tid. The therapist attempted to visit the patient on the inpatient unit twice and she refused to see him. However, on the 15th day of hospitalization after 5 days on lithium carbonate, the patient requested that the therapist visit her, and they met briefly on the inpatient unit.

The patient was simultaneously rageful and contrite. She spontaneously noted the enormous discrepancy between her early feelings toward the therapist and the totally negative views she had of him now. She was very impressed by this disparity and also noted that although the therapist was worthless, she was also missing him somewhat. She was contrite about her preadmission behaviors, very upset and concerned about them in retrospect, and thanked the therapist for hospitalizing her when he did. She ended the session with an embarrassed grin, saying, "You're obviously a totally worthless person, but I hope you will take me back into treatment." The therapist replied that, from his side, he never had had any question that the treatment would continue after the hospitalization, and he was pleased that she had made this decision. The patient was discharged 2 days later and resumed outpatient treatment.

The hospitalization marked the nadir of the entire treatment, and her subsequent course was slowly, sometimes imperceptively, upwards, interrupted by frequent regressions and emotional storms. Two months after the hospitalization, she began working as a waitress in a local restaurant, leaving the part-time volunteer job she'd had. Three months later, she left the waitress job and began working as a "girl Friday" in a local business establishment. Three weeks thereafter she began an affair with her employer, a married man 20 years her senior. She consistently denied any further involvement with drugs; acting out, when it did occur, was a minor variant of the previous behaviors. She drove her automobile too fast, crossed streets carelessly, and occasionally engaged in minor self-mutilations. None of this was such as to cause the therapist concern about her safety. She often criticized and derided the therapist, but it usually had a note of humor in it, as though she didn't totally believe it. Note the following dialogue from the 178th session:

PATIENT: Eddie (the boss) is really good to me. He listens to me, he tries to understand, he takes me to nice dinners, and we had a wonderful weekend away last week. I really feel happy with him, even though I'm concerned that he just wants sex from me. But that doesn't really seem true either, at least I don't think so. The sex is pretty good, he's gentle and understanding, and I love to be held and caressed. But I can't come, at least not with him. I never had that trouble before, so thanks for another big favor. By the way, somebody at the halfway house mentioned that maybe the drugs are doing it. Could that be true?

The anorgasmia could be drug related, but is just as likely due to the incestuous overtones of the relationship, and the fact that it so clearly represents a displacement from the transference.

THERAPIST: It's possible, but I'm honestly not sure what's interfering with your ability to have an orgasm.

PATIENT: I really felt that the lithium made a difference and calmed me down, but I'm not sure that I still need the nortriptyline. I think I'd like to stop it.

THERAPIST: I think that's something to be considered. I wouldn't stop it abruptly, but let's talk about it some more and if it still seems like a good idea, we can begin to slowly taper the nortriptyline. I'm glad that you're able to enjoy the relationship with Eddie, but I'm also curious why, with all the men in the world, you chose a married man to get involved with.

PATIENT: Ha, you're jealous, I knew it. You decrepit old bastard, you probably haven't had it in 5 years. Look stupid, Eddie's there and he really cares about me. A bird in the hand . . .

THERAPIST: Well I understand what you're saying, but I still wonder what prevents you from getting involved with a more appropriate guy. Incidentally, I trust that you're using adequate birth control when you're with Eddie.

PATIENT: He doesn't like that stuff, so we use rhythm. I know the old joke about, "What do you call people who use rhythm?" But that's what I'm doing and I'll thank you to mind your own business.

THERAPIST: I would be a lot more comfortable if you were using a more reliable method of birth control. Eddie may not like condoms, but there are diaphragms, etc. I think you ought to think about that.

PATIENT: Yeah, I'll think about it.

The displaced transferences, both loving and hateful, becomes even clearer. The associated guilt is acted out in her attitudes toward effective contraception, and possibly in the anorgasmia.

Three weeks later the patient announced she was pregnant. She thought she might want to keep the pregnancy, but Eddie insisted she have an abortion. She decided to comply with his wishes, but in the process, Eddie's wife found out about the affair, raised a ruckus, and Eddie told her that he could no longer see her. The result was a one-night binge with alcohol, followed by severe slashing of both forearms.

The dialogue below is from the next session. The patient entered with both forearms covered with bandages. The therapist had previously learned that she had cut herself deeply enough to require 30 sutures.

PATIENT: I don't know what happened to me last night, I don't even remember most of it. When Eddie told me he couldn't see me anymore, my whole world collapsed; the bottom fell out of everything. I went back to my place and I was trying to think about all this and I couldn't concentrate. I started getting very upset and nervous. I went out to have a drink to calm myself, but I had too many. I went back to my place and I sat there feeling totally lost and alone, and rageful and furious, and like I wanted revenge. I started to feel more and more depressed, and more and more angry, and I didn't know who I wanted to kill, me or Eddie. And then this crazy thing happened. Every time I thought of Eddie, I saw your face; it got totally confusing. I didn't know whether I wanted to kill me, you, or Eddie, or all of us. I couldn't believe it, you and me and Eddie were all mixed up in my mind as though we were all one person.

Why you? You didn't get me pregnant, you didn't walk out on me. I got more and more confused, and then I had this crazy thought. Eddie was my left arm and you were my right arm, and I got my roommate's razor blade and I began to slash you and Eddie. Blood was flowing all over the place, and I imagined it was your blood and Eddie's. And I kept thinking to myself, "Why am I angry at you?" I was slashing and screaming and crying, and eventually one of the staff heard me and came in and stopped me. She took me to the emergency room and I got fixed up.

I went home but I couldn't sleep. I felt calmed down, but very sad this morning. Now I feel exhausted, hung over, and totally played out. Why was I so angry at you, and why did I get you and Eddie so mixed up?

THERAPIST: I guess because you felt that I too had promised you something, had led you on, and . . .

The fact that Eddie represents a displaced transference figure, suggested in earlier dialogue by the patient's response to why she chose a married man, "Ha, you're jealous, I knew it," represents a wish on the part of the patient that the therapist experience the rejection that she has experienced from him. Of course, the relationship with Eddie is also a displacement of her intense loving transference feelings.

This tends to be confirmed by the patient's description here. She, Eddie, and the therapist are all confused in her mind, particularly after Eddie rejects her, as she feels rejected by the therapist. This confusion, frequently combined with depersonalization and/or derealization, commonly occurs in borderline patients when they self-mutilate. There is a regressive loss of ego boundaries, and she slashes Eddie and the therapist by slashing herself. "I imagined it was your blood and Eddie's."

PATIENT: (*Interrupting*) You did. I wanted you all for myself, and you never would be that. I know you never said you would, but I wanted you to, and now I feel that I need you more than ever. I feel alone and devastated, and I know you're still with me, but I felt that you had totally deserted me.

God, was I sick and confused last night. But now I just feel empty and sad and very needy. I'm afraid you'll stick me in the hospital again. But I don't need that. I feel a strange kind of calm in the middle of all my exhaustion. I wanted you to feel toward me the way I felt about you, and I never felt you did. I know you were doing your job but it wasn't enough. I felt that in some crazy way Eddie was a kind of substitute for you. I'm very embarrassed to say this, but occasionally when I was with Eddie I would picture your face instead of his.

Please don't stick me in a hospital. I would like to ask you one favor though, could you see me an extra time tomorrow? I think there's something very important going on here, but I'm too exhausted and hung over to get it. I would really appreciate an extra session tomorrow.

THERAPIST: That would be fine, and I would agree with you that there's no reason for you to be in the hospital. Please don't try to prove me wrong by escalating this behavior again, but I don't think you need to do that, and I agree with you that something extremely important happened.

PATIENT: I realize now how enraged I've been with you for such a long time because you didn't feel toward

As the patient continues, there is clear evidence of self-examination and curiosity about herself. "Why was I so angry with you, and why did I get you and Eddie so mixed-up?" came from the patient, but could just as well have come from the therapist. It represents some identification with the therapist and his constant attitudes of curiosity and wish to understand. But it also demonstrates the patient's wish to understand herself, one indicator for considering a switch to a more exploratory treatment.

In addition, the patient is now more comfortable with her dependency feelings, correctly states that she doesn't need to be in a hospital, and requests an extra session, acknowledging the therapist's helpfulness.

This is a clear expression of ambivalence toward the therapist, which is evidence of

me as I felt toward you. And yet you were the one who stuck by me through all of this shit. I feel grateful for that, at the same time that I still feel deserted and furious at you.

THERAPIST: I'm very impressed by your awareness of the connections between Eddie and myself. But do you think this all really started with me?

PATIENT: I don't know what you're talking about.

THERAPIST: Do you think I was the first man to disappoint you?

PATIENT: Oh no, you're not gonna give me that daddy garbage. Oedipus, schmoedipus. My father was never there; he just hid out in the library and got himself drunk. No, no, no. It all started with you.

THERAPIST: I'm not sure I agree with that, but that's the way it feels to you now. Although I'm sorry that you cut yourself up so badly, I certainly agree that you've come to some very important realizations about yourself and your feelings. I think you should be pleased with yourself about that, and I'm happy to meet an extra time tomorrow when you're not so hung over, and we can try to get clearer about what happened.

significant change in her splitting tendencies. Precursors of this change can be found in the clinical material above.

The therapist praises the patient's awarenesses of her feelings toward the therapist, as well as her open and honest way of talking about it.

His attempt to address genetic issues regarding feelings toward her father is not consistent with the techniques of dynamic supportive psychotherapy, unless the therapist intends a "pseudogenetic inexact interpretation," a benign projection, which this does not appear to be because of its probable accuracy. However, he rapidly drops the issue and returns to the reality of their extra meeting the following day.

In the next session, the issues were talked about again, with the patient steadfastly denying that it had anything to do with her father because he was never available and he never promised anything. The therapist did not press the point. The patient remained subdued and sad. She talked repeatedly of her gratitude and her rage toward the therapist. She also noted that she often felt a "kind of sad and empty solidness," which surprised her. The subdued sadness occasionally alternated with angry critical attacks on the therapist, but the attacks lacked their previous intensity. Throughout it all, she also insisted that she needed the therapist and the therapy, and occasionally expressed gratitude "for sticking with me through all this garbage."

The patient left her job at Eddie's company and secured a position as a mental health worker at a local psychiatric institution. She began to talk about returning to college to finish her undergraduate degree and thought about becoming a psychiatric social worker. She functioned well in her new position and after a while began dating a young man who also was a mental health worker at the institution and was planning to continue on to a graduate degree in psychology.

The previous patterns of depression, sadness, and rage at the therapist continued but they lacked their former intensity. When she got into difficulties with her new boyfriend, she would drive fast or occasionally drink too much or smoke marijuana, but these episodes were mild and self-limited. She passed the college courses she was taking and began to talk seriously of a graduate degree in the mental health field.

At about the 30th month, she first brought up the issue of stopping. She had left the halfway house and was living with her new boyfriend. That relationship appeared to be going reasonably well, and the entire psychotherapy had a less intense feel to it.

The therapist's first response, in his own mind, to the mention of termination was to wonder what the patient was avoiding. However as they continued to discuss the pros and cons, he felt that the termination idea was not primarily an acting out of resistance; rather it represented an ambivalent wish to move on and to invest more in the new boyfriend. Most of her previous patterns of difficulty were still evident, including the significant use of projection and denial; sometimes her thinking became confused, but all of this was without its former intensity and self-destructiveness. After repeated discussions of the pros and cons of stopping, over about eight sessions, the patient and therapist agreed to stop in 6 months. This decision marked the end of the Middle Phase, and the beginning of Termination.

FINAL THOUGHTS

Psychotherapy has often been compared to chess, with clearly spelled-out opening moves and end-game tactics, and a very variable middle game/phase. This metaphor is accurately applied to POST.

The Middle Phase constitutes most of the psychotherapy, but it is unpredictable in its developments. Its main task is the working through of the major adaptational difficulties of the patient, but these difficulties can assume an endless variety of forms. Thus, it is the Middle Phase of POST that requires the utmost in skill and creativity from the supportive therapist.

CHAPTER 8

The Termination Phase of Treatment

The phase of Termination begins with the setting of a termination date and ends with the last meeting. Its main tasks are dealing with the patient's reactions to the impending separation, and with the recrudescence of problems and symptomatology that occurs in reaction to the upcoming separation.

Termination itself in dynamic supportive therapy is frequently less definitive than in exploratory treatment and may not occur at all with chronically psychotic patients, particularly when maintenance medications are necessary. Acting out, and other resistances to the pain of separation, tend to be more accepted in supportive therapy than in exploratory treatments. Stopping before the agreed upon date, or decreasing the frequency of sessions by patient request, are permissible when they are not clearly self-destructive. This is consistent with the supportive therapy strategy of evaluating the adaptive/maladaptive values of each resistance and not undermining those not clearly maladaptive. Similarly, when the therapist feels that the probable alternative to resistant behaviors is an interminable treatment, he will respond acceptingly to those behaviors.

Access to the supportive therapist does not end with the termination of the treatment episode. The therapist clearly communicates that his door is always open, either for occasional sessions at times of crisis or for a further episode of treatment if necessary.

These comments should not be taken to minimize the fact that many patient behaviors during the Termination Phase of a supportive treatment are markedly maladaptive and are vigorously undermined; for example, the patient who wishes to stop immediately after a termination date is set. This response is always maladaptive and needs to be clarified, confronted, and undermined. As always in supportive therapy, the therapist's evaluation of the adaptive/maladaptive ratio of any resistant behavior will determine whether he responds with acceptance and support, or with questioning, skepticism, disapproval, and undermining.

CLINICAL MATERIAL

The decision to terminate in this case was made at the 30th month (about 225 sessions), and a date was set 6 months (about 50 sessions) in the future. In the early weeks following the setting of the termination date, little change was apparent in the patient. Her functioning at work, at school, and with her boyfriend appeared unaffected. What was notable was a relative trivialization of her verbal material in the sessions. The patient spent a lot of time talking about patients she was involved with at her job, her coworkers, and her college courses. The therapist's calling attention to this change in the quality of the session material led to sarcastic responses, minimization of his comments, and further trivia. This reached its peak in the fifth week after setting the termination date.

Session 236

The session was filled with impersonal and trivial material. At about the midpoint, the following dialogue occurred:

PATIENT: I think I would like to cut down our sessions to once a week. I don't feel like much is happening here, I am very involved in my outside life, and I just don't feel very interested in what's happening here. I would really like to cut down to one session per week. It will save me money and time, and I think we should do it.

THERAPIST: I would tend to see that request in the context of the increasing impersonal nature of what you have been talking about here. It seems to me that cutting the frequency in half is another way of pulling out, and I am concerned that you are avoiding feelings that you would better deal with

Before a quarter of the 6-month termination phase has elapsed, and in the context of trivial and impersonal material, the patient proposes a radical decrease in the session frequency. The therapist states his opinion that the patient is in a very resistant state and that decreasing the frequency is another aspect of that resistance. For those reasons, he responds negatively to the patient's proposal. This leads,

directly. I will keep an open mind about the idea of cutting back, but in the present context I feel that it would be a bad idea. What are your thoughts about what I have said?

PATIENT: You just want to keep me here. You know that I'm doing better, it's very clear, and you want to keep me here for your own reasons. You know, Doc, all relationships have to end sometime. I am losing interest in this treatment and I want to go, and you want to keep me here and I don't understand why. Do I have to buy my way out of here by getting you another patient to take my place? Do you need the money? What's the story with you? I am feeling better, things are going well in my life, and I want to get out of here, and you won't let me. This is your problem, not mine.

THERAPIST: I would certainly agree that you are doing much better in many areas of your life. However, I also feel that you are running from something. I could let you do that, but I honestly don't think it's in your best interest. I would suggest that we keep our regular schedule for now and see what happens.

PATIENT: That really pisses me off! What will you do if I only come once a week? Are you going to tie me down and make me come here?

THERAPIST: I can't do that obviously. I can only give you my best opinion, and that is that, at the moment, we should not change the schedule.

expectably, to a paranoid outburst from the patient, though with some humor, but the therapist stands his ground.

The patient reluctantly agreed, but with much derision and sarcasm. Two weeks later her life was in disarray. It began with a fight with her boyfriend, to which she responded by becoming intoxicated. She missed some time at work, and her work performance deteriorated rapidly to the point where her supervisor was concerned and raised questions about her functioning. Bickering with her boyfriend became constant. After a particularly bad fight the patient again drove recklessly up local highways, got drunk, and came home and cut her arms, superficially this time, not requiring suturing.

Session 241

PATIENT: Now you've done it. I told you to let me out of here, and you wouldn't, and look what's happening now. Every time I listen to you I just get into more trouble. I feel like hell, my relationship with Sam is shakey, and my supervisor at work is questioning whether I can do the job. I wanted to get out while the getting was good. Why did you stop me? Do you want me to destroy my whole life before you let me out of here?

THERAPIST: Well, what's happening here? Why is everything falling apart all of a sudden? Of course I am not happy with what's going on in your life, but there must be a reason.

PATIENT: Yeah, there's a reason. I didn't want to come here any more. I wanted out and you made me stay. That's the reason!

THERAPIST: It is true that I had questions about the change in what you were talking about, the impersonal quality of it, and your wish to cut down the sessions. I didn't understand what was happening then. But what's happening now?

PATIENT: It's your fault. Why did you want me to stay? I could've gotten out of here and avoided all this trouble.

The correctness of the therapist's response is clear almost immediately, as the patient's life and function become increasingly disorganized. Quarrels with her boyfriend lead to a return of the patient's self-mutilating behavior. However, this time the cutting is much less dramatic.

The patient blames her increasing difficulties and symp-

Why wouldn't you let me go? It's all your fault. I wanted to go and you wouldn't let me leave. . . . (*Suddenly begins sobbing violently*) You wanted to leave and I wanted you to stay. . . . Oh God, I got that all backwards. I wanted to leave and you wanted me to stay. . . .

THERAPIST: That's quite a striking slip.

PATIENT: Now you've done it. Now I am totally falling apart. . . . (*crying and sobbing*) I wanted to leave cause you wanted to stop. . . . No that's not right. I wanted to stop. . . . But why did you go along with me? . . . You were supposed to say, "No don't leave, never leave, I need you to stay here". . . . But you went along with stopping and you broke my heart. I wanted to leave you before you left me, so I had some control over it, or at least I felt like I had some control. How could you let me stop? How could you let me go? I hate you for that. . . . I want to leave you like you are leaving me. . . . I want to leave you before you leave me. . . . I love Sam, but it's you I want . . . and you were willing to stop, you were willing to let me go . . . and that meant you

tomatology on the therapist, a return of paranoid and externalizing tendencies. The therapist maintains a stance of curiosity and repetitively poses the question, "What's going on here now?" Suddenly there is a breakthrough of powerful affects and a striking slip. She reveals her intense disappointment that the therapist was willing to set a termination date. Now her trivial associations and negativism make sense. "You went along with stopping and you broke my heart." "You broke my heart and I will never forgive you." "How could you let me go? I hate you for that."

didn't give a shit . . . so I don't want to give a shit . . . and I didn't want to see you anymore. . . . I didn't want to talk to you . . . you broke my heart and I will never forgive you.

THERAPIST: I don't have a lot to add. You're spelling it out pretty clearly. You experienced my agreeing to stop as the final rejection, and you wanted to get even by rejecting me and leaving early. And you talked about things other than yourself and wanted to cut down the sessions so you wouldn't have to deal with all those feelings, and to punish me. As you said, to reject me as I had rejected you and before I could reject you. I really have nothing to add. You spelled it out quite accurately, at least it seems so to me. I'm really very impressed.

PATIENT: I don't want words and I don't want your praise. I wanted you, I wanted you to want me the way I wanted you, and you never did, and you never will, and I hate you for that. I hate you because I cared so much about you, and you would never give me the time of day. You didn't even care enough about me to yell and scream at me as I do to you. You just kept your professional stance and your fucking distance. You've broken my heart, I will never forgive you, and life will always be empty and blah.

THERAPIST: I am not only impressed by your ability to spell this out. I am also very touched by what you are saying and I appreciate it a lot. But remember how we set up this treatment—that we'd work together to try to get your life on a better level, not to have a love affair. That was our job

The therapist is complimentary to the patient about her ability to describe the issues so clearly. Here he shares with the patient his emotional reactions to her powerful statements about her feelings. He continues by reminding

and those were our goals, and of course this is painful and disappointing and enraging to you, but this is what we met to do in the first place. Can you accept that?

the patient about the realistic set-up of the treatment.

It seems to me that the therapist could have stopped after expressing how he was touched by, and appreciative of, what the patient was saying. The remainder of this therapist intervention seems to me unnecessary, and even negative, in that it dilutes the intensity of the interaction.

PATIENT: Sure I remember it but it's empty and intellectual. It doesn't make me feel any better. All I feel now is a great emptiness and sadness, and the feeling that with everything going well for me in my life, it just isn't worth the game. I feel now like I'll always be sad and I'll always feel empty.

In succeeding weeks the acting out diminished in intensity and the issues elucidated above were discussed repetitively and from every vantage point. The associated affects gradually decreased in intensity.

Shortly after the midpoint of the 6-month termination phase, the patient again brought up the issue of decreasing meetings to once a week. This time her stated reason was that she was frightened of stopping and felt that it would be easier to gradually cut down. After some discussion, the therapist agreed and sessions were decreased to once weekly. There was no further recrudescence of acting out or other symptomatology during the final weeks, nor did the patient appear to react to the diminished frequency.

The termination agreement included the offer that the patient could return as needed in the future or didn't need to return at all, except that the therapist suggested that they meet 6 months post termination; the patient agreed to this. This dialogue is from the final session of the treatment:

THERAPIST: As I said before, although we are stopping, the door is always open for you to return if you need to.

We have also agreed to meet in
6 months, and I think we should set
that appointment time before you
leave.

Well we've come a long way together, and this is our final regular session. It wouldn't be like me if I didn't
ask you about your thoughts and feelings at this time.

PATIENT: In role to the last minute! I'm
sure glad I'm not your daughter or
your wife. I could fall off my bike and
come to you with my knees cut open
and bleeding looking for comfort and
help, and you would probably say,
"What are your feelings about that?"

No, I want to be serious about this. I
thought a lot about this last session.
First of all I feel sad, in a gentle sort of
way, soft-like, not very depressed,
and not particularly angry. I feel that
there was so much that I wanted here
that I never got, but I also feel that I
can live without it or at least survive
without it. But it would have been
really nice; that's the sadness.

I also feel very grateful to you. For
all that I yelled and screamed and
gave you a hard time, and bothered
you at home, and for all my joshing
you for your psychiatric bullshit, the
fact is that you always stayed with me,
you never deserted me or exploited
me, and even though you enraged me
most of the time, I have to admire
your honesty and your stick-to-itness.
I used to think you were a brilliant and
wonderful therapist; I'm not so sure
about that anymore. But I do know
that you were always straight with me,
you stuck by the rules that we set, you
were always professional, and mostly

... (*tears up*) ... mostly I am just feeling so much better. My life is really reasonably okay now. I still see the old problems. I still get drunk too often. I see myself playing my old borderline games with my boyfriend and with other people ... but Doc, I've got to tell you, in comparison to where I was 5 years ago, I am very different. I am in a whole new place, and I am grateful to you for that. You did it for me, you made it possible for me to feel and act like I have recently, and I am tremendously grateful to you.

THERAPIST: I am very touched by what you are saying, but I really don't totally agree with you. First of all, I agree that you are enormously different from what you used to be, and I am very pleased for you, and I am very pleased to have been able to help you with that. But as I said in one of our very first meetings, this was a collaborative effort, and to the extent to which we are successful the credit belongs to both of us, just as to the extent to which we are not successful the responsibility belongs to both of us.

So what I am trying to say here is that I am very grateful for what you have said to me, but I also think that you should be pleased and proud of what you have accomplished and, I guess put most accurately, what we've accomplished, what we were able to do together. I put it that way because neither of us could have done it alone and we both should share the credit, 50, 50.

PATIENT: I remember you saying that at the beginning of the treatment. I

I find this long patient statement one of the most moving descriptions of the feelings of a patient for her psychotherapist that I have heard or read. In the last analysis, the important things to her were the therapist's honesty, his sticking with her, and his maintenance of the professional role in the face of major provocations. The patient is so articulate, so capable of describing intense and complex affects with such sensitivity, that I think I now understand what the therapist found appealing about her initially.

The therapist also seems affected by what the patient is saying. He states that he is, but he also seems more alive, perhaps in response to the intensity of the patient's feelings, or perhaps because he is having his own emotional reactions to the termination. He accepts her praise and loving feelings reasonably comfortably, but reminds her of the collaborative nature of the work and that she deserves 50% of the credit for the outcome.

didn't believe it then, and I am not sure I believe it now, but it's very kind of you to say that. And yet I know there is some truth in what you are saying because if I had, for example, run and quit the treatment when things got tough as I had before, obviously you couldn't have helped me. It feels to me like you have done something really terrific for me, but I can see it somewhat in the way that you're putting it also. In any event, whether it's you, me, or us, I am very grateful to you and for your role in this. Thank you very much.

THERAPIST: Thank you for staying here during times when it was almost impossible for you. I have been very aware in recent months of feeling pleased for you, and for me, at the progress that we were able to make together. So thank you for your part in it. Now before we both dissolve in a puddle of sentimentality, let's set that date for 6 months down the road so that we don't forget it. . . .

In his last intervention, the therapist becomes even more alive and emotionally available. He thanks the patient for not quitting at times of intense stress, he tells her of his feelings of pleasure at her progress, and thanks her for her role in that. He gently kids himself, which is a nice note, and then returns to role.

I find the interaction in this final session extremely moving in general. Both participants seem very much "in tune" with each other. At the end, I find myself feeling admiring toward both participants, but particularly toward the therapist, who has been able to treat this very difficult patient with impressive success.

POSTSCRIPT

The meeting in 6 months actually consisted of two sessions. In general the patient had continued her positive course. She was doing well at college, and the relationship with her boyfriend, although troubled, appeared to be a lasting one. The patient reported transient depressions, occasional drug and alcohol bingeing, never long lasting, and occasional head banging at moments of maximum frustration. These symptoms existed in a general context of doing well at her job and beginning to seriously consider a career as a psychiatric social worker. She reported that subjectively she felt fairly comfortable, but this appeared to depend absolutely upon the stability of the relationship with her boyfriend. When that relationship was threatened, the patient would head bang, drink, and act out in her usual style.

It was not clear why there was a second session; the first ended in the middle of relating some incidents and the patient suggested a second meeting. She again talked quite rationally about the frustration and nonreciprocation of her loving feelings, and her reactive rage and self-destructiveness; she appeared to have achieved some mastery of the material. She also seemed somewhat further away from it emotionally. She reported a dream in which the therapist, her current boyfriend, and her father seemed to be all mixed together, and commented, "I guess that suggests that you were right about my father in the first place. I thought about that dream a lot, and I have vague memories of some good times with him and wanting more of them, and some feelings that he had not always been withdrawn from me, so I guess there was something to what you were saying. I am really not sure."

Near the end of the second session, the therapist asked if she thought it was worthwhile to meet again in another 6 months. The patient replied, "No, I don't want to do that. I know I can call if I need to, and I would rather leave it that way. I feel sad about not knowing when or whether I will ever see you again, but it feels to me like that's the right thing, and I would prefer it."

FINAL COMMENTS

This is an impressive treatment and outcome for any psychotherapeutic treatment of a Borderline Personality Disorder patient. A caveat is in order. The case report should not be seen as implying that this positive result can be expected from the dynamic supportive therapy of BPD patients. This is a single case, and there is not enough experience with this treatment applied to these patients to say anything about outcome.

I don't know all the reasons why the treatment went so well. The patient seemed ready to be serious about the work and about change in herself; the therapist was very skilled and empathic. There was probably also a good patient/therapist "fit."

The case report does demonstrate that significant change, and probably change in basic psychic structures, can occur in a primarily supportive psychotherapy. This is consistent with Wallerstein's (1986) findings.

ISSUES
IN TREATMENT

CHAPTER 9

The Therapist's Countertransference

C ountertransference issues are particularly complex and problematic in the psychodynamic supportive therapy (POST) of the Borderline Personality Disorder (BPD) patient. Two major factors are primarily responsible. First, the patient's psychopathology and its manifestations in interactions with others, particularly the intense, labile, and frequently acted-out transferences induce powerful and confusing counter-reactions in the therapist. Second, the nature of POST, its less fixed guidelines for intervention, and the fact that appropriate techniques include advice, suggestion, praise, limit setting, and so forth, leaves the supportive therapist especially vulnerable to acting out of the countertransference. Thus, from both standpoints, the patient's pathology and its expression in the therapeutic relationship, and the character of the psychotherapy, supportive treatment of the BPD patient is a virtual "mine field" for countertransference acting out. I view the potential for countertransference acting out as the major technical difficulty in all dynamic supportive psychotherapies, and nowhere are these problems more likely to occur than with BPD patients.

For these reasons it is crucial that the supportive therapist, and particularly when treating BPD patients, be maximally aware of his own character style, problems and idiosyncracies, his unresolved conflictual areas, and the specific behaviors that should serve to warn him that he may be acting out countertransference issues. In the hands of unskilled and uninsightful therapists, supportive psychotherapy includes the alarming possibilities of all kinds of pathological therapist behaviors. These include not only such gross examples as physical and sexual intimacies, but more commonly the acting out of the therapist's needs to rescue, to control, to overgratify, to tell the patient how to live, and so on.

THE CONCEPT OF COUNTERTRANSFERENCE

In its most general sense, "countertransference" refers to the conscious, preconscious, and unconscious responses of the therapist to the patient. More specifically, the term is currently utilized in two different, but overlapping, ways. In its broad, or totalistic, meaning it encompasses all of the emotional responses that the therapist experiences with the patient. In its narrow, or classical, sense it refers to the therapist's transferential reactions to the patient and his transferences, that is, the therapist's analogue of the patient's transferences. Initially viewed as a problem within the therapist and an obstacle to the treatment, it is currently seen as inevitable in all psychotherapies, without a negative connotation.

The broad definition tends to be utilized by therapists who treat sicker patients, with the implication that the therapist's emotional responses are primarily responsive to the patient's transferences, projections, and projective identifications. Therapists treating neurotic patients tend to use the narrow definition; the patient's transferences are not so intense and primitive, and the therapist can focus more on his own irrational responses. Both definitions of the term are acceptable, and it is important to specify in which sense the term is being used.

The concept of countertransference was introduced by Freud in 1910 (Freud, 1910). He viewed it as a problem in the therapist that interfered with the analysis and therefore needed to be minimized or eliminated. It was probably his main reason for recommending regular returns for more psychoanalysis for the analyst. He urged the analyst to become maximally aware of his countertransferences, both through self-analysis and via more psychoanalytic treatment. Winnicott's (1960) view of countertransference was similar to that of Freud. He saw it as ". . . . the neurotic features which spoil the professional attitude and disturb the course of the analytic process. . . ." (p. 9).

In a related vein, other writers argued that countertransference was most usefully viewed as the exact analogue in the therapist of the patient's transferences. Annie Reich (1951) wrote ". . . . the patient represents for the analyst an object of the past onto whom past feelings and wishes are projected just as it happens in the patient's transference situation with the analyst" (p. 76). Lucia Tower (1956) said, ". . . . Transferences and countertransference are unconscious phenomena, based on the repetition compulsion, are derived from significant experiences, largely of one's own childhood, and directed toward significant persons of the past emotional life of the individual" (pp. 227-8).

The broad definition of countertransference was introduced by analysts of the British school. Michael Balint (1965) viewed countertransference as the totality of the analyst's attitudes and behaviors toward the patient, including the professional attitude. Heinrich Racker (1953, 1957), promoting the broad, totalistic view, wrote, "It is precisely this fusion of present and past, the continuous and intimate connection of reality and fantasy, of external and internal, conscious and unconscious, that demands a concept embracing the totality of the analyst's psychological response, and renders it advisable, at the same time, to keep for this totality of response the accustomed term 'countertransference'" (p. 310). However, he continued, "Where it is necessary for greater clarity one might speak of 'total countertransference' and then differentiate and separate within it one aspect or another. One of its aspects consists precisely in *what is transferred* in countertransference; this is the part that originates in an earlier time and that is especially the infantile and primitive part within total countertransference" (1957, pp. 310-11). Thus, Racker argued for the broad view, but at the same time differentiated the narrow view from the remainder of the broad concept.

The issues and controversies surrounding countertransference are summarized by Douglas Orr (1954) and Otto Kernberg (1965). Those who favor the narrow or classical definition criticize the totalistic one as confusing and nonspecific. Those who prefer the broad totalistic view criticize the narrow concept as still implying a negative value to countertransference and for not sufficiently appreciating its usefulness in clarifying more subtle aspects of the transference.

In my view, there is merit in both concepts. The danger of the totalistic view is the over-reading of countertransference reactions as due totally to projections into the therapist from the patient, rather than separating the contributions of the therapist from those of the patient. The usefulness of the therapist's emotional responses for understanding the patient is well accepted, and countertransference no longer has the negative connotation it had previously. Rather, it is universally viewed as valuable data, whether about the patient or about the therapist, and as inevitable in psychotherapy as is transference.

The capacity to accurately perceive and experience countertransference reactions, and to differentiate the therapist's contributions from the projections of the patient, are probably the strongest argument for an analytic experience for all dynamic psychotherapists. Whether the countertransference is best utilized in the broader sense, or whether it is preferable to confine it to the therapist's transferential reactions to the patient and to use a third term, such as "reaction to the transference"

(Rockland, 1989), remains a personal preference. However the term is used, countertransference reactions constitute extremely important data, whether primarily about the patient or the therapist or, as is usually true, about the complex interaction between the two.

COUNTERTRANSFERENCE
IN THE SUPPORTIVE THERAPY
OF BORDERLINE PATIENTS

As noted above, dynamic supportive therapy of the borderline patient makes accurate awareness of countertransference issues doubly important. The greatest danger of supportive psychotherapy is its furnishing a rationale for "wild" psychotherapy, and nowhere is this more likely to occur than in the treatment of the borderline patient.

The BPD patient's desperate need for love and approval, the corresponding propensity for violent and rageful reactions when these wishes are frustrated, and the primitive defenses and propensity to act out can place enormous pressures on the therapist. For example, he may be tempted to supply inappropriate amounts of gratification to compensate for earlier deprivations, to perpetuate the patient's admiration and idealization, or to protect himself against the onslaughts of primitive rage that result from frustrating the patient. The patient's ability to create anxiety in the therapist by impulsive acting out, particularly self-destructive acting out, further adds to the difficulty of the therapist's task. It is in the supportive psychotherapy of the BPD patient that the therapist's ability to utilize countertransference reactions without acting them out, that is, to use support, advice, praise, or limit setting *only as required by the patient's ego deficits*, and not to gratify conscious or unconscious wishes of the therapist, receives its most challenging test.

It is the borderline patient's tendencies to present intense, chaotic, and contradictory transferences (splitting); to express these transferences via behaviors rather than verbally (acting out); and to deny feelings or parts of themselves and to put them into the therapist (projective identification) that lead to such intense countertransference reactions in their therapists. The impact of these countertransference experiences on the therapist can be positive or negative. If they are perceived clearly and not denied or minimized, and do not flood the therapist affectively so that his working ego is overwhelmed, they can be the source of crucial data about the patient. If, however, they are denied, minimized, or distorted, or overwhelm his working ego, he will respond less than optimally; for example, by withdrawing empathic contact from the patient or by acting out countertransference issues.

The therapist may observe himself atypically withdrawing, unaware that he is protecting himself from the patient's projective identifications. Alternatively, he may find himself affectively overwhelmed, rageful, discouraged, depressed, or experiencing inner chaos and disorganization. Impairments in the function of the therapist's working ego are best handled by introspection during the session and further self-analysis afterwards, trying to sort out, understand, and master the irrational aspects of his affective reactions. For further elaboration of these issues, see Rockland (1989, pp. 116–17).

CLINICAL MATERIAL

Countertransference problems may occur across the therapist's practice, or they may occur only with certain types of patients or with one individual patient. Every therapist has her own unresolved wishes, conflicts, and needs, and these will lead to various kinds of countertransference difficulties unless she is constantly alert to their affective and behavioral consequences.

The specific forms that these countertransference difficulties can take are as innumerable as there are therapists. Thus it is extremely important that each therapist be keenly aware of her own irrationalities and how they can distort the treatment. She must remain alert to her particular "red flags," signals that she is acting out countertransference reactions. She may observe that she is acting in a more gratifying manner than usual, or conversely is more withholding and aloof. She may be unusually combative and hostile, or conversely so conflicted about aggressive impulses that any confrontation or limit setting is experienced as a hostile attack on the patient. She may find herself running over the session time or wanting to end the session early. She may wish to treat only well-functioning patients due to excessive anxiety about primitive, unmodulated affects, or conversely treat only very sick patients to satisfy nurturing, rescuing, and regressive fantasies. Each of these behaviors are instances that signal the therapist that countertransferences are probably distorting the treatment relationship.

As examples of generalized countertransference difficulties influencing several or many patients, consider the following material from the treatments of two mental health professionals.

Clinical Example 1

This 42-year-old psychiatrist reported increasing complaints from his wife about his lack of availability to the family because of frequent, prolonged evening telephone calls from patients. On further query, all of the calls were from four female borderline patients, each of whom called the therapist one to several evenings per week with "emergencies." These emergencies consisted of transient depressions, feelings of emptiness, implied threats of drug use or promiscuity, thoughts about hurting themselves, and occasional suicidal threats. The therapist felt justified in responding to these calls, each of which lasted up to 45 minutes, and believed that his willingness to do so was keeping the patients out of serious harm or even out of a hospital. At the same time, his resentment was apparent in the demeaning manner in which he described the patients. He also felt torn between the demands of his wife and family and the demands of his patients, and felt resentful toward his wife for not understanding the exigencies of his work.

In his own treatment, he was often scathingly critical of the therapist, feeling that the therapist was not sufficiently interested in him and viewing himself as superior to the therapist in his devotion to his patients. These transferences were similar to feelings toward his wife, whom he felt demanded more than she was willing to give and did not appreciate him adequately as a husband and doctor. It gradually became clear to him that he found the evening phone calls gratifying as well as wearing; the patients appreciated and needed him as no one else did. He also became aware that he was very frightened of hostile attacks from the patients, felt he would do anything to avoid such attacks, and much preferred the more modulated criticisms of his wife.

His awareness of the gratification, and of the fears of attack that he came to view as a condensation of real patient hostility and the projection into them of his own hostilities, allowed him to begin to set more realistic behavioral limits. He became increasingly cognizant of his narcissistic fragility, inordinate needs to be admired and needed, and his guilty fearfulness and rage when these needs were frustrated. As he set more realistic limits with his patients, the marital relationship improved, although he never received from his wife the degree of admiration and idealization he sought; what he got was "adequate but pale" compared to what his patients gave him.

As he limited the behaviors of his patients, his ragefulness, devaluation, and wishes for admiration intensified in his own treatment. Thus, the cessation of the countertransference acting out not only improved the treatments of his patients and his marital relationship, but allowed those issues to develop to their full intensity in the transference. It was clear that his behavior with patients had also functioned as a powerful resistance in his own treatment. It will not surprise the reader that although his borderline patients complained bitterly about his newfound limit-setting abilities, the clinical results were positive.

Clinical Example 2

This mental health professional, in treatment primarily for widespread narcissistic character pathology, began to discuss the fact that she was still treating almost all the patients that she had begun treatment with 14 years previously. Although in each case she could rationalize the patient's need for further treatment, she was also aware that her behavior was quite unusual. The behavior became less ego-syntonic as she became increasingly puzzled and concerned about it.

As the therapist repeatedly examined this behavior in her treatment, it became clear to her that she could not terminate a patient until she was "totally cured." She was unable to set realistic treatment goals and invested each patient with the fantasy that with more psychotherapy they could finally become "perfect."

With further exploration, she became aware that she was projecting her own wishes for perfection into each of her patients. If she could turn out perfect patients, she could maintain the fantasy of her own eventual perfection. Each patient represented a narcissistic extension of her own perfection; she could not terminate with them until they reflected that perfection. Further working through of these issues, first with her patients and then in her views of herself, allowed her to set more realistic treatment goals and to permit patients to terminate with imperfect outcomes.

These two examples illustrate the impact of unresolved conflicts and character pathology on countertransference difficulties extending across several patients or whole practices. These countertransference problems are best treated by a psychoanalytic or intensive psychotherapeutic treatment for the therapist. They illustrate again the crucial need for every dynamic psychotherapist to have an intensive psychotherapeutic experience for himself. The alternative is the kind of problematic psychotherapies illustrated here, or worse, destructive treatments carried out by psychotherapists who deny any need for their own psychotherapy.

We will now examine the kinds of countertransference reactions that can arise with different types of BPD patients. Each type is discussed briefly and then the potential countertransference problems are illustrated with clinical examples. Although each kind of interaction is presented separately, in reality patients frequently demonstrate several of the paradigms, either simultaneously or sequentially.

THE HOSTILE, DEVALUING PATIENT

Hostile transferences, both overt and covert, are omnipresent in borderline patients. Some are hostilely demeaning from the earliest sessions of the treatment, while in others these reactions develop after an initial period of positive or idealizing transferences. They can be extremely threatening to the therapist, and especially to inexperienced therapists already struggling with questions about their competence. The patient's devaluations reverberate with the therapist's feelings of incompetence, thereby increasing his anxieties and fears of incompetence as he struggles against his tendencies to view the transferences as reality.

Even for the experienced psychotherapist, however, the attacking, intensely devaluing borderline patient can be a disturbing and painful experience. Some of these patients appear to possess an uncanny awareness of the therapist's "soft spots" and an impressive ability to accurately attack in areas of particular therapist sensitivity. It is difficult for the mature, and certainly for the beginning, psychotherapist to experience the patient's hostile and devaluing attacks without withdrawing emotionally or responding with counterhostility. Beginning therapists often deny or minimize patient hostilities by focusing on the "hurt little girl" beneath the "facade" of hostility and destruction. This view has a kernel of truth but is primarily a defensive rationalization that serves to minimize patient ragefulness and to aid therapist denial.

The ideal response of the therapist is to neither deny nor to minimize what is being directed at or projected into him, nor, on the other hand, to be so affectively overwhelmed by the attacks and projections that his ability to work effectively is seriously compromised. In other words, the therapist experiences his countertransference affects in their full intensity, while simultaneously taking "a step back" to examine and to understand the interaction and the projections. His next task is to tease out of his total affective experience what "belongs" to himself in order to highlight what originates in the patient and is being projected into him.

Because patient and therapist contributions are usually combined in complex ways, this task is more difficult than it might appear. The patient's projections of negative part self and part object images into the therapist can provoke not only intense, but also regressive, counterreactions in the therapist. That is especially so when there is some impairment of ego boundaries in the patient that can induce experiences of chaos and confusion in the therapist, so that he, in turn, becomes increasingly unclear about who is doing what to whom.

In spite of these complex interactions, the experienced therapist can usually achieve a reasonable separation of patient from therapist issues. However, when inexperienced trainees present material that demonstrates confusion about what derives from the patient and what from the therapist, this should not be surprising to supervisors.

A common problem in the handling of countertransference is the therapist automatically attributing all of his affective reactions to the patient; for example, "if I am angry, you are projecting that anger into me." Although this is always partially true, especially in the treatment of sicker patients, it is also incomplete and oversimplified. There are always two people interacting in the room, and each makes her irrational contributions to the transference/countertransference matrix. It is tempting to view the therapist's affective reactions as wholly due to projections, but this oversimplifies an interaction that is, in fact, extremely complex. This is true, even though the borderline patient's projections and behaviors are generally the most powerful influences on what the therapist experiences.

Clinical Example 3

This 24-year old BPD female was in once per week supportive psychotherapy for complaints of inability to maintain a relationship with a man, intermittent promiscuity, and drug abuse. The treatment was characterized by hostile attacks on the therapist from the outset. The attacks on the sincerity, professionalism, intelligence, and skill of the therapist alternated with threats to act out sexually or with substances; they were not carried out, although they had been acted on innumerable times in the past. The therapist's hypothesis about the patient's behavior was that it resulted from the projection into him of a helpless, attacked "little girl" self-image, and then attacking it (him) as the powerful, critical, and hostile maternal object image, thereby converting the intrapsychic conflict into an interpersonal one. His formulation was supported by a significant decrease in the patient's self-destructive acting out while she was repeatedly attacking the therapist in the treatment. The material below is from the 15th session.

The patient began this session, as she had most others, by attacking and criticizing the therapist. He was insensitive to her needs, self-centered, and out only for himself, not very intelligent, and didn't understand her. The therapist noted a muted response in himself; it was far less intense than he had experienced previously in response to this behavior. He wondered whether he had heard it too many times so that it was losing its impact on him. Or was he tired and therefore not fully responsive emotionally? Or no longer taking the patient as seriously? Was the patient presenting the material with less intensity, more "going through the motions"?

He intervened by asking the patient if she had any further thoughts about her view of him as stupid, insensitive, and self-centered. This further enraged the patient, and she insisted that this was simply reality and that the therapist was demonstrating his stupidity and defensiveness by asking for further thoughts. We pick up the dialogue at about the 20th minute.

THERAPIST: I'm puzzled by the intensity and the certainty with which you hold to these views of me. How would we understand why you'd see me so negatively when in fact I'm your doctor and trying my best to be helpful to you? Your descriptions of me don't jibe with my own views of myself. Are you absolutely convinced that this is what I'm really like? Can you take a step back and be curious at all about what you're feeling?

This intervention produced another series of attacks on the therapist. However, in the middle of the tirade the patient said that if she really saw the therapist only in such negative terms, she would be foolish to continue treatment with him. This response, plus similar responses in the past, reassured the therapist that her reality testing was intact. However, the ferocity of the attacks continued.

The therapist continued to examine his own emotional responses and became aware that his muted feelings represented denial of the intensity of the patients criticisms, but more strikingly denial of increasingly angry feelings in himself at the unfairness of her accusations. As he became increasingly aware of his anger at her, he no longer felt affectively muted and was also aware of feeling hurt. He also had the thought that he wished the patient would leave treatment if she continued to act so hostilely. He then made his next intervention.

THERAPIST: I'm also aware, as I sit here experiencing a whole range of reactions to your attacks, that your description of me is strikingly similar to the way you berated your boss in the last session.

This intervention attempted to deflect negative transferences out of the treatment situation by pointing out parallels in the relationship to another key figure in the patient's life.

The patient appeared somewhat more contemplative and responded that she was quite aware of her tendencies to be extremely critical and attacking of all the authority figures in her life. She became mildly depressed, quiet, and slightly tearful. Simultaneously, the therapist observed a decrease in his angry and rejecting feelings. He then offered a third intervention, a deliberately inexact interpretation (Glover, 1931).

THERAPIST: Your attacks on me, and the feelings that you are trying very hard to produce in me sound very much like your early experience with your mother, and the ways that her criticisms made you feel. Perhaps you are trying to show me something about those early interactions, for example, how hostile and destructive your mother could be.

This intervention is an inexact interpretation because, although it contains historical truth, it redirects the patient's attention to the past (instead of the present) and to the mother's harsh criticisms (instead of her own). It takes the focus off the here and now of the therapeutic interaction, the patient's hostile attacks, her identification with the destructive mother, the projection of her "helpless child" self-image into the therapist, and so forth. It also exemplifies a benign projection, externalizing the focus to the past, and the aggression to a person other than the patient, thereby diminishing the patient's guilt and anxiety.

The therapist's ability to observe his reactions to the patient's transferences, to be curious about their initially muted quality, to become aware of his rage and hurt, and to use that awareness to help reestablish an effective working ego illustrate the effective use of countertransference reactions. His ability to offer the patient's projections back to her with understanding, with some "detoxification" or neutralization of the primitive aggression demonstrates useful therapeutic work in the context of a supportive psychotherapy.

Note that although the therapist was fully aware of the patient's projection of the "helpless child" self-image into him, and her then attacking as the "malignant mother" object image, he did not make this the focus of his interventions, as might likely have occurred in an exploratory therapy. Instead, he first focused on the reality of the treatment relationship, then on parallel phenomena in the patient's external relationships, and finally offered an inexact interpretation. These are all appropriate and common supportive interventions.

Compare this well-handled case with the difficulties the therapist gets into in the next vignette.

Clinical Example 4

This 33-year-old male borderline patient was in once a week supportive therapy for identity diffusion, inability to hold onto a job, difficulties in interpersonal relations, and a mild chronic depression. He also attacked and devalued the therapist and the therapy, but in a more subtle manner. His devaluations took the form of repetitive latenesses, frequent missing of sessions, a tendency to fill the time with trivial irrelevancies, and chronic complaints that the therapist was not sufficiently giving and accepting, and compared very poorly with his previous therapists. He had been in several previous psychotherapies, all short-lived, and each unilaterally terminated by the patient with bitter complaints about the therapist.

His complaints about the therapists probably represented projections of his own withholding behaviors and negative attitudes. The therapist fully experienced the devalued and withholding images projected into him, but could not take any distance from the induced affects. Instead he felt increasingly guilty and inadequate, and began to act out his resentment by starting sessions late. His formulation of the patient's difficulties centered around early deprivations, and his treatment plan was to accept and gratify the patient enough to satisfy his complaints, thereby "correcting" the childhood privations. Consistent with this, he responded to the patient's complaints by attempting to give him more. He talked more, ran over the end of the session, and eventually kept the next session open so that he could give the patient even more time if the patient "needed" it.

Thus he accepted the projections into him of the patient's internalized withholding images as realities, supporting this view by theoretical rationalizations. At the same time, he acted out both his resentment (starting the hour late) and reaction formations against the resentment (running over the session time, talking more).

To the surprise of the therapist, but probably not to the reader, these strategies led only to increasingly intense attacks on the therapist and the treatment. Finally, the patient threatened to quit, the therapist redoubled his efforts, and the patient left in a vitriolic attack on the therapist. At that point the therapist, a trainee, came for supervisory help and the above story unfolded.

I believe that what happened here is that the therapist's attempts to deal with the patient's projected withholding maternal representation by more giving and gratification, rather than his being able to take some distance from the countertransference affects, to understand them, and to return them to the patient in a verbal and "metabolized" form, led the patient to feel increasingly misunderstood, more angry and devaluing, and the vicious circle gradually worsened. This vignette also illustrates the futility and naiveté of attempting to compensate for childhood deprivations by making restitution, rather than by focusing on the self and object representations that result from the inadequate environment and are then reexternalized in the transference.

THE IDEALIZING, SELF-DEVALUING PATIENT

Borderline Personality Disorder patients with significant narcissistic features sometimes present transferences in which the therapist is idealized while the patient demeans and devalues herself. This is usefully viewed as the result of the splitting of self-images; the grandiose and idealized self-image is projected into the therapist, while the devalued and demeaned self-image is experienced by the patient. This view is supported by the rapid shifts that can occur in the patient's view of both participants; minor disappointments by the therapist suddenly cause him to be viewed as a devalued object, while the patient grandiosely and contemptuously details his shortcomings.

The situation is best managed by the therapist's cognizance of both aspects of the split self-image, that which is experienced and that which is projected. He focuses on the patient's unrealistic views of both herself and the therapist, gradually undermining the idealization of the therapist and devaluation of the self and constantly working toward an increased integration of the patient's split self-images. This clinical situation and the therapist's effective use of his countertransference reactions are illustrated in the following vignette.

Clinical Example 5

This 28-year-old woman with recurrent major depressions and Borderline Personality Disorder was first seen while suffering from a Major Depressive Disorder. The depression was severe enough to warrant the use of tricyclic antidepressants; they had been effective in previous episodes and were rapidly effective again. Vegetative signs and difficulties in concentration and memory improved markedly, but the patient continued to experience considerable dysphoria, in spite of adequate TCA plasma levels. Thyroid function was normal, and T_3 and lithium augmentation did not produce further improvement. Because of the recurrent nature of her depressions, the patient was maintained on the tricyclic at acute treatment levels and a twice weekly supportive therapy was begun.

The patient's propensity for idealization, increased by the gratitude she felt for the therapist's presence during the depression and the successful pharmacotherapy, lead to a markedly idealized transference. The therapist's positive aspects were exaggerated beyond any reality, while his negative aspects were totally denied. The patient's dysthymia appeared to be related to the devalued self-representation she experienced, while the idealized self-representation was projected into the therapist. The therapist was surprised when, on several occasions, a minor shortcoming of his, for example, beginning a session 5 minutes late or being slightly preoccupied, led to a transient but virulent attack on him in which he was viewed as worthless. These attacks were inevitably followed by tears, guilty recriminations, the feeling that she was "crazy" to have such negative feelings toward such a wonderful therapist, and a rapid return to the idealizing transference position.

The material below is from the 30th session. The patient is pursuing a familiar train of associations, focused on her inadequacies and how poorly she compares with the "wonderful" therapist. This had been the theme of the 3 previous hours and the therapist had already made several interventions similar to those below.

THERAPIST: I want to thank you again for your very flattering descriptions of me, but I'm also aware of some discomfort about how you see me. I am trying my best to be helpful to you, but there are also times when I feel confused about what's going on and other times when I'm not as tuned in and as empathic as you describe. In fact, it seems to me that no real person could live up to the picture you're painting of me. Again I'm curious—why would you view me in such an unreal perfect way?

PATIENT: I don't think it's unrealistic, you're really wonderful. You understand me all the time, you're always accepting of me, and you're the best therapist I could imagine, at least for me.

THERAPIST: Well, again, thank you. But this view of me is way overdrawn, it doesn't jibe with my own views of myself, and in fact I can't imagine any actual person being as wonderful as you describe. Again, I'm wondering why you'd draw such an overblown portrait.

PATIENT: (*Suddenly enraged*) You are perfect, you stupid asshole! You're perfect because I want you to be perfect, because I need you to be perfect. I need a perfect therapist. Only the very best therapist could understand me. Besides, you have to be perfect; I want to be treated by a perfect doctor so then I can be perfect myself. You are perfect, goddamn it, and your false modesty only convinces me that you have a problem, and that you can't see yourself as realistically as I do.

THERAPIST: Well, now I seem to be a perfect person with a problem. This seems to me a contradiction in terms. Why would either of us have to be such totally perfect, unreal people?

PATIENT: Look, you idiot, I was everybody's perfect, cute little doll when I was a kid, and if I'm not perfect then I'm nothing. I'm a piece of crap, like I feel I am, and if I need you to be perfect because then someday I can be perfect, then I need it. And who the hell are you to tell me that I'm wrong in my view of you?

THERAPIST: I want to point out how quickly your view of me changed from being perfect, to perfect with a problem, to being an idiot and an asshole. Those are pretty extreme and one-sided views. There's no grey area, there's no room for trying your best but failing, for having imperfections. Your views of yourself are also swinging wildly between seeing yourself as worthless and then demanding, quite arrogantly, that I have to be exactly what you want me to be. Are you as struck as I am by these rapid oscillations between perfection and worthlessness, both in your views of yourself and of me?

PATIENT: You can argue all you like, I just don't believe it. If I choose to see you as perfect then you are perfect, and I don't give a damn what you say!

THERAPIST: Now here again you're being quite grandiose, telling me that I have to be how you see me, no matter what I really am. And as we're talking, it strikes me that your descriptions of other people tend to follow similar extremes. Most of the people you talk about are either very admirable or totally worthless. So that what you're doing here with me in the session is also reflected in your views of other people in your life, like your sister and your boyfriend and some of your co-workers. This tendency to see yourself and others in totally black or white terms seems to me to be a problem. Can you understand what I'm talking about, and why I think it's so important?

The patient became quiet, appeared somewhat saddened, and then predictably began to berate herself.

PATIENT: You're right. I feel terrible about what I'm doing to you. And you're right, I do it with everybody. I'm not worth anything, I'm totally bad. I just want people to be what I want them to be, and I have no real interest in what they really are. People exist to meet my expectations, and to fulfil my views of them, and I honestly don't give a damn who they really are. That's terrible, I'm a terrible person. I'm not worth anything!

THERAPIST: Well, here again, now you've swung back to the worthless extreme and are seeing yourself as totally bad. Soon you're going to put me back on the pedestal, telling me that I'm even more perfect because I'm not only perfect but also humble. Do you see what I'm driving at, do you see how your views of yourself and of others keep swinging back and forth between extremes? Do you see what a problem this is, and how it gets you into trouble with all the people you want to be close to?

In this vignette, the therapist experiences the patient's projected grandiose and omnipotent self-image, confronts the discrepancies between her projections and his own more realistic views of himself, and uses his countertransference reactions to better understand the patient's splitting operations. He then translates his awareness into words and plays it back to the patient, repetitively focusing on the splits into all-good and all-bad self and object images. Obviously this interaction has to be repeated many times before the patient can begin to take it in, identify with it, and make it her own, thereby beginning to modify the split in her self and object images. The therapist utilizes his countertransference reactions effectively, confronting the patient with the realities of himself and of the relationship. He also employs the tactic of displacing transference out of the treatment situation by pointing out parallel themes in the patient's relationships with significant others.

Contrast the serious difficulties that arise in the next case when the therapist does not deal appropriately with his countertransference.

Clinical Example 6

This 31-year-old borderline married mother of two was in weekly supportive psychotherapy for extramarital promiscuity, intermittent substance abuse, and ego-dystonic explosive outbursts, aimed primarily at her husband and children. The therapist was a slightly younger, unmarried male resident. From the earliest sessions, the patient related to the therapist as an idealized and adored person, seemingly without any negative aspects. The therapist was understanding, extremely sensitive, loving, and even at times "adorable." She consciously compared him to her favorite younger brother with whom there had possibly been some childhood sex play.

From his side, the therapist felt mildly discomforted by the patient's image and her feelings toward him but also found them gratifying and reassuring, particularly when contrasted with the negative transferences of several of his other borderline patients. He rationalized his not confronting, or otherwise dealing with, her idealizing transference by arguing (to himself) that idealization of the therapist should not be undermined as long as the patient requires it.

The therapy continued for several months, the patient idealizing and adoring the therapist, and the therapist basking in the positive transference, neither confronting it nor questioning it in any way. Occasionally he would discuss the treatment with his peers but did not seek any supervisory help. He joked "when patients hate you that's transference, but when they love you that's just good judgment."

The therapist was totally shocked when, in the 16th session, the patient announced her plans to leave her husband to begin dating the therapist. He became acutely anxious and immediately confronted the patient with the reality of the treatment relationship.

THERAPIST: Wait a minute here, this is crazy! We are meeting together to try to deal with your problems, and you want to change this into a romantic relationship. That's totally inappropriate, and I'm shocked by your plans.

PATIENT: You are the one that's outrageous! You have been leading me on for months now, and then when I want to take the next logical step you're suddenly scared, reminding me of all kinds of realities. What are you, some kind of a fag? Are you afraid of me? Are you afraid of a real woman? Either you start going out with me or the treatment stops right now, and I'm starting a malpractice suit against you for leading me on.

By this time the therapist was panicky, incapable of dealing effectively with the patient in any way. He fumbled through the remaining minutes of the session and rushed off for emergency consultation. The sequence described above was elucidated in the supervision. The supervisor's comments focused on the therapist's difficulties in dealing appropriately with his countertransference reactions to the patient's idealizing and erotized transferences. The therapist was advised to tell the patient that he had erred in not confronting her with the discrepancies between the realities of the treatment relationship and the treatment goals, on the one hand, and her idealized and erotized transferential distortions of him, on the other. It was also suggested that he immediately set limits on the patient's behavior, telling her that she was not to make any impulsive changes in her marital and family situation.

The therapist remained panicky, fearing that he had revealed his incompetence and that he would become the target of a malpractice suit. The supervisor responded by reminding him that he was a beginning therapist, that the error, though serious, was understandable, and that it did not cause the supervisor to consider him incompetent. Further, the supervisor believed that the malpractice threat was probably a temper tantrum and unlikely to be carried out. He also suggested that the therapist and patient try to resume working together, but if they did not feel this was possible, transfer to another therapist would be considered.

The therapist and patient met only one more time. The patient reiterated her threats and refused further treatment with the therapist, or any other therapist. She left and was lost to follow-up; there was no malpractice suit.

This vignette illustrates the dangers of allowing an intense idealizing, and in this case also erotized, transference to persist without repetitive confrontation and undermining. In this case, unfortunately, the patient's transferences were complementary to the narcissistic needs and inexperience of the therapist and furnished him with excessive gratification. We cannot know whether regular confrontations of the transferences would have led to a workable treatment. Certainly, however, this was a therapeutic disaster—terribly upsetting for the young, inexperienced therapist and a poor treatment experience for the patient. Skilled supervision from the beginning could have, in all probability, avoided this unfortunate experience for both participants.

THE SELF-DESTRUCTIVE PATIENT

Attacks upon the self by self-mutilations, impulsive suicidal threats, acts and gestures, and a myriad of other self-destructive acts are extremely common among patients with Borderline Personality Disorder. They result from intense and poorly modulated rage turned against the self, strong propensities for acting out, widespread use of primitive defenses, and the desperate need for objects that characterize these patients. They frequently follow disappointments in the therapist or in other key figures, and thus tend to be viewed, in a somewhat derogatory fashion, as "manipulative."

It is true that often these behaviors are conscious manipulative attempts to force specific behavioral responses from the therapist, or to produce affects such as guilt in him, but it is also true that the manipulative nature of these behaviors is exaggerated and that they frequently represent attempts to self-treat intolerable feeling states (Lebenluft, Gardner, & Cowdry, 1987). Whether or not the behaviors are *primarily* motivated by the wish to elicit responses from the therapist, they generally do have a powerful effect upon him due to the frightening and often highly dramatic nature of the acts.

Theoretically, one could view the overemphasis on the manipulative aspects of these behaviors as a defensive countertransference reaction in the therapist(s). He can rationalize that his irritation is justified by the manipulativeness of the patient and can defend himself against potentially more painful countertransference affects, such as helplessness, guilt, incompetence and inadequacy, or feeling badly for the patient that she is so desperate. None of this should be construed as minimizing the fact that these behaviors always have transferential determinants, and that they are frightening and difficult to deal with, particularly for the young, less experienced therapist. In addition, of course, the anxiety of the therapist is multiplied many fold when the self-destructive acts raise questions of possible lethality.

The patient's self-cutting, self-burning, pill ingestions, and other self-destructive acts, such as promiscuity, exposure to AIDS, reckless driving, and excessive alcohol or drug intake, all have significant impacts upon the therapist. His ability to handle his countertransference reactions to these behaviors, and to use them constructively to advance the therapy, is essential for effective treatment.

In most cases the therapist can anticipate self-destructive acting out from the initial evaluation of the patient, particularly from the history that such behaviors have occurred in the past. The initial contract (see Chapter 5) is the crucial first step in structuring a psychotherapy that can be effective in the face of the patient's self-destructive acting out. The contract terms must be set carefully and in detail, making clear the responsibilities of each participant should such acts occur.

Conditions under which the patient will require hospitalization, for example, loss below a predetermined weight in the anorectic, or need evaluation in an emergency room, for example, pill ingestions or self-cutting, are structured into the contract. For nonlethal behaviors, such as wrist scratching or arm burning, the patient can be told that the therapist cannot prevent these acts and therefore will not respond acutely to them. Rather, he will continue to help the patient to understand them and hopefully to master them, or to learn less destructive ways of dealing with the painful affects that motivate them.

Only when effective limits and structures are built into the initial treatment contract is the therapist free to fully experience and effectively utilize his countertransference reactions to elucidate the patient's behavior. Otherwise, his energies will be dissipated in frantic responses to the patient's crises. This will not be further discussed here; it is dealt with in Chapter 5.

The following two clinical vignettes describe BPD patients who call their therapists in the evening claiming an emergency, and portray in detail the discomfort they are experiencing. Both also threaten to cut their forearms, behaviors they had acted out on many prior occasions. In both cases, the initial contract included the agreement that the therapist could not prevent such behaviors, and that any self-cutting required medical and psychiatric evaluation in an emergency room. The focus in both vignettes is the therapist's handling of the countertransference reactions induced by the phone calls and his subsequent behaviors.

Clinical Example 7

This 25-year-old single female was in weekly supportive therapy for repetitive forearm and wrist scratching and slashing, identity diffusion, intermittent substance abuse, and severe difficulties in interpersonal relations. She was extremely distraught during the phone call, having had a fight with her boyfriend, was feeling suicidal without serious intent, and announced that she was about to begin slashing her forearms.

The therapist, with the terms of the initial contract clearly in mind, was aware of the following feelings. He felt mildly irritated with the patient for calling him at night. He felt some pressure to help the patient avert the threatened behavior and guilty that she was feeling so badly; maybe it was partly due to his shortcomings. Finally, he experienced some temptation to abrogate the contract, to have a lengthy phone conversation, or even to set up an emergency session. At that point he realized that he felt somewhat confused and told the patient that he wanted 5 minutes to think about the situation and would call her back.

The therapist wondered about his temptation to abrogate a contract that he believed in and into which he had put serious effort. He found himself thinking about times in his own life when he had experienced feelings of desperation, of his characterologic tendencies to feel over-responsible for patients, and of the genetic roots of those tendencies. Only then was he able to integrate the intellectual knowledge of what was appropriate behavior with his affective responses to her call. (His request for 5 minutes to think about it also furnished a model for the patient of not acting immediately on one's feelings, and taking some time instead to think about them.)

He returned the patient's phone call. She was furious about the delay and had already begun some preliminary superficial scratching. The therapist reminded her of the terms of the contract and said that he had been aware of some temptation to abrogate it, but was convinced that it was in the best interests of both that they hold to the contract precisely. He asked if there were any other behaviors she might consider, such as jogging to exhaustion, plunging her arm into ice-cold water, or repetitively flicking the skin of her arm with a rubber band; the patient refused all such suggestions. Her rage intensified; she was furious that he had "hung up on her" and she began further cutting during the phone conversation. The therapist expressed his regrets that she was feeling so badly, reiterated that there was nothing that he could do at the moment to prevent the behavior, reviewed the indications for evaluation in an emergency room, and in a kind but firm manner told her that they would talk further about this at the next appointment. The patient screamed, "Now I'm going for the artery!" The therapist reiterated that he was sorry she was feeling so badly and would see her at their next session.

Clinical Example 8

The patient had almost identical presenting symptomatology to the previous patient, and a similar contract had been instituted at the start of the treatment. However, this therapist was never totally convinced of the value of the contract and had felt somewhat coerced by his supervisor's insistence that a contract was an essential part of the treatment. Thus, when a similar phone call occurred, the therapist was already in a state of ambivalence about the contract.

The patient described increasing difficulties at work, culminating in a bitter argument with a coworker, feeling utterly discouraged and alone, and announced her intention to begin cutting herself. The therapist experienced mild irritation, but also rapidly increasing anxiety, guilt, overconcern, and over-responsibility for the patient's safety. He impulsively suggested an immediate emergency session, and they agreed to meet at the therapist's office in 30 minutes.

The therapist arrived promptly, but the patient did not appear. He waited 15 minutes, experiencing increasing anxiety, and finally telephoned the patient at home; he was surprised when there was no answer. His anxiety increased even further when several more phone calls to the patient's home over the next hour were also not answered. At that point the therapist was terrified about the patient's safety and imagined her bleeding to death in an alley. He also felt furious, that he had been manipulated, and guilty and foolish about undercutting the contract.

He reached the patient at work the following day and was amazed by her good spirits and flippancy. She told him that she had felt better immediately after he offered the session and had gone out to a party. When asked why she hadn't called to tell him that she was feeling better and to cancel the emergency session, she in turn was surprised that he would expect such a call. The therapist felt extremely foolish, furious at the patient, embarrassed by his behavior, and incompetent.

Fortunately, this case was in regular supervision, and the therapist was able to examine the incident and his reactions. He discussed his tendency to feel over-responsible for his patients, his rage at the patient, his feelings of incompetence, and his ambivalence about the contract. He was able to confront the patient about her behaviors in the next session and to respond appropriately when the same behavior recurred several weeks later. His inappropriate responses were a positive learning experience for the therapist and also a significant factor in his decision to begin his own psychotherapy.

These two vignettes illustrate once again the critical importance of the therapist's ability to "read" his countertransference accurately and to differentiate his idiosyncratic and irrational responses from reasonable reactions to the patient's transferences. Only then can he utilize his countertransference reactions adaptively to further the treatment, rather than acting them out with all of its associated technical difficulties.

OTHER PROBLEMS

There are several other clinical situations in the treatment of the BPD patient that are particularly likely to lead to countertransference difficulties. The patient who threatens repeatedly to quit the treatment often stimulates irrational counterreactions in the therapist. These include his responsibility for saving the treatment, over-responsibility for the patient, personal reactions to desertion, feelings of inadequacy about technical skill and competence, and similar responses specific to the character and psychodynamics of the therapist.

When psychotropic medications are part of the treatment, counter-transference problems are very common, whether the medications are prescribed by the therapist or by another physician. When the drugs are prescribed by another physician, disparagement or idealization of the psychopharmacologist, or competition with him for the patient's positive regard, are common countertransference issues. Where the therapist prescribes the medications, countertransference issues can be manifested as negative feelings about the medication, overvaluation of the medica-tion, feelings of failure and inadequacy demonstrated by the need for medication, competition between therapist and medication, excessive attention to side effects, or conversely failing to appropriately educate the patient about the pharmacologic aspects of the drug.

In a more general sense, the decision to utilize medications may result from irrational feelings of psychotherapeutic failure and incompetence. Intense opposition to all medications can derive from irrational attitudes about drugs or from psychotherapeutic omnipotence and grandiosity. Medications should always be prescribed for clear and specific indica-tions, in clinically appropriate dosage, and with definite target symp-toms. They should not be prescribed casually, or in inadequate dosage, hoping for a placebo effect.

Other clinical situations likely to produce countertransference prob-lems include silent and withholding patients, who can induce the thera-pist into a reactive silence or into talking too much to fill the emptiness. Chatty and trivializing patients, or those who externalize inner conflict and whose verbal material consists mainly of negative descriptions of others, can also produce problematic counter-reactions in their therapists.

FINAL THOUGHTS

Several of the points made in this chapter deserve repetition. First, countertransference does not have negative implications, and it is as ubiquitous as is transference. It provides crucial information about the patient and/or about the therapist, but it also can be a major source of difficulty when handled inappropriately.

Second, whether one prefers the broad (totalistic) or narrow (classic) concept of countertransference, the therapist must make every effort to separate what belongs to the patient, his transferences and projections, from what arises within the therapist, his transferential distortions. Since these are almost always complexly intertwined, the task can be extremely difficult. To focus only on the therapist's irrational contributions to countertransference is to ignore a very valuable source of data about the patient, especially in the treatment of more disturbed patients. On the other hand, to attribute all countertransference reactions to patient projections into the therapist is to oversimplify what is a complex interactive phenomenon, and even possibly to be destructive to the patient.

Third, the therapist ideally will fully experience countertransference affects, without either minimizing them or becoming so overwhelmed that his working ego is dysfunctional. In the latter instances, he is likely to withdraw empathic contact from the patient or to act out his countertransference reactions. These problems are particularly common in the supportive therapy of BPD patients.

Finally, the ability to process countertransference usefully, to distinguish patient from therapist contributions with reasonable accuracy, and to maintain both empathic contact and an effective working ego are powerful arguments for a psychoanalytic or intensive psychotherapeutic experience for the therapist. Supervision and consultation are very helpful in aiding the therapist to deal constructively with his countertransferences, but when countertransference difficulties are repetitive and widespread, further treatment is probably indicated for the therapist.

CHAPTER 10

The Impulsive, Acting-Out Borderline Patient

Acting out is most precisely defined as the expression of transference memories, conflicts, and affects in behaviors instead of being remembered, experienced, and verbalized during a psychoanalysis or psychotherapy (Moore & Fine, 1968). However, this rigorous definition has gradually been diffused by application of the term to related phenomena. For example, people who tend to express psychic conflicts via behavior are often described as "acting out," regardless of whether they are in a psychotherapy. This seems reasonable; just as transferences are omnipresent in or out of the treatment situation, so can they be acted out inside or outside of psychotherapy. In this more general sense, usually applied to aggressive or antisocial behaviors, "acting out" tends to have a pejorative connotation. Thus, at present, "acting out" is an imprecise term; only the rigorous definition, the conversion of transference memories into behaviors in the treatment situation, is universally accepted.

Acting out, as a defensive style, is often associated with somatization; both are nonverbal expressions of psychic conflict. Both may be associated with alexithymia, and both are problematic in any dynamic psychotherapy because conflictual material is thereby rendered unavailable for verbalization and for understanding. Somatization is the more difficult problem because there is little conscious control, while acting out is at least partly under conscious control. This allows the therapist to bring his influence to bear directly upon the acting-out behaviors when there is a sufficiently positive transference. Somatization is not prominent in Borderline Personality Disorder (BPD) patients, though it may be present, while acting out is extremely common and is the source of many of the most difficult situations that are encountered in the treatments of these patients.

Why is acting out, particularly impulsive acting out, so common in the borderline patient? In part the answer is tautologic. DSM-III-R criteria for BPD include (2) impulsiveness in at least two areas that are potentially self-damaging; (5) recurrent suicidal threats, gestures, or behavior, or self-mutilating behavior; and (8) frantic efforts to avoid real or imagined abandonment (p. 347). The qualifier "frantic" suggests desperate attempts to powerfully impact the other person, and this is frequently accomplished through acting out.

In addition, a percentage of adult borderline patients, around 25% according to Andrulonis et al. (1980), suffer from Attention Deficit Disorder, Minimal Brain Dysfunction, or other mild organic impairments. These patients tend to be verbally inarticulate and prone to express conflicts and dysphoric affects in behaviors. Yet another view of the BPD patients' strong potential for acting out is based in the assumption that the BPD core conflicts are closely associated with preverbal and early verbal experiences. Preverbal contents cannot easily be translated into words and therefore are frequently expressed in behaviors.

Whatever the etiologic issues, the borderline patient's propensity for acting out in the session and/or in her outside life via drugs, promiscuity, eating disturbances, attacks on the patient's own body, and so on, creates difficult management problems in the treatment of these patients. The acting out is often frightening, upsetting, or enraging to the therapist, inducing intense countertransference reactions.

The focus thus far has been on relatively gross acting out. In addition, BPD patients often indulge in more subtle acting out in the session. For example, the patient may withhold information, expressing distrust of the therapist or the wish to deprive the therapist. Devaluations of the therapist via subtleties of language or tone of voice may be difficult to perceive. Repeatedly paying the bill late is an obvious example of acting out, but always paying it in the very next session may also represent a less overt instance of acting out.

CLINICAL EXAMPLE 1

This 47-year-old man was in treatment for identity diffusion, outbursts of rage at his wife and children, and chronic difficulties at work due to abrupt swings in his feelings toward his superiors. He was always on time, never missed a session, paid each bill at the very next session, and talked freely, although his verbal material tended to be trivial and filled with bitter complaints about the important people in his life. He never complained when the therapist was late for the session, insisting that the waiting time was a bonus that he filled with productive introspection.

When the therapist expressed curiosity about his compliant and excessively agreeable behavior, the content of the patient's material changed abruptly. He revealed extreme skepticism about the usefulness of any psychotherapy and the feelings that his treatment was a total waste of time and the therapist a charlatan. His "good behavior" resulted from deciding that he might as well "play the game" since the whole treatment was a waste of time anyhow. When the about-face in attitude was queried, he again rapidly reversed himself, insisting that the psychotherapy was extremely helpful and his negative feelings totally irrational, not to be taken seriously. His "good patient" caricature was an example of acting out in the treatment session. It was a pattern of behaviors that defended against the opposite feelings in the transference and ultimately against marked splitting tendencies and identity diffusion.

GUIDELINES FOR MANAGING ACTING OUT IN SUPPORTIVE THERAPY

The specific behavioral forms assumed by the acting out are informative about the conflicts or affects being expressed. However, the conversion of transferences, psychic conflicts, and affects into behavior does not make it easily available for exploration, understanding, and "insight." In exploratory psychotherapy, acting out is always a resistance, to be limited, undermined, and hopefully understood, while every attempt is made to inhibit acting out and to promote verbalization.

In supportive therapy, however, the crucial role of the adaptive/ maladaptive balance in deciding how to respond to any psychic phenomenon includes acting out; that is, acting out is responded to as is any other resistant or defensive behavior. Although the acting out of the borderline patient is usually both self-destructive and maladaptive, and is undermined to ensure the survival of both the treatment and the patient, some instances of acting out are best left alone or even encouraged in supportive psychotherapy.

Consider, for example, the borderline patient involved in an intense power/control struggle with the therapist. During the session, the patient agrees to comply with the therapist on several major issues, but then attempts to control the ending of the session by leaving several minutes early. In a supportive therapy, the therapist might decide that the patient, having complied on the important issues, will be allowed to control the length of the session by leaving early. This is certainly an acting out by the patient. But it is without significant harm to the patient or to the treatment, salves the patient's injured narcissism, reestablishes some patient control, and therefore can be more adaptive than maladaptive on balance.

Or consider the patient in the termination phase of a supportive treatment who withholds feelings about termination while frantically pursuing new friends. This acting out of resistance is undermined in an exploratory treatment, and the patient is encouraged to talk directly about his feelings regarding termination. In a supportive therapy, the therapist is more tolerant of the patient's not talking about termination, and though he would encourage verbalization, he might also encourage and support the patient's efforts to replace the therapist with other people. The different responses are determined not only by dissimilar attitudes toward the handling of resistances, but also by the differing qualities of the terminations in the two treatments; that is, termination is less definitive in supportive therapy.

The theoretical point should be clear. In an exploratory therapy, the emphasis on introspection and insight makes any acting out a more or less negative factor. In supportive treatment, the therapist evaluates each acting-out behavior in terms of its adaptational valence and deals with it accordingly. Depending upon its adaptive/maladaptive balance, he will ignore it, support it, or undermine it. This theoretical issue is important, even though almost all acting out by BPD patients is in fact maladaptive, requiring active limit setting and undermining.

The management of acting out in the supportive therapy of borderline patients is accomplished in several steps. First is the detailed clinical evaluation of the patient. Careful attention is directed to any history of acting-out behaviors because these patterns tend to be repetitive. The evaluator is very interested in historical evidence of past suicide attempts and gestures, self-mutilations, substance-abuse and eating disorders, dangerous driving, and so forth. In the assessment of these behaviors, the evaluator is especially interested in the impulsive nature of the acts. Do they appear to occur unpredictably, without clear precipitants or mood states? If not, what kinds of external events or internal states tend to precede them? Is the behavior carried out immediately, or does the patient struggle to delay or control the behavior? The practical importance of these issues is that the impulsivity so common in borderline patients, the almost immediate translation of thoughts and affects into behaviors, requires especially careful attention to structures and systems that hopefully will safeguard both the patient and the treatment.

Another important issue relates to how the various acting-out behaviors have been handled in previous treatments. The evaluator is particularly concerned about the success or failure of past interventions, that is, what worked and what didn't work for specific behaviors.

The second step in the management of acting out is the construction of a treatment contract prior to the beginning of the psychotherapy. Previous acting out, particularly behavior that has created major problems in previous treatments, requires detailed attention. The treatment contract is not unilaterally created by the therapist and presented to the patient as a *fait accompli*. Rather, therapist and patient engage in active discussion and negotiation around such questions as, "How are we going to deal with behavior x or behavior y to ensure that it does not destroy your treatment, as it has in the past?" The patient's ideas and feelings are taken seriously, but do not by themselves determine the final terms. The therapist must be comfortable with the structures, convinced that they deal effectively with the acting out, and do not place unrealistic burdens or intrusions on him. They should take reasonable account of the exigencies and idiosyncratic features of his professional life. For example, the therapist who travels and is away often must take realistic cognizance of this in setting up the details of the contract. Similarly, a therapist with professional commitments to an academic or administrative position should discuss the impact of this fully with the patient and include these realities in structuring the contract.

The therapist does the patient no favor by agreeing to contractual arrangements that gratify the patient but will cause himself practical difficulties, intrude unduly into his private life, or in any way cause him to feel resentful. These feelings will fester, make accurate countertransference perceptions difficult, tend to be acted out in the treatment, and can lead to a total breakdown of the treatment relationship.

Examples of contractual terms that furnish limits for specific behaviors include (1) setting minimum weights for anorectic patients; (2) setting minimum electrolyte values, as part of regular medical checkups, for severely bulimic patients who purge; or (3) dealing with suicidality or suicide threats by using the local emergency room for evaluation and treatment of suicidal crises.

The third step in the management of acting out is the therapist's evaluation of each patient behavior in terms of its adaptive/maladaptive valences. Examples are furnished above of behaviors that certainly are examples of acting out, but are judged to be more adaptive than otherwise and therefore are ignored or supported. Also as noted above, most acting out by borderline patients is maladaptive and is therefore addressed by limit setting and undermining; examples of these are provided as well.

Fourth, the therapist deals directly with maladaptive acting-out behaviors in the psychotherapy. Interventions such as limit setting or prohibitions on certain behaviors, and praise for decreased impulsivity and increased control, are widely utilized. The therapist uses his psychodynamic understanding to identify frequently utilized primitive defenses, to demonstrate their role in the maladaptive acting out, and to clarify, confront, discourage, and undermine them. He reminds the patient of the terms of the treatment contract, of the realities of the treatment relationship, of each participant's responsibilities and roles in the treatment process, and of the treatment goals, all in the service of diminishing and controlling acting out.

Environmental structures built into the treatment, such as regular AA or NA attendance for substance abusers, are rigidly maintained and enforced. The terms of the original treatment contract are repeated and reinforced. The roles of splitting, projective identification, denial, and other primitive defenses in promoting acting out are constantly emphasized. Negative transferences, generally powerful contributors to acting out, receive constant attention. Where the acting out is seriously self-destructive or life threatening, hospitalization is necessary. The therapist should not be hesitant about insisting on hospitalization, making clear to the patient that it is her behavior that is making hospitalization necessary. (See pages 226–27 for an example of these issues and of the countertransference difficulties that often complicate the situation.)

Hospitalization does not signify a failure of the outpatient treatment, although it may sometimes result from faulty handling of transference and countertransference issues. It is more reasonably viewed as an integral part of some treatments, used sparingly but not avoided when clinically necessary, with the understanding that therapy will resume when the patient is discharged. In some cases, the therapist hospitalizes the patient with the message to the inpatient staff that he does not wish to continue the treatment after discharge. Frequently this is the unfortunate result of excessive patient gratification, of inadequate attention to therapist needs, of denying the aggression and sadism of the patient, or of inadequate structuring of the treatment; that is, of the acting out of irrational countertransference reactions.

In cases where the patient's acting out is unconflictedly ego-syntonic and intractable, the therapist should not hesitate to terminate the treatment or to insist on inpatient treatment. Attempting to carry out a psychotherapy while the patient is regularly getting intoxicated, for example, is an antitherapeutic farce. It is far more respectful to the patient to point out that her behaviors are making outpatient treatment impossible at this time, and therefore it will be terminated. This decision is usually accompanied by a statement to the effect that when the patient is able to accept behavioral limitations and structures, for example, to cease the substance abuse, the clinical situation will be reevaluated and treatment may then be possible. This is not emotional blackmail. Rather the patient's reality testing, self-esteem, and judgment are aided by the therapist's not participating in a pseudopsychotherapy, implicitly joining the patient in the devaluation of the treatment, the therapist, and of the patient herself that is being acted out.

On the other hand, behaviors such as self-cutting or self-burning, however much they may discomfort the therapist, may be the patient's most effective way of coping with unbearable psychic pain at present; they are accepted, and the acceptance is communicated to the patient. The therapist remains keenly aware that there are multiple meanings to all such acting-out behaviors. They are utilized to increase understanding of the patient's internal conflicts, while at the same time the patient is encouraged to express the conflicts, feelings, and transferences in words rather than in action.

CLINICAL MATERIAL

Acting Out in the Session ("Acting In")

Acting out in the treatment hour can take many forms. Repetitive latenesses, extended silences, and late paying of the bill are common examples, as are more flagrant acts, such as threatening or even attacking the therapist or the therapist's property. Other examples are loudly slamming the office door on entering, tracking mud, or dripping blood on the carpet, or burning cigarette holes in the furniture.

Clinical Example 2

This 21-year-old female met all eight BPD criteria and was referred for supportive psychotherapy following cocaine detoxification. She regularly attended meetings of NA and AA. One aspect of the initial contract had specified that psychotherapy would cease if the patient resumed substance abuse.

The patient entered the office hesitantly, slammed the door loudly, sank into her seat, and glared silently at the therapist. He asked what was wrong, reminded her of their agreement that she was to say whatever came to mind, and commented that she appeared distraught and angry. She remained silent, but her angry glaring alternated with what appeared to be embarrassment and anxiety. The therapist commented on her change in facial expression, continued to be curious about her silence, and stated that he wanted to be helpful to her but had no way of knowing what was bothering her. At about the 15th minute the patient said, "I'm depressed"; when the therapist asked for more data about her feelings, the patient again fell silent. We pick up the dialogue at the 20th minute.

THERAPIST: You're obviously very upset and you seem to be angry, embarrassed, and anxious all at the same time. You seem to be wanting something from me, but I have no way of knowing what you want except that you said you felt depressed. I have reminded you about saying what's on your mind. I have reassured you that I want to be helpful, but I cannot do the work by myself. You are certainly free to continue to suffer by yourself, but if you do want help from me you'll have to tell me what's going on.

PATIENT: You can't leave well enough alone can you, you stupid bastard! OK, well here goes, and after I tell you, you can kick me out of treatment. I did cocaine again for the first time in 3 months; I did it last night. I was out with my boyfriend, everybody was doing it, and I went along. I'm very embarrassed, I feel like a jerk. Well, there it is. When do we end? Right now, at the end of the session or next week? Don't keep me in suspense, give me the bad news.

THERAPIST: It is true that we agreed that a return to using cocaine would make treatment impossible. However, I do not consider one slip a return to drugs; I was talking about the regular use of cocaine. I explained to you why that would make the treatment a waste of time. But I'm curious how you heard that as "one strike and you're out."

PATIENT: That's what I thought you said. I thought either no cocaine or no treatment; I was sure this was the end. I was furious at you so it wouldn't hurt so much to stop, and also I feel like a total idiot.

THERAPIST: I wonder if this isn't an example of a tendency on your part to see things in all-black or all-white terms. Regular drugs would make treatment impossible because your painful feelings would be covered over by the drug. But you have tried very hard, and I don't think that one slip necessarily says anything about the outcome of the treatment. How did it happen that you did the cocaine last night? You've been out with this group before and it didn't happen.

PATIENT: Right, I'm with these people every week, and every other time I was able to avoid the drugs. But last night my boyfriend was bugging me, egging me on, and threatening to leave me if I didn't have "just a little," and once that happened, I was gone.

God, what a relief! I was sure it was all over. I was sure, one slip and I'm finished. But you're also right, I do tend to see things in extremes and that's what I'm doing here. I'm so relieved. I feel very grateful to you. I think if the treatment had stopped now, like this, it would have been the end of me; back to drugs big time. I wonder why I do see things in such extreme ways. That's pretty weird. . . .

This vignette illustrates the patient's acting out, first outside the session and then in the session. The door slamming and silent glaring exemplify acting out in the session, that is, the conversion of transference affects into behaviors instead of words. The material also demonstrates how hard the therapist may have to work to help the patient convert behavior into talk.

Note that the therapist neither responds to the patient's silences with retaliatory countersilences, nor does he feel obliged to fill the session with words. Rather, he attempts to remain empathically in touch with the patient, sharing his confusions and observations, trying to understand whatever verbal or nonverbal communication does come from the patient, while simultaneously giving her the message that affects are more usefully expressed verbally than in behaviors.

Clinical Example 3

This 220 pound borderline woman was in treatment for identity diffusion, uncontrolled binges without purging, severe interpersonal difficulties, and marked affective lability. Over the previous three sessions, there had been gradually increasing rage at the therapist. He did not care enough, was self-centered, wouldn't allow her to touch him, and was not helping her enough. The therapist responded by repeatedly confronting her with the discrepancies between her wishes and feelings, and the realities of the treatment relationship; he had also drawn several parallels between her transference feelings and her rages at family members and coworkers.

This session began as a temper tantrum and crescendoed. The therapist attempted, once again, to point out the realities of the treatment relationship, the goals of their work together, and the many parallel situations in the patient's outside life. This appeared to have no effect on the patient; she dismissed it as "more psychiatric crap" and continued to escalate. The therapist noted that he was feeling increasingly anxious.

The patient began yelling that the therapist's unwillingness to have her touch him was his problem; he was too uptight, too Freudian. "Why don't you drop your psychiatric act and be more human?" We pick up the interaction 15 minutes into the session.

THERAPIST: I hear what you're saying, but I must also tell you that the volume of your voice and the intensity of your rage are making me quite uncomfortable, and they're making it difficult for me to concentrate on what you're saying to me. Please try to lower your voice so that I can be comfortable enough to continue being useful to you.

PATIENT: I don't give a damn about your discomfort, only my discomfort! It's all your fault anyhow because you won't allow one little touch.

The volume of her voice increased still further, and she rose out of her chair and began advancing on the therapist. His anxiety markedly increased, and he was unsure whether he was about to be physically attacked. He also stood up and felt slightly more comfortable. The patient continued to advance so that they were less than 2 feet apart and continued her vitriolic tirade.

THERAPIST: At this point, you are quite out of control. If you can't sit down and talk in a more reasonable tone of voice, I am ending the session right now and we can talk more about this next time. What is clear to me is that, right now, your behavior and my discomfort make any useful work impossible.

The patient remained where she was, the volume of her voice decreased, and she appeared confused and disorganized but still enraged. At that point the therapist took her upper arm, walked her back to her chair, and sat her down. He resumed his seat and asked her what she was feeling.

The patient held her arms around herself and began rocking back and forth, moaning. She cried, "I'm so alone, I feel so alone, I feel so terrible, what am I going to do?" From a very frightening adult, she abruptly changed into a pitiful small child, crying and attempting to soothe herself. The therapist pointed this out and wondered if it had anything to do with his taking her arm and directing her back into her chair. The patient continued her inconsolable rocking and moaning for several more minutes and then spoke.

PATIENT: I can't stand feeling so alone. I know I'm not really alone when I'm with you here, but it feels to me like I'm only with you if I can touch you. I know that's not acceptable to you, but sometimes my feelings are too strong to resist. I appreciate your stopping me, I appreciate your taking my arm and getting me back into the chair, and most of all I appreciate your not ending the session or kicking me out of treatment. But these feelings are so intense, they seem so impossible to satisfy. That's the kind of feeling that makes me eat. If there were food here, I would have gone for that instead of you. I just feel a great nothingness inside if I can't eat or touch someone. . . .

In this vignette, the supportive interventions of focusing on the realities of the treatment relationship and of diverting negative transferences out of the treatment situation were ineffective in controlling the patient's escalating behavior. The therapist shared his subjective discomfort, telling her that the level of anxiety she produced in him by her behavior made it impossible to be helpful to her. When verbal limit setting was not adequate, the therapist took the patient's arm, physically limiting her behavior and simultaneously gratifying her wish to be touched. After several minutes of inconsolability, the patient was able to resume the therapeutic work.

It will not surprise the reader that this interaction occurred several more times over the succeeding 3 months, but with decreasing intensity. After that, the patient appeared to derive adequate emotional gratification from the usual treatment relationship, and she could talk about feelings of emptiness and wishes for physical contact without acting on them.

Acting Out Around Medications

The borderline patient treated with combined psychotherapy and psychopharmacology frequently engages in acting out around medications, the specific behaviors partly determined by whether the medication is being prescribed by the psychotherapist or by a separate psychopharmacologist. When the psychotherapist is not an M.D., the latter arrangement is, of course, necessary. When the psychotherapist is an M.D., he may or may not prescribe the drugs, depending on factors such as his comfort with pharmacologic agents, anxieties that prescribing drugs will unduly complicate transference/countertransference issues, or, conversely, convictions about the advantages of having medication and psychotherapy delivered by the same person. The arguments for the latter arrangement are that (1) only the psychotherapist has the detailed data, the patient's verbal material in the session, to most skillfully evaluate medication effects, and (2) splitting is inevitable in the two-doctor arrangement and should be avoided if possible. However, either setup presents the patient with numerous opportunities for acting out.

Clinical Example 4

This 32-year-old borderline man initially presented with a severe depression. Treatment was begun with nortriptyline, blood levels were within the therapeutic range, and the depression responded in the usual time frame. Prior to prescribing the drug, the M.D. therapist had explained the time lag of TCA response, the common anticholinergic side effects, the desired range of drug blood levels, and the importance of taking the medication as prescribed. The dose was 100 mg h.s., two 50-mg tablets.

Six weeks later during the weekly supportive treatment, the patient mentioned that he was taking between zero and three tablets in the mornings, depending on whether or not he felt depressed that day. The therapist again explained the importance of taking the prescribed dosage and keeping the blood level within the therapeutic range. He emphasized that the medication did not have immediate antidepressant effects and that the patient's way of taking it did not make pharmacologic sense. The patient stated that he understood fully and would comply with the prescribed dosage regime.

Two weeks later, he again mentioned that he was taking varying amounts of medication in the morning depending on his mood. By this time it was clear that the patient's idiosyncratic dosing would not respond to education alone, and the therapist asked why he insisted on taking the medications in a medically irrational manner. The patient again reassured the therapist that he understood the need to take it as prescribed, that he saw the irrationality of his dosing schedule, had simply been a "wise guy," and would now comply with the therapist's prescription.

However, a month later, the patient again mentioned that for the several previous weeks he had been taking the medication sporadically. The therapist had noted moderate depressive symptomatology and had asked the patient several times whether he was taking the drug as prescribed; the patient had reassured him each time that he was. Now he was informing the doctor that he had both lied to him and was not taking the medication as prescribed. It was clear that these behaviors had to become a focus of therapeutic work.

The following picture gradually emerged. First, the patient did not believe that the medication had relieved his depression; rather, he had gotten better spontaneously, through "willpower." He had gone along with the doctor's belief in the effectiveness of the medication and the medication regime so as to not cause conflict between them. Because he did not believe that the medication had been the active agent, it did not seem important to take it on a regular basis. On the other hand, when he felt depressed he became frightened and would then take either the two, or up to four, pills.

The major issue, however, was transferential, in that he felt controlled by the doctor and by the medication; this was very threatening to him. His idiosyncratic pill taking was a hostile and rebellious action. Because the medication was not the active agent, and because the doctor was controlling him with the drug, taking it only when he chose to seemed reasonable to him.

The therapist made several interventions. He agreed that control issues were a major issue for the patient, but forcefully stated that it was a poor idea to make the medication the locus of that struggle. Second, he had no question that the nortriptyline had played a major role in the patient's recovery; part of the difficulty had been a "chemical imbalance" that required medication. He also reminded the patient that since he had been taking the medication erratically, his depressive symptomatology had partially recurred. Lastly, he told the patient that he must take two tablets each day, but that it was up to the patient when he took them; that is, if he wanted to take two tablets in the morning that was fine. The therapist added that he would measure nortriptyline blood levels on a regular basis and that if they were not in the therapeutic range, or if the patient continued to take medication on his own schedule, he would no longer prescribe it. "Although I understand your fears about being controlled by me, in fact you are controlling me and putting me in an impossible situation by taking the medication I prescribe according to your whim. I am not willing to do that, and I will not prescribe medication for you unless you take two tablets a day; but the time of day you take them is up to you. Also, I believe that if you do not continue nortriptyline in appropriate dosage you will become depressed again, and I don't think that's an experience you will enjoy."

Essentially, the therapist was insisting on adequate dosage (clinically essential) while allowing the schedule to be determined by the patient (not clinically essential). Periodic nortriptyline blood levels remained in the therapeutic range, demonstrating that the patient was taking the medication in the correct dosage. As expected, the control and power issues moved into other areas and were a major theme of the psychotherapy.

The addition to the two-person patient/therapist system of a third person, the psychopharmacologist, always has significant impact on the treatment. It is a situation ready-made for splitting, and this can be expected to occur. In one scenario, the psychopharmacologist is the good, powerful doctor who makes the patient better, while the psychotherapist is a "big talk, do nothing" impotent. In the contrasting scenario, the therapist is the warm, giving, humanistic, good doctor, while the psychopharmacologist is a cold, symptom-oriented, uncaring pill dispenser. Both these outcomes of splitting operations are common, and they complicate the treatment of the borderline patient, as well as furnish important material for the treatment.

Clinical Example 5

This 28-year-old borderline female was referred for psychopharmacologic consultation by her psychotherapist because of a mixed anxious depression that impeded her function at work. Although the patient had made progress in the areas of identity diffusion and interpersonal functioning, the anxious depression had not responded to the once weekly supportive psychotherapy. The psychopharmacologist felt the patient was suffering from an atypical depression and placed her on the MAOI phenelzine.

Four weeks later there was a significant improvement in the patient's affective symptomatology and associated improved work performance. The following dialogue occurred in the 54th session.

PATIENT: I'm feeling a lot better and work is going better; those pills are really helping. It's no big deal to watch myself with the foods. I don't like cheese much anyhow. Dr. A. (the psychopharmacologist) is a doll. He's really interested and caring. He's happy that I'm feeling better and I really don't see why I should continue my psychotherapy. You're disinterested and cold and withdrawn, and you don't seem pleased enough when I'm doing better. I think I'm just going to continue the pills and stop our sessions. I don't need you anymore, and compared to Dr. A. you're not helping me at all. I don't think you ever helped me. You listen, you talk occasionally, sometimes you help me understand things, but he's the one that really fixed me. He's wonderful, I'm crazy about him, and he makes you look useless.

THERAPIST: I'm certainly pleased that the medication is helping you to feel better. However, I don't believe that medication alone will help you with your confusions about yourself, what you want to do with your life, and your difficulties with other people. Also, I'm struck by the parallels between how you're describing Dr. A. and feelings you've had toward me in the past. It seems as though all your positive feelings have left this relationship and are now attached to Dr. A., while I am seen as useless, cold, and disinterested. In no way am I minimizing the fact that the medication has been helpful to you; it helps your depression and anxiety, it makes you feel better, but it doesn't solve all of the problems that brought you here originally. We have made some progress on them, and there's further work to be done. How is it that Dr. A. is seen in such highly positive terms while I appear to be without any redeeming features?

PATIENT: Why doctor, I do believe you're jealous! You have people in your life that are more important than I am, and now you're jealous that I have someone who's more important than you are. Control yourself, doctor, I think you're splitting.

THERAPIST: (*Laughs*) I really don't feel that way. The medication and the psychotherapy are helping with different aspects of your difficulties, and although they overlap to some extent, neither treatment is sufficient by itself. I'm more struck by how Dr. A. is being painted in all-positive terms, myself in all-negative terms, while you decide that all you really need now is medication. I'm curious about that.

PATIENT: Well, I still think you're jealous. I must say I'm getting a big kick out of this. Eat your heart out Doc, I'm in love with Dr. A. But we've talked a lot about my tendency to make impulsive decisions, and I still trust you and take seriously what you say. So I'll stay here for a while anyhow. . . .

A month later, with the patient continuing to do well on the phenelzine and the psychotherapy also moving along well, the patient was enraged with Dr. A.

PATIENT: That son of a bitch! I was fooling around with a little cheese, I had some pizza, and he started on me about headaches and strokes, and how I'm going to end up paralyzed. He doesn't give a damn about me, he doesn't care about my feelings. Mostly I think he's afraid of a malpractice suit. Boy, do I feel like a jerk! You're the one who really cares about me, the one who sticks by me when I give you a hard time, while that jerk is all over my case.

THERAPIST: Well, this is a turnabout from last month. Suddenly Dr. A. is all bad and I'm the good guy. It seems to me that Dr. A. was totally appropriate in warning you about eating cheese and truly concerned for your safety and well-being. But again, what's most striking to me is how everything has now flipped 180°. Now I'm the "doll" and Dr. A. is the bastard, and we see the same extreme feelings, but switched around.

I hope you're as struck as I am by your tendencies to either idealize or to make nothing out of people, not viewing others as mixtures of good and bad. And let me also point out that you do the same with yourself. Your views of yourself swing wildly from wonderful to worthless, with very little "middle of the road" feelings, and I wonder if this isn't connected with your confusion about who you are.

PATIENT: You've made your point a hundred times. You don't need to keep beating a dead horse. I get it. . . .

Acting Out Outside of the Session

Acting out outside of the therapy hours can take a myriad of forms: various eating or substance-abuse disorders; promiscuity; shoplifting; a variety of self-mutilations; suicidal threats, gestures, and attempts. They represent attempts by the patient to communicate distress to others, to force responses from others, or to alleviate dysphoric affects. Frequently they serve all three functions simultaneously. It is important to stress the role of these behaviors in relieving psychic pain because they are often viewed only as "manipulative" attempts to coerce the therapist, to express rage at him, or to drive him crazy. As with all psychic phenomena, acting-out behaviors are multiply determined and do contain significant interpersonal determinants and communications; but they also serve intrapsychic functions and sometimes those are primary. Cognizance of both sets of factors will help the therapist to maintain empathy with the patient and to feel less angry and/or threatened by the behavior.

Lebenluft, Gardner, and Cowdry (1987) quote extensively from accounts by self-mutilating borderline patients; their material suggests that attempts to relieve unbearable affects or experiences such as depersonalization are at least as important as interpersonal motivations in producing these behaviors. One gets the impression that patients often cut or burn themselves primarily because they have discovered from experience that nothing is as effective in relieving severe psychic pain.

An early aim in a supportive therapy might be to help the patient find another way to produce physical pain that is less destructive and without permanent sequelae. For example, patients who scratch or cut their forearms sometimes find that exercising to exhaustion, plunging their arm into painfully cold ice water, or repeatedly snapping a stiff rubber band against the forearm produces inner relief almost as well as the more dramatic and disfiguring cutting. But whether or not he can help the patient find a less destructive alternative, the therapist ideally will maintain empathy and tolerance for these behaviors, realizing that from the patient's point of view she often is doing the best she can to relieve intolerable feelings.

Other kinds of acting out can be seriously life threatening. Driving 90 miles an hour at night on the wrong side of the road, crossing streets with one's eyes closed, taking a potentially lethal dose of drugs, and then phoning someone—all can inadvertently destroy or maim the patient. In these cases, strict limit setting is instituted, using all of the authority and "clout" at the therapist's disposal to prevent the patient from "accidentally" killing herself. When these interventions are not effective, the patient will require hospitalization for her own safety.

The patient's acting-out behaviors often cause intense affective reactions in the therapist. These countertransference (broad view) responses are various combinations of realistic anxiety about the patient's safety, realistic responses to the patient's sadism, and irrational transferential (countertransference, narrow view) factors in the therapist. The greater the contribution of therapist irrationality and neurotic conflict to his total response, the more difficult it is for him to respond appropriately, to use his countertransference reactions to help elucidate the patient's behaviors, and then to share these understandings with the patient.

The following vignette illustrates the complex relationships between a patient's escalating self-destructive acting out and the therapist's problematic countertransference reactions that made it difficult for him to respond appropriately and effectively to her behaviors.

Clinical Example 6

A young borderline woman began an escalating pattern of self-mutilation and increasingly dangerous self-destructive acts. She scratched her forearms, burned her thighs, and took 90-mile-per-hour rides on local highways. Then she began crossing busy streets with her eyes closed, not reflecting a grandiose delusion about her own invulnerability, but rather her version of Russian roulette. All of these behaviors were described gleefully to the therapist. His best attempts to understand with the patient why she did these things, what she was trying to communicate to him, her attempts to sadistically control and punish him, what she felt before the behaviors, and so on came to nothing. She was clearly getting pleasure and gratification both from hurting herself and from relating her behaviors to the therapist.

He felt helpless and rejecting, and became aware of the magnitude of his rage when he had the thought, "Why doesn't she succeed already?" He felt sadistic urges to shake and hit her, and simultaneously was aware that permitting these behaviors to continue was an antitherapeutic submission to her sadistic displays. He felt protective urges to bring her home and take care of her as a helpless waif. He wanted to save her, to kill her, to survive with her through these behaviors, and to refer her to another therapist and free himself of her.

All of these feelings represented combinations of realistic reactions to her behaviors and irrational responses based in his early life experiences and neurotic struggles. He sought consultation from a senior colleague whose treatment suggestions, in turn, were defeated by the patient as she continued her self-destructive behaviors.

As the therapist struggled with his conflicted feelings and anxieties, with the help of the consultant, he became aware of a grandiose fantasy that was strongly influencing his treatment of the patient. "I will succeed against all odds. I will accomplish what no ordinary therapist can. I will become my parents (patient's) hero and savior, the favorite child, loved above all others."

As this fantasy became increasingly conscious, and then mastered, in all of its ramifications and genetic antecedents, the therapist was finally able to tell the patient that her behavior was making outpatient treatment impossible and that she could be effectively treated only inside a hospital. He felt so strongly about this, he told her, that if she would not sign into a hospital voluntarily, he would recommend involuntary commitment. He was fearful that the patient would feel rejected, or attack him, and was surprised when the patient sighed with relief and said, "I kept hoping you would blow the whistle on me. I couldn't believe that anybody would tolerate what I have been doing. You should have hospitalized me weeks ago."

This example illustrates the intense countertransference feelings, rational and irrational, that can be stirred up by a patient's frightening self-destructive acting out. The focus here is on this therapist's struggles with his countertransference, but comparable reactions to borderline patients' acting-out behaviors are very common.

The manifestations of acting out outside of the session by BPD patients are limited only by the patient's "creativity." However, the behaviors do tend to fall into a number of categories, and these are illustrated below.

Suicidal Threats, Gestures, and Acts

Of all the acting out that is so common in borderline patients, suicidal threats, gestures, and attempts are usually the most anxiety provoking and the most countertransferentially problematic for the therapist. The initial diagnostic evaluation will determine whether the patient has a major depression and requires antidepressant medications or hospitalization. But there are many borderline patients for whom suicidal threats and behaviors are a way of life, and most are not responsive to medication. These patients constitute a difficult dilemma for the therapist. He doesn't want to reward manipulative and coercive suicidal threats with extra phone calls or sessions, but he does feel some responsibility for the patient's safety.

Thus, after evaluating the severity of the patient's depression, the therapist's next task is assessment of the threats and gestures; specifically, what is the potential for lethality or serious harm? However, this too can be complex. Some patients successfully suicide by accident, while others, seriously intent on self-destruction, are saved by their own ineptitude or luck. One therapist's struggles with this difficult problem is illustrated in the vignette below.

Clinical Example 7. This 25-year-old borderline female had a long history of suicidal gestures and attempts, of varying degrees of lethality. The more serious attempts occurred while the patient was clinically depressed, while the gestures tended to occur between episodes of major depression when she was dysthymic. She had, on various occasions, taken close to lethal doses of drugs, jumped from a second-story window breaking her leg, and attempted to hang herself. In addition, her behaviors included driving at dangerous speeds, driving while severely intoxicated, and walking through dangerous neighborhoods in the middle of the night.

During the initial evaluation, serious consideration was given to long-term inpatient treatment, but this was not feasible. Her suicidal behaviors were necessarily the focus of the contract setting. The agreement was made that if the patient were feeling seriously suicidal and felt she couldn't control her behavior, she would immediately go to an emergency room for psychiatric evaluation. On the other hand, if she felt suicidal but could control her behavior, she could make one 15-minute phone call to the therapist. All of this was discussed with the patient in great detail, and she agreed with the reasonableness of the arrangements. The rationale for these arrangements was that the therapist did not want to reward suicidal behavior, yet the patient needed psychiatric evaluation—therefore the emergency room option. He did want to reward her not acting on suicidal feelings—therefore the 15-minute telephone contact.

During the third month of a twice weekly supportive psychotherapy, the patient called the therapist in the evening for the first time and said she was frightened of how suicidal she was feeling. She did feel that she could control her behavior and therefore had called the therapist rather than going to the emergency room. During the phone conversation the patient was rational, very sad, and desperate, but also confident that she was in control of her behavior.

Within an hour after the phone call, the patient took a nonlethal dose of her mother's benzodiazepines and was taken to an emergency room for gastric lavage. The therapist was notified, she was observed overnight, and released in the morning. The dialogue is from the next session.

PATIENT: I know that you know about my pill taking because they told me at the hospital that they called you.

THERAPIST: Yes, that's true. What happened?

PATIENT: After I talked to you I got increasingly depressed, and I couldn't control myself any longer.

THERAPIST: Then why did you not at that point go to the emergency room as we had agreed?

PATIENT: Because I didn't want to go to any goddamn emergency room! You're my doctor and it's your responsibility. You talked to me for 15 minutes and I appreciated that, but then I'm on my own again. I didn't go to the emergency room because I didn't want to go to the emergency room. I refused to go to the emergency room. When I'm suicidal, you're supposed to be there for me. It's coming to me, it's owed me. You can't send me off to see some other doctor when I'm feeling at my worst. What kind of treatment is that? You're gonna treat me when I'm feeling OK but when I feel suicidal I have to go to see somebody else? That's nonsense and I won't do it!

THERAPIST: You know that you've had many previous experiences like this, and in each case your suicidal behavior led to the end of your psychotherapy, to a hospitalization and then a new psychotherapist. We set up this system to safeguard this treatment. It was not done without careful thought, and we felt it had a fair chance of working to keep the treatment viable. Furthermore, this arrangement is something you agreed to, and seemed to feel was reasonable, while now you are attacking it as unfair. Why didn't you question it at the time?

PATIENT: To be honest I was afraid that if I did you wouldn't take me into treatment, and so I tried to see it your way. I wasn't lying to you, but it never made sense to me. And it still doesn't and I'm not gonna do it. It seems totally crazy to me that you who are my doctor will not see me at the times when I'm most upset. To me that's totally ass-backwards and unfair.

THERAPIST: I can understand your feeling that way, and I can see your point of view. But the fact is that this is how we set it up, and I believe that this is the only system that will work for us. I believe that very strongly. So I guess you have a choice. You can agree to hold to the original contract terms, whether or not they make sense to you; you're welcome to talk about it as much as you like, especially why it seems unfair and crazy to you. But if you call me when you can't control your behavior, or if you can't control your behavior and don't go to an emergency room, the treatment will stop at that point. I know it seems unfair to you, but I insist on this and you have the choice of accepting it or finding another doctor.

PATIENT: I don't like it, I think it stinks, but I don't want to stop treatment with you and start with another doctor. I will abide by the rules and I understand if I don't, treatment will stop. So I will . . . but I don't like it. . . . I'm very angry about it . . . and I think it's completely crazy. . . .

The next vignette illustrates another kind of suicide-related behavior, the patient whose threats and gestures are so histrionic that they are not taken seriously until he almost destroys himself by miscalculation.

Clinical Example 8. This 23-year-old homosexual male musician met criteria for Borderline, Narcissistic, and Histrionic Personality Disorders.

He had a long history of suicidal threats and gestures whenever he was frustrated in his professional or love life. Two previous psychotherapies were both short lived, terminated by the therapist because of poor motivation, sporadic attendance, and frequent suicidal threats and gestures. These parasuicidal behaviors were so frequent and so often reactive to minor frustrations and discomforts that his family and friends no longer took them at all seriously. The patient's presentation of them also gave the impression that he regarded them frivolously. They appeared to have become an ego-syntonic part of his behavioral repertoire, although he did feel that they were somewhat strange behaviors.

The therapist asked why the patient continued these behaviors when they no longer elicited much interest or concern from those about him. He also insisted that the contract setting include the proviso that should the patient feel seriously suicidal he would go immediately to the nearest emergency room for psychiatric evaluation. The patient agreed without argument, treating the whole issue very lightly, in spite of repeated confrontations of his seeming lack of concern about the behavior.

In his once weekly supportive therapy, the threats and gestures continued in reaction to any frustration in the treatment sessions or his outside life. The patient would dramatically announce that he was seriously thinking of killing himself, while his affect and histrionic manner made it clear why others did not take the behavior seriously. Usually the threats were followed by no behavior whatsoever, although on several occasions the patient swallowed enough aspirins to cause him to throw the pills up again.

The main theme in the treatment was the patient's omnipotence and entitlement, which existed together with the feeling that he was small, weak, and unable to tolerate any frustration. In other words, "I'm too weak to handle frustrations," together with "I'm too important to have to deal with frustrations." These contradictory self-images, together with their complementary object images, were clarified and confronted repeatedly without any change in the patient's behaviors. He often came late to sessions and frequently expressed attitudes of derision toward the treatment and the therapist while demeaning himself. For example, he wondered why the therapist would waste time with a "flaming fag" like himself and accused the therapist of being interested only in the fee. Attacks on the therapist gradually escalated and were understood as representing projections into the therapist of his devalued and omnipotent views of himself.

About 5 months into this once weekly supportive treatment, at a time when the therapist was increasingly wondering whether he could have any impact upon the patient, the patient unexpectedly made a suicide attempt with a combination of Vodka and street drugs. According to his conscious plan this was another gesture; he had expected his roommate/ lover home shortly. However, the roommate was unexpectedly delayed and the patient was not found until 24 hours after the ingestion. He was in a deep coma, and the panicky roommate called the therapist who arranged medical hospitalization. The patient spent 3 days in an ICU, had several grand mal seizures, and then recovered. The therapist arranged a transfer to a psychiatric unit.

When the therapist saw the patient on the psychiatric unit, he was impressed by the striking change in the patient's demeanor. He was sober and distraught; he never had believed that his behavior could have serious consequences, and he was shocked at the near lethality of his attempt. There was a dropping away of the denial and a significant decrease in his feelings of omnipotence. Psychological testing did not reveal any organic sequelae of the overdose. Over the succeeding 2 weeks the patient looked increasingly depressed and was started on fluoxetine by the hospital physician.

The once weekly outpatient psychotherapy resumed; although there were occasional suicidal threats, the behaviors were now ego-dystonic. The psychotherapy took on a more serious tone, centered around his grandiosity, entitlement, rage, and feelings of inadequacy and worthlessness. There was a gradual decrease, and then extinction, of suicidal threats and behaviors, together with an increased ability to tolerate frustrations and the unavoidable narcissistic blows of life.

In this case, the ego-syntonic suicidal threats and gestures became increasingly ego-dystonic after the patient almost succeeded in destroying himself. It was the therapist's belief that the patient's near death acutely and dramatically undermined his omnipotence, leading the patient to become both depressed and more amenable to psychotherapy. It is an example of a borderline patient who really never expected to harm himself, whose threats and gestures had become part of his lifestyle, but who nevertheless almost succeeded in killing himself.

Self-Mutilation

Clinical Example 9. The patient is a 29-year-old single woman with a history of multiple self-cutting episodes; she had not cut herself since starting psychotherapy. She has been in once a week supportive psychotherapy for 3 months. The patient enters the session dressed in short sleeves, though it is winter; there are prominent superficial cuts on both forearms. She sits silently, staring expectantly at the therapist. After 2 minutes, the therapist begins.

THERAPIST: I can't help noticing the cuts on your arms.

PATIENT: (*Silence*)

THERAPIST: How did it happen that you cut yourself?

PATIENT: (*Silence*)

THERAPIST: (*After 3 minutes*) I get the feeling that you want me to say more.

PATIENT: (*Silence*)

THERAPIST: (*After 3 more minutes*) I want to remind you that you are supposed to be expressing whatever is on your mind.

PATIENT: Fuck you!

THERAPIST: It's clear that you are angry with me, but I have no idea why. I can't read your mind.

PATIENT: (*Silence*)

THERAPIST: It seems to me that the silence too has an angry, punishing quality to it.

PATIENT: Angry? I am furious. I called you last night and you never called me back. Where were you when I needed you, you bitch?

THERAPIST: I did call you back, but you seemed intoxicated, and you were ranting and raving. I couldn't understand what you were saying. I told you that I would see you at our regular time today.

PATIENT: You called me? I don't remember.

THERAPIST: That raises another issue. We agreed at the beginning that any significant substance abuse would make treatment extremely problematic, if not impossible, and that if it happened, you would return to AA on a regular basis.

PATIENT: Fuck you and AA.

THERAPIST: (*After 3–4 minutes of silence*) You appear to be so angry with me that even my telling you that I called you seems to have no impact.

PATIENT: Go to hell! I called you when I needed you and you weren't there, and that's why I got drunk. It's your fault, not mine!

THERAPIST: The reality is that I would have called you back sooner had I gotten the message sooner. But another part of the reality is that I can't be available all the time. I called you when I got the message.

PATIENT: (*Silence*) I had a terrible time (*more softly and with less anger*). I started to get terribly anxious, and I felt I was jumping out of my skin. That's why I called you, I thought maybe talking to you might help. But you are always busy with something more important. I started to drink, but the anxiety got worse, and then I got depressed and I was cursing you for not being there and me for needing to talk to you. I hated me for needing you, and you because I needed you, and you obviously don't give a damn! I started to feel unreal—horrible!—it was unbearable. So I took a razor and started to slice my arms. It was crazy, I hardly felt anything. But I started to feel a little better, and the more I cut the better I felt, and I kept saying "Fuck you," "Fuck you" with each slice, and I didn't even know if I was saying it to you or to me. I stared at the blood, and I felt better—the unreality went away and I felt I didn't need you anymore. Who needs you? You don't give a damn anyhow! (*The patient visibly calms down as she talks, and ends looking slightly angry, somewhat sad, with tears in her eyes.*)

THERAPIST: It sounds terrible. I am sorry you had such a painful time of it.

PATIENT: (*Angry again*) Thanks a bunch, that's a big help!

THERAPIST: Again, I am sorry you had such a rough time and that I didn't get back to you for several hours, but that's the reality of it. I also think that you can do better right now than to continue your tantrum. What was going on last night that led to the anxiety?

PATIENT: Same old shit. I had a fight with my boyfriend. He stomped out of the house, and I started to get terrified, then anxious and depressed.

THERAPIST: So the episode started with a rejection, and then you tried to reach me, and then felt rejected by me, and things escalated.

PATIENT: Yeah, I guess so. Very helpful! I knew all that before you said it. I felt so good with him, loved and warm, and then he left, and bango!

THERAPIST: What was the fight with him about?

PATIENT: I was complaining that he wasn't around enough, he didn't show me enough attention, and he didn't love me enough. His answer was to leave.

THERAPIST: It's clear that you are very sensitive to any rejection, particularly by men you care about. But why so intense a reaction?

PATIENT: When I feel let down, it's like I disappear as a person. Like I am nothing, nothing and worthless, a worthless piece of shit.

THERAPIST: So when you feel loved, you feel whole and good, but if someone lets you down, perhaps particularly a man, you plunge into the depths.

PATIENT: (*Silence*)

THERAPIST: We are getting near the end of our time, I am concerned about the drinking. Please do your best to stop it, but if you can't you must return to AA on a regular basis. I am also concerned about the cutting. Can you think of any other way to deal with those unbearable feelings if they happen again?

PATIENT: (*Silence. Increasingly sullen, and angry again*)

THERAPIST: Your whole attitude changed when I said we had to stop soon, and you're getting angry and silent again. I guess you experience it as another rejection. Do you have any ideas about alternatives to cutting yourself?

PATIENT: (*Silence*)

THERAPIST: Let's talk about that next time. While cutting your arms isn't the end of the world, it would be good if we could find some less self-destructive way for you to deal with the rage and despair that you experience when you feel rejected. For now, I guess it's the most effective relief you have found. But I hope we can find some better way of handling those awful feelings—behavioral, maybe psychopharmacology; we'll see. You might think about it. Now we need to stop.

PATIENT: Fuck you.

THERAPIST: I will see you next week.

Here the therapist is faced initially with a silent patient who is simultaneously communicating powerful nonverbal affects. His first interventions exemplify dealing with patient silences in the session. Later, the patient's drunken state during the telephone call is confronted, and the therapist makes it clear that significant deviations from the abstinence of the original contract will not be tolerated. However, as illustrated, occasional lapses are accepted and handled by trying to understand why the patient got drunk at that particular time.

The therapist spells out the realistic conditions of their work together and sets limits on the patient's behavior in the session: "I also think that you can do better right now then to continue your tantrum." Limit setting regarding substances is illustrated, as well as the therapist's attempt to help the patient find a substitute for cutting, while remaining tolerant of the behavior. Finally, the patient's angry acting out at the end of the session is accepted, while the patient is assured that the therapist will still be there at the next session.

I find the patient's description of her arm cutting particularly poignant. It demonstrates how the dramatic acting out of self-destructiveness expresses the patient's disappointment and rage at the therapist, and simultaneously is an attempt to diminish unbearable inner affects. Note the depersonalization, the anesthesia during the cutting, how effectively the cutting relieves psychic pain, and the transient loss of ego boundaries and merger with the therapist.

Substance Abuse

Clinical Example 10. This 29-year-old BPD junior executive came for treatment primarily because of problematic interpersonal relations and feelings of inner confusion and emptiness. He mentioned in passing that he occasionally engaged in bouts of drinking, about once every 8 months, with unclear precipitants. He had a past history of severe alcohol abuse during mid to late adolescence, together with abuse of other substances. The possibility that substance abuse would become a serious problem in the treatment was addressed during the contract setting, and therapist and patient agreed that should periods of drinking occur with any regularity, and particularly if they increased in frequency, he would immediately attend AA and make every effort to maintain sobriety.

In the treatment, as the patient began to deal with his internal confusions, his difficulties in maintaining relationships with appropriate women, and feelings of inner emptiness and deadness that were unbearable to him, he began an escalating pattern of alcohol abuse. At first he kept this information from the therapist, rationalizing that he could control the drinking by himself and would tell the therapist after he was back in control. However, he announced it behaviorally by arriving for a session in an intoxicated state. When his unusual behavior in the session was confronted, the patient revealed the whole situation, which had been going on at that point for 2½ months. He talked of fears of becoming dependent on the therapist and the importance of being able to handle his problems by himself. The therapist pointed out his ambivalence about dependency and self-control, as revealed by appearing in the session intoxicated while trying to keep the information to himself. He also stated that he would not continue the session at that time because of the patient's acute intoxication; they would discuss the issues again in the following session.

The next session was very stormy. The therapist held to the terms of the contract and insisted that the patient try to become abstinent and begin attending AA meetings regularly. The patient argued that the therapist was making too much of the problem and that he still felt that he could control it by himself; his coming intoxicated to a session was only a temporary lapse of judgment.

The disagreement continued into the next session. The therapist stated that he certainly respected the patient's attempts to handle his own difficulties, but they had set up contractual agreements for just this situation, and those initial agreements needed to be honored. When the patient asked what would happen if he absolutely refused to attend AA and continued trying to handle his drinking problems by himself, the therapist replied that such an abrogation of the original contractual agreements would lead to the immediate discontinuation of the psychotherapy. The patient resentfully agreed to attend AA.

Over the next several weeks the patient attended AA meetings but derogated them continually. They were not helpful, the other people were of a different social class; they were "real" alcoholics, bums, nothing like himself. The patient decided to investigate alternatives to AA and found a private group run by a competent mental health professional; the clients were more similar to himself. He asked if the original contract could be modified to replace AA by the group. Having satisfied himself that this was a reputable program, the therapist agreed to the substitution. The patient continued in the substance-abuse group and gradually returned to the occasional drinking, which was addressed in the psychotherapy.

Treating the substance-abusing patient in supportive therapy, or in any psychotherapy, involves the therapist's taking an unambivalent stand against the use of substances. Coming to a treatment session intoxicated is a dramatic demonstration of the problem, and the therapist does not attempt to carry on any psychotherapy while the patient is drunk. There must be a program in place for dealing with the substance abuse. This is an absolute requirement because any significant intake of substances makes effective psychotherapy impossible. The therapist need not feel ambivalent about the stance that he will terminate the psychotherapy unless the patient makes every effort to control the substance abuse. Any other position leads to a pseudotreatment, in which the participants act as though they were in a serious psychotherapy, while the patient's affects and conflicts are displaced, covered over, and acted out in the substance abuse.

Eating Disorders

Clinical Example 11. This 20-year-old borderline female had been hospitalized for severe bingeing and purging. In addition to the Bulimia Nervosa, she suffered from severe identity diffusion, unstable affects, unstable relationships, occasional use of street drugs, and occasional shoplifting. She was treated with the MAOI phenelzine in the hospital, achieved a good symptomatic response to the bulimia on 60 mg a day, and was discharged from the hospital to begin once weekly outpatient supportive psychotherapy.

A treatment contract was successfully negotiated in regard to the substance abuse and shoplifting, but the patient adamantly refused to discuss the bulimia and how it should be handled should it recur. She was absolutely sure that the symptoms would never return and held to this position in spite of repeated efforts to undermine the denial. Unable to achieve a resolution in this area, the therapist agreed to the patient's request that they supplement the contract regarding the bulimia only if it became clinically necessary.

Six months into the once weekly treatment, which was proceeding smoothly with a positive and mildly idealized transference, the patient experienced an unexpected and very traumatic rejection by a boyfriend. She began bingeing and purging again almost immediately and now was agreeable to discussing the management of these symptoms. The therapist increased the phenelzine from 60 to 90 mg per day, but this produced only slight improvement in the symptomatology. The contract was amended to include weekly examinations by an internist, including weekly serum potassium determinations. Outpatient treatment would continue so long as she remained medically clear and maintained potassium levels within the normal range. Should her medical condition deteriorate, hospitalization would be necessary. These conditions were accepted by the patient, and the therapy was continued as before.

She began to deal with her feelings of desolation and emptiness, and her rage at the boyfriend. After 6 weeks, during which there were several extra sessions requested by the patient, the bulimic symptomatology gradually decreased and then ceased altogether. Medical visits became unnecessary and there were no further episodes of eating-disordered behavior during the remainder of a quite successful psychotherapy.

Eating disorders, both bulimic and anorectic, commonly occur together with Borderline Personality Disorder. In the management of anorexia, minimal weight criteria are specified at the beginning of the treatment, with the agreement that inpatient treatment will become necessary should the patient's weight fall below those levels. In the case of bulimia, the contract terms depend upon its severity. Occasional episodes of bingeing and purging do not constitute a threat to the patient's physical safety and are compatible with outpatient treatment. However, severe bingeing and purging can lead to serious medical complications. The patient may lose enough weight to be in danger on that basis, while severe electrolyte imbalances are potentially lethal. Should either of these medical complications occur, inpatient treatment is necessary. The therapist makes every effort to build limits and structures into the initial contract, designed to protect the patient from life-threatening medical complications while keeping himself comfortable enough about the medical risks to treat her effectively.

Promiscuity

Clinical Example 12. This 23-year-old single borderline female began an escalating pattern of promiscuity at about the sixth month of a once a week supportive treatment. She began going to neighborhood bars to pick up men, many of questionable reliability, and then had sex with them, usually without condoms. On several occasions she was beaten up, once severely enough to require treatment in an emergency room. The therapist became increasingly concerned, both about AIDS and about the possibility that she could get herself killed and expressed these concerns in the 26th session.

THERAPIST: As I hear more about your frantic rushing off to bars and picking up guys, having unprotected sex, and all the violence, I am feeling increasingly concerned about your safety; both the possibility of AIDS and of someone killing you one of these nights. What are your thoughts about these behaviors?

PATIENT: I'm finding it increasingly impossible to stay home alone at night. I get such terrible feelings of aloneness and emptiness, I begin to feel unreal and then I run out to the bar. I appreciate your concerns. I'm very worried about what I'm doing too.

THERAPIST: Do you have any ideas about why this behavior is reaching such frantic proportions now?

PATIENT: No, I really don't understand. I've always had trouble being alone, but I've never felt the kind of franticness I feel now. I think a lot about you, you know, and maybe it has something to do with coming here. I often don't find these sessions pleasant. I'm aware of wanting you to talk more, to see you more and be with you more, and maybe it's all connected.

THERAPIST: Well I have a couple of thoughts about that. What would you think about meeting twice a week rather than once?

PATIENT: I thought about that too, but I didn't think it was allowed in this kind of treatment. I would love that, and it wouldn't be any problem for me.

THERAPIST: I have another thought too. Sometimes it's helpful in dealing with feelings of loneliness to have a pet. I don't know how you feel about pets, whether you think it would be comforting to you. . . .

PATIENT: *(Interrupting)* I love animals, especially dogs. I feel like a jerk for not thinking of that myself. I think that's a great suggestion.

THERAPIST: But the *quid pro quo* for increasing our sessions is that you stop the frantic rushing to bars, picking up the first man you meet. I have no desire to interfere in your sex life, but you're taking great dangers with your health, and even your life. I'm glad to meet twice a week, but you must agree to stop these dangerous behaviors. When you do have sex, I strongly suggest that you insist on condoms. I hope the dog works out for you. I haven't seen you looking so positive for a long time.

PATIENT: I am, I feel hopeful for the first time in a long while. I was also getting more and more worried about my behavior, and I do think I'll be able to control it. I think the dog will help a lot with my feelings of loneliness. . . .

The danger in the therapist's offering more frequent meetings is an increase in the patient's dependency on the therapist; frustration of those wishes could lead to an increase, rather than the desired decrease, in acting out. In this case that did not occur. The patient stopped the barhopping and promiscuity, and became very involved with her new pet. The trade-off of the acting out for the increase in sessions appeared to work well, without untoward effects.

Using pets to help borderline patients with feelings of loneliness or inability to be alone has not been adequately stressed in the literature. Yet, in my experience, the use of pets as transitional objects (Modell, 1963) to help with feelings of loneliness can be quite successful. The choice of a pet reflects the psychodynamics and character style of the patient, but that is beyond our focus here.

I became aware of the potential usefulness of pets while treating a 35-year-old woman of schizoid character with severe Anorexia Nervosa. At the start of the treatment, she had been amenorrheic for 8 years and weighed 80 pounds. Because of concurrent research interests, her vaginal cytology was followed by an endocrinologist; the cytology was that of an 80-year-old woman.

This was a very difficult and painful treatment. Before there was any evidence of change in the psychological area, her vaginal cytology began to change toward more age-appropriate findings. At that time, she purchased a small dog that immediately became a crucial love object for her. Her investment in the dog was the most intense attachment she'd ever experienced. I believe that the dog was a transitional object in the process of cathecting human objects again. (I will leave speculations about the transference aspects to the reader.) She loved the dog as though it were a baby and often referred to it as "my baby." Her weight gradually increased, and her cytology became age appropriate at the 18th month of treatment. Shortly thereafter she began regular menstrual periods and 6 months later conceived the first of two children.

The many symbolic meanings of the dog for this patient are beyond our focus, but I was convinced that the dog was a vital link in her increasing connections to people, and in her becoming endocrinologically normal, beginning to menstruate, and becoming pregnant. In this connection, note also the use of the bird as a transitional object in the detailed case description above (Chapter 7).

Shoplifting

Clinical Example 13. This 28-year-old borderline male medical student came to treatment primarily for problems with identity diffusion and chaotic interpersonal relationships. There was relatively little evidence of acting out in this patient, except for a history of repetitive shoplifting during mid-adolescence which had continued for 2 years and then ceased spontaneously. He had never been caught and believed that this behavior was all in the past and would never recur. Because of the patient's strong feelings about this, the issue of shoplifting was not addressed during the contract setting. For reasons of schedule, an every other week supportive therapy was begun.

Unexpectedly, in the setting of an increasingly dependent and moderately idealizing transference, the patient suddenly began shoplifting again. He took items of clothing that he didn't need; often he gave them away to the Salvation Army afterwards. The behavior was ego-dystonic to him and had an extremely compulsive quality. It appeared to be a final common pathway for feelings of inadequacy, deprivation, inner emptiness, mild depression, and existential meaninglessness, plus unclear transferential elements.

The therapist wondered aloud why the behavioral pattern had re-emerged at that time, reminded the patient of the consequences of his behavior, and attempted to set limits on it; the shoplifting decreased only slightly. The patient himself became increasingly concerned about the behavior, its connection to his dysphoric feelings, and its effectiveness is relieving those feelings. He also felt guilty and that it was "crazy" behavior; he was fully aware of the effects on his career were he to be caught. The behavior was acting out, but unlike most acting out in BPD patients, it appeared to be more like a neurotic symptom. Thus limit setting, etc., would not be expected to be effective, and further progress would require increased focus on his intrapsychic life and on the transferences. At that point, the patient suggested an increased frequency of sessions to twice a week; his schedule now made it feasible and the therapist agreed.

The therapist switched into a more exploratory mode. The dependent and idealizing transferences became the central concerns, and it became clear that feelings of deprivation, intense wishes for the therapist's love and admiration, and guilty and conflicted reactions to those wishes were being displaced and condensed in the shoplifting behavior. The conflicts were confronted, clarified, and interpreted, leading to a significant decrease in the behaviors, although they continued occasionally. During one shoplifting episode, the patient was apprehended by department-store security police. He was terrified and guilty, and began to cry; probably because of his reaction and his medical student status, he was released with threats but no consequences. The fright over this episode put a total halt to his shoplifting, and the now exploratory psychotherapy continued on a twice a week schedule.

The acting out in this case is somewhat unusual in that (1) the patient was monosymptomatic in his acting out and (2) the acting out seemed more like a neurotic symptom; it was compulsive, ego-dystonic, and guilt laden. This type of acting out requires different handling from ego-syntonic behaviors, and I believe that the patient's guilt and conflict about the behavior were correctly viewed as indicating a switch to a more exploratory therapy.

Missing Treatment Sessions and Stopping Prescribed Medications

Clinical Example 14. This 24-year-old borderline female was referred for outpatient treatment after a 3-week inpatient treatment for a major depressive disorder, during which she was begun on lithium carbonate and nortriptyline. The patient was quite dysfunctional and unable or unwilling to work because of her psychiatric symptoms; she had almost no social supports and very few positives in her life. The initial contract did not address the issue of her psychiatric medications, but focused instead on serious antisocial features in the patient's lifestyle.

Immediately after the evaluation and contract setting, the patient abruptly and unilaterally stopped the medications, phoned the therapist to say that she was too depressed and anxious to come to sessions, and asked if he made house calls. The therapist replied that this was not reasonable and asked the patient why she had stopped her medications; she had just been discharged from the hospital and appeared to be getting increasingly depressed, perhaps secondary to stopping the medications. The patient did not answer directly; she promised to think about it, but did not restart the medications or attend sessions. Over the next 2 weeks she became more depressed and dysfunctional, and finally acutely suicidal. She again called the therapist and asked him to arrange rehospitalization for her. The therapist felt conflicted. The patient had seemingly brought this upon herself and was not attending sessions. On the other hand, she was so dysfunctional that it was questionable whether she could engineer her own hospitalization. His conflict was temporarily solved when the patient had a friend help her to get readmitted.

The medications were restarted in the hospital and within 3 weeks the patient was as she had been prior to stopping the medications. At that point, she recontacted the outpatient therapist, asking that the treatment begin again when she left the hospital. He again felt conflicted and agreed to discuss the issues with her on the inpatient unit. His attempts to understand her previous behaviors with her met with little success. They did agree to augment the initial contact in that the patient would continue medications as prescribed and not make unilateral judgments about changing them. The therapist reassured her that he would take her wishes seriously regarding medications, but that the final decisions had to be his. He raised the issue of the missed sessions and wanted to structure that into the contract too, but she adamantly refused, insisting that it would not be a problem again.

Immediately following discharge, the patient began missing sessions regularly. The therapist confronted the attendance issue and stated forcefully that treatment could not be effective when the patient was missing significant numbers of meetings. He insisted that this issue too had to be structured into the treatment contract; the patient reluctantly agreed. They agreed that if she continued to miss a significant number of sessions (the exact number left vague), it would signify that the treatment was not viable at this time, and therefore it would stop.

The therapist began to focus on the transference issues involved in the absences. The patient had two diametrically opposed self-images: (1) She was worthless and deserved nothing, and (2) she was very special, shouldn't have to work to support herself, and deserved to have the therapist make house calls when she was too upset to attend sessions. In addition, issues of control, negativism, and the wish to destroy her treatment were clarified. The patient attended more regularly but continued to miss a significant number of sessions, complaining either that she was too emotionally upset or too physically ill to leave her home.

The absences occurred now about once every five sessions, leading the therapist to question whether the treatment should continue. This was not done in a punitive fashion; rather, he again stressed that regular attendance was necessary for an effective treatment. Was she trying to destroy hers? This intervention had the effect of decreasing absences further, the patient missing about one session in ten. The therapist felt that this was an adequate schedule for continuation of the treatment, but continued to focus repeatedly on the splitting, the self-destructive and self-entitled determinants of her attendance. The treatment continued in that fashion to the present, with gradual slow improvement in attendance.

Irregular attendance and unilaterally stopping prescribed medications are common acting-out phenomena in the treatment of the BPD patient. These behaviors commonly reflect struggles over control (also illustrated in this chapter, pp. 220–22). The therapist can allow the patient some leeway in terms of medication schedules, but should remain firm about the necessity for taking the medications in the prescribed doses. Regarding erratic attendance, I agree with the above therapist's approach. Psychotherapy is not likely to be effective when sessions are sporadic, and the patient acts out transference issues by not appearing for sessions. The issue is confronted quickly and forcefully. It is preferable to stop the treatment, rather than to have patient and therapist engage in a psychotherapy in which the patient's erratic visits express devaluation of herself, the therapist, and the treatment.

FINAL THOUGHTS

The specific behavioral manifestations of acting out in the treatment of the borderline patient are very variable from patient to patient. The most common types of acting out by BPD patients are illustrated above. The management of acting out in the supportive therapies of these patients follows certain general guidelines: limit setting, prohibitions, reality testing, praise for improved behaviors, encouraging less self-destructive behaviors, discouraging impulsivity, encouraging verbalization instead of action, and clarification, confrontation, and undermining of the negative transferences and primitive defenses that drive the acting-out behaviors.

However, in spite of the therapist's best efforts, acting out often continues unabated. In its more dramatic forms, it is likely to cause marked countertransference difficulties for the therapist. It is sometimes helpful for the therapist to remember that acting out in his universe may be the best the patient can do in hers. Nevertheless, short hospitalizations are often necessary to safeguard both the patient and the treatment.

CHAPTER 11

Treatment Time and the Borderline Patient: An Underappreciated Strategy*

SAMUEL PERRY

The difficulties in treating borderline personality disorders are widely reported in the psychiatric literature and are well appreciated by clinicians who have struggled with the intense, perplexing, and disruptive transference–countertransference reactions characterizing the course of therapy with these patients. What has not been adequately appreciated is that the management of the treatment's time—the length and frequency of sessions and the established duration of therapy—can help reduce the inherent frustrations experienced by both borderline patients and their therapists.

This underappreciation is not surprising. Until recently, time has not been viewed as a separate component of psychotherapy. Instead, the intensity and duration of outpatient treatment have traditionally been considered dependent upon other variables, most notably the treatment's techniques and goals; the therapist's training and orientation; and the patient's motivation, expectations, and financial resources (Perry, 1987). However, the issue of time in psychotherapy has recently been challenged not only by third-party payers but, more interestingly, by brief dynamic therapies (Davanloo, 1978; Malan, 1976; Mann, 1973; Sifneos, 1972) that have encouraged us to view the use of time as a more independent component with its own therapeutic impact. Applying the innovative approaches of these time-limited psychotherapies and the ac-

*From the *Journal of Personality Disorders*, 3, pp. 230–239. Copyright 1989 by The Guilford Press. Reprinted by permission.

cumulating data regarding differential therapeutics (Frances, Clarkin, & Perry, 1984; Perry, Frances, & Clarkin, 1985), this paper discusses the rationale and benefits of using time as a therapeutic strategy with borderline patients.

PSYCHODYNAMIC CONSIDERATIONS

In establishing the time frame for the treatment of borderline patients, the therapist should consider five interrelated dynamics. First, feeling empty, lonely, and unduly deprived, these patients are typically convinced that they "never get enough"—enough attention, love, admiration, commitment, whatever. Second, lacking a firm sense of object constancy and identity, they experience separation as an abandonment, with only a limited recognition that both they and the nurturing figure exist when apart. Third, given their fragile ego and overwhelming drives, they are prone to both formal and temporal regression when not provided sufficient external structure, with a resultant disorganization in thinking and a return to more primitive modes of viewing relationships as either all good or all bad. Fourth, in response to feelings of deprivation, fears of abandonment, and the regressive pull of treatment, a sense of entitlement and unfiltered primitive rage emerge that threaten the therapeutic alliance. And last but equally important, borderline patients have the uncanny ability to make therapists feel totally responsible for their plight, not only responsible for curing the problems, but responsible for causing the problems as well. The countertransferential guilt, confusion, and resentment have been experienced by us all. While the therapeutic use of time offers no panacea to these difficulties, it can be extremely useful.

LENGTH OF SESSIONS

Establishing the length of sessions becomes a paradigm for the more major considerations of the treatment's intensity and duration. Admittedly, the length of sessions holds little intellectual interest and is supported by even less systematic research. Freud saw his patients on the hour with a brief time in between for a breather and notetaking; and even nonanalysts have been influenced by this "50-minute hour," which for logistical and financial reasons has now become shortened by most private psychotherapist to 45 minutes. Some have suggested that for supportive therapy the length could be shortened further to 20 minutes (Castelnuovo-Tedesco, 1965) or even 5 minutes (Zirkle, 1961); and at the other extreme, some have suggested "marathon" sessions to wear down defenses or to meet the needs of a crisis (Bellack & Small, 1978; Caplan, 1964; Ewing, 1978). The points to be made here are that the evidence supporting the value of the traditional "hour" is not very convincing and that, given the dynamic considerations of the borderline patient outlined here, there are good reasons for not rigidly adhering to this convention and routinely prescribing a 45-minute session.

Compared to establishing the frequency of sessions and the treatment's duration, discussing the length of sessions provides a less emotionally charged opportunity to educate the patient about the requirements and goals of therapy, how the patient's "personality" may be challenged by the unavoidable constraints of time, and the therapist's confidence that the patient will be able to meet these expectations. More specifically, after the first few sessions of an extended consultation, the therapist will have data from both the history and interactions with the borderline patient to note difficulties in object constancy and separation. Initially, these may be quite subtle: a hesitancy to leave the office or, defensively, "no thoughts" about the preceding session; a casual remark that a piece of furniture or the papers on the therapist's desk have been slightly rear-ranged (as if time should have stood still between sessions and neither party had a life separate from the other); or a phone call between sessions to make contact with the "excuse" of checking on the hour of the next appointment or of making a change in the time that was not really necessary. The therapist will also note subtle indicators of a potential malignant regression: intense and premature erotic and idealizing trans-ferences, either in dreams or fantasies; feelings of detachment or deper-sonalization during silent pauses; or the patient's preoccupying concerns about what the therapist is *really* thinking (as if the therapist's manifest interest and caring serve to mask his or her actual disinterest or financial exploitation). And finally, in response to the borderline patient's apparent fragility, immediate consuming attachment, and simultaneous distrust, the therapist may begin to feel a need to prove his or her integrity by focusing on the patient's every word, self-consciously monitoring his or her own statements, and, at the same time, wishing to be more spontane-ous and free of the patient's implicit control, yet fearing that to act on such wishes would have dire consequences.

The contradictory feelings evoked in the therapist are reflections of the borderline patient's internal experience. This understanding of initial countertransference responses will enable the therapist confidently to discuss the prescribed session length and its rationale. The therapist can begin by negotiating a mutually convenient time, then stating when the sessions will begin and end. With most outpatients there is an implied understanding that the sessions will start and finish on time; but with borderline patients this agreement not only must be made more explicit, but also must be explained in terms that specifically address five overlapping therapeutic needs that have been identified during the initial evaluation. First, the fixed scheduling will provide a beneficial structure for the patient, whose internal and external worlds are experienced as unstructured or even chaotic. Second, having a fixed time allotment will highlight the patient's expressed feelings of deprivation, thereby providing an opportunity for these feelings to be explored while reducing the expectation that more time with the therapist will somehow in itself magically remove the chronic sense of emptiness and "never getting enough." Third, adherence to stopping on time will positively reinforce the patient's capacity to tolerate the termination and offer an opportunity to examine this difficulty that has been evident in the patient's history and during the consultation process. Fourth, having a fixed time–fee arrangement will help address implied concerns about the therapist's "secret agenda" or "real intent" by openly clarifying from the start that his or her motivations are indeed partly financial. Fifth, the designated length of sessions will be chosen in accord with the capacities and difficulties that the patient has both described and illustrated during the initial evaluation.

Given the dynamics of borderline patients, one cannot expect that the foregoing rationale will be easily accepted; but if relevant examples are given in a nonjudgmental manner, the therapist can convey not only his or her general expertise in treating such problems but also specific understanding of the individual patient. For example, the therapist can state the anticipation that the patient may experience the termination of some sessions as abrupt and abandoning; but since these are the very feelings for which the patient is seeking help, the two of them must work together not only to understand such feelings, but also to find ways that reduce the distress accompanying any separation. The aim here is to reframe termination of sessions so that it is not seen as an obstacle but rather as a therapeutic opportunity. Similarly, the therapist can state that he or she anticipates that from time to time the patient may doubt the therapist's integrity and be convinced that the fixed time–fee arrangement is evidence of an exploitative and uncaring approach; but again, since these are familiar feelings in other relationships, the clarified and open professional arrangement will offer a rich opportunity to determine the derivatives of this distrust and ways of preventing exploitation in relationships that are less well defined. In the throes of an initial idealizing transference, such comments may seem to fall on deaf ears, yet they serve as predictive interpretations that will provide a rudder to negotiate transferential storms that lie ahead.

Relatively more questions are likely to be asked at the start about why the particular length of session was selected. This can be explained not only in terms of the chosen goals and technique of the therapy, but also in terms of the patient's capacities and "personality problems," a tactful euphemism for malignant regressive potential. Within limits, the actual length of the session is less important than adherence to the prescribed time. As a general guideline, borderline patients who have difficulty making emotional contact, such as those with prominent schizoid, obsessive, or narcissistic traits, often require sessions longer than the usual 45 minutes; whereas those with affective instability or poor impulse control, such as those with prominent histrionic and antisocial traits, often find briefer sessions of 20 to 30 minutes sufficiently supportive and engaging without being too emotionally disruptive. Those with prominent paranoid traits fall midway along this spectrum, experiencing the longer sessions as potentially too intrusive and shorter sessions as perfunctory. More than particular character traits, however, the prodromal indicators of malignant regression noted during the initial evaluation provide the best guide and offer acceptable specific explanations to the patient. Finally, the patient may be informed that the length of sessions may be changed as the treatment progresses, but only after the rationale for such a change has been adequately discussed.

FREQUENCY OF SESSIONS

No systematic studies have examined how treatment outcome of borderline patients is affected by frequency of sessions, and the data from outpatient studies of mixed populations in psychotherapy are somewhat contradictory. In a review of 16 of these studies, Orlinsky and Howard (1978) concluded that more intensive therapies generally caused no harm and that some patients did better if seen more than once a week, a conclusion consistent with earlier reports (Graham, 1958; Imber et al., 1957). However, at least eight studies (Heilbrunn, 1966; Heinicke, 1969; Kaufman et al., 1962; Kernberg et al., 1972; Lorr et al., 1962; Rosenbaum, Friedlander, & Kaplan, 1956; Van Slambrouck, 1973; Zirkle, 1961) of diverse patients in very different settings found that improvement was not related to frequency of sessions and, of interest here, a study (Graham, 1958) conducted four decades ago documented that adult psychotic outpatients did less well if seen twice rather than once a week, supporting the clinical impression that severely disturbed patients may have difficulty with a therapeutic relationship that is too intense.

Therapists with a particular expertise in conducting psychoanalytically oriented character reconstruction with borderline patients recommend three to five sessions per week (Kernberg, 1984; Masterson, 1976), but for more supportive psychotherapies and psychopharmacotherapies, one or two sessions per week is suggested to prevent unmanageable iatrogenic regression and transference psychoses. Again, the rationale for this decision and the challenges it will pose to the patient should be explained early in the course of treatment. The therapist can convey that, given the patient's feelings of loneliness and deprivation, the prescribed frequency will at times be experienced as inadequate, with the resulting wish to increase the number of sessions and to phone the therapist between sessions either for nurturance or for reassurance that the frustrating rage (expressed or not expressed) has not jeopardized the relationship. The patient may even feel compelled to evoke some crisis in an attempt to force the therapist to intervene between sessions, such as making a suicide attempt requiring a hospitalization that would express both the wish to have the therapist "more involved" and the anger over his or her prescribed limitations. The therapist must establish from the start that such attempts are a product of the patient's impulses, that in no way are they therapeutic, and that the patient is fully capable of preventing such feelings from disrupting the treatment. These points, although phrased empathically, cannot be made too firmly. The patient (and the therapist) must be convinced that trying to make contact between sessions is a manifestation of the patient's problems and not their solution, that the time frame has been chosen for clear therapeutic reasons, and the patient and therapist will therefore work together to ensure that this crucial aspect of treatment is not sabotaged. If it is, the therapy simply will not be as effective and, given the ultimate benefits of treatment, this risk is not worth taking.

Inevitably, borderline patients will test the therapist's resolve with missed appointments, phone calls, suicidal threats, and trips to the emergency room. These must never be allowed to escalate and must be promptly interpreted, *not* as an indication that more "treatment" is necessary (the patient's view), but rather that the patient is refusing treatment. The patient may argue, often most compellingly, that the therapist has set the time frame for his or her own needs rather than the patient's. This argument can be countered by nondefensively stating that because the therapist's personal needs are in complete accord with the patient's therapeutic needs, this makes the time–fee arrangement ideal. Further, failure in adhering to the therapeutic time frame can be presented as being similar to a failure to take prescribed medication, discuss problems with the therapist, or pay the fee. In short, treatment cannot and will not proceed under these terms. Friends and family members also may need to be informed of the rationale for the prescribed time frame so that if and when it becomes necessary to stop treatment or refer the patient for emergent care, often at a time when the patient appears most disturbed and even suicidal, they—and at some level the patient—will understand that clinical experience has repeatedly indicated continuing treatment under such circumstances would hold no value and might even be more harmful. If this lesson is learned when the first therapist stops treatment because of the patient's noncompliance with the prescribed time frame, it is less likely to be repeated with the second.

DURATION OF TREATMENT

The statements in the preceding section may seem unduly harsh and inconsiderate of the borderline patient's psychopathology until put in the context of the following recommendations regarding treatment duration. As opposed to the paucity of studies regarding frequency of sessions, more general and specific data are available to guide the decision about treatment duration. At first glance, the general research literature regarding outpatient psychotherapies would tend to favor the prescription of a relatively brief therapy lasting a few months. Three large and respected reviews (Butcher & Koss, 1978; Luborsky, Singer, & Luborsky, 1975; Smith, Glass, & Miller, 1980), despite using very different methods, failed to demonstrate a significant advantage of longer treatments; however, the outcome studies used in these reviews favored the initial impact of briefer therapies because the studies measured symptom relief rather than personality problems, because behavioral techniques were heavily represented, and because briefer treatments were favored by a regression to the mean (patients were seen at their worst and were bound to improve) (Frances et al., 1984). More directly relevant to the decision here is a review of studies more varied in technique that found the duration of treatment significantly correlated with greater therapeutic benefits (Orlinsky & Howard, 1978). In addition, a more recent meta-analysis (Howard et al., 1986) of studies involving over 2,400 patients indicated that by eight sessions of psychodynamic or interpersonal therapies, approximately 50% of patients are measurably improved, and approximately 75% are improved by 26 sessions (for example, once weekly for 6 months). More specific data regarding treatment outcome of Borderline Personality Disorders have begun to emerge in the past few years (Gunderson, 1989; McGlashan, 1983; Stone, Hurt, & Stone, 1987). Although these follow-up studies did not focus on treatment duration, they are helpful in guiding the decision in that they indicate borderline patients, as a rule, improve with time, experiencing the most difficulty during their third and fourth decades, then "settling down" in middle life.

In discussing treatment duration, the therapist can begin by educating the patient about the general and specific data that have been summarized. When appropriate, family members should be included in this discussion. Two points should be emphasized. First, although results of treatment cannot be predicted with absolute assurance for any one individual, studies indicate that most outpatients improve with psychotherapy (Andrews & Harvey, 1981; Butcher & Koss, 1978; Luborsky, Singer, & Luborsky, 1975; Smith, Glass, & Miller, 1980) and that for the majority of these patients, at least some improvement has occurred by 6 months (Howard et al., 1986). Therefore, in the absence of notable improvement midway through the first year, the therapist will consider referring the patient for consultation and/or a change in technique, format, setting, medication, or therapist. These possibilities underscore the therapist's flexibility and comfort with recognizing his or her limitations, and diminish the predisposition toward pathological idealization and the view that the therapist and patient are locked into an immutable dyadic involvement.

Second, the therapist can point out that although the distress bringing the patient into treatment at this time appears acute, the evaluation has disclosed that the present crisis is actually a reflection of a chronic personality problem that is extensively described in the psychiatric literature, is characterized by intermittent difficulties during the early adult years, and is very likely to improve with time. Therefore, a cardinal aim of treatment will be to provide support during periods of difficulty over the years and to help reduce self-destructive acts and injudicious decisions, especially impulsive financial, vocational, or interpersonal decisions that will have an irreversible damaging effect on the patient's life. This prescription of intermittent continuous therapy (Perry, 1987), consistent with the medical model of treating chronic illnesses characterized by periodic exacerbations, not only implicitly reinforces the belief that the problems are treatable and will improve with time, but also helps diminish the borderline patient's fear of abandonment and need to contact the therapist between sessions by evoking various "crises." In addition, labeling the difficulties as "personality problems" indicates that the patient is not controlled by a "disease" for which the therapist bears total responsibility to "cure," but rather that the patient is capable of adhering to the designated time frame and other requirements of treatment. Although understandably challenging, this cooperation will enable the patient to overcome the identified lags in personality development, and to acquire a more consolidated sense of self, acceptance of limitations in oneself and others, improved impulse control, and tolerance of common distressful feelings, such as anxiety, grief, loneliness, boredom, and anger.

After prescribing intermittent continuous therapy and supporting its rationale, the therapist can address two seemingly contradictory concerns that are often raised directly or indirectly by borderline patients in response to this recommendation. First, the prospect of a "lifelong" treatment and "growing old together" may at first increase feelings of hopelessness. This defeatist view of having a refractory condition can be countered by explaining that chronicity is not necessarily associated with severity. Just as many medical patients have relatively mild chronic conditions, such as rashes or headaches, that are characterized by intermittent exacerbations and that require periodic symptomatic care, many patients with personality problems are also sensitive to certain stressors and can benefit from supportive advice during those times. Drawing upon personal clinical experience and the extensive psychiatric literature, the therapist can state with confidence that the expectation that treatment will have a well-defined termination can actually be a dis-service to patients with personality problems. Such expectations can lead to feelings of disappointment, frustration, and bitterness toward themselves and their therapists when the difficulties do not completely resolve. Hope comes not from trying to reach unrealistic goals, but rather from the assurance that, when conflicts are most pressing and accessible for change, help will be available and continued growth will therefore not be disrupted.

As opposed to the concern that treatment will be too long, borderline patients may simultaneously be concerned that the prescribed duration will not be long enough, fearing they will be unable to tolerate the intermittent separations. Noting material from the patient's history and from the premature intense involvement with the therapist during the initial evaluation, the therapist can explain that planned "treatment holidays" of several weeks, months, and eventually years will help reduce the patient's tendency to lose his or her own identity when involved with another, permit the patient to acquire more autonomy and confidence as the benefits of previous treatment are consolidated, clarify what treatment is or is not currently accomplishing, and distinguish treatment goals from life goals that are outside the purview of psychotherapy (Ticho, 1972). A useful analogy may be that a crutch is necessary when a leg is sprained or broken; but if it is used for too long, muscles may become weak, or even wasted, and impede potentially healthy functioning.

Although intermittent continuous therapy is the preferred duration for most borderline patients, a subpopulation with less malignant personality organization may be candidates for long-term exploratory psychotherapy in which both patient and therapist anticipate that character reconstruction is feasible and that a distinct ending to treatment will then occur (Kernberg, 1984; Kernberg et al., 1972; Masterson, 1976; Stone et al., 1987). This approach requires enabling factors rarely present in borderline patients (Perry et al., 1983) and an expertise beyond the training of most therapists. At the other extreme is a subpopulation of borderline patients for whom some have contended that the prescription of no treatment is the recommendation of choice (Frances, Clarkin, & Perry,

1984; Perry, 1987; Perry, Frances, & Clarkin, 1985). These are patients whose self-destructive and provocative actualization of the transference assumes a delusional intensity and induces repeated negative therapeutic reactions (Bergin & Lambert, 1978; Strupp, Hadley, & Gomes-Schwartz, 1977). Feeling partly responsible for this deterioration, the therapist may attempt to overcome his or her guilt with increased therapeutic zeal in the belief that more time—length and frequency of sessions or treatment duration—will at some future point turn things around despite impressive evidence to the contrary. Because such patients with recurrent treatment failures typically present when their situations appear most desperate and chaotic, the consultant may find it extremely difficult to recommend no further treatment; therefore, before concluding that a change in setting, format, technique, intensity, duration, medication, or therapist will very likely be of no avail and may even be iatrogenically harmful, the consultant may wish to obtain a second opinion, reducing the possibility that the recommendation of no further treatment has arisen from countertransference feelings.

This discussion of no treatment as the duration of choice ends this article with a humbling recognition that for some borderline patients we have at present no effective therapy; however, this acknowledgment is more than offset by the optimistic view that in recent years we have acquired a detailed understanding of their phenomenology and dynamics, and that we are beginning to obtain an increasing amount of systematic data regarding their life course and responses to various techniques and psychotropic medications (Gunderson, 1989; McGlashan, 1983; Stone et al., 1987). The application of this understanding to the prescribed time frame can be remarkably effective in providing the structure and hope necessary for both borderline patients and their therapists.

CHAPTER 12

The Role of Medication in the Treatment of Borderline Personality Disorder

HAROLD W. KOENIGSBERG

Medication may have a useful place in the treatment of borderline patients. Recent clinical studies have provided evidence that borderline patients can achieve symptomatic and behavioral benefit from pharmacological treatments. While there is as yet no consensus about a single drug of choice, certain medications appear to benefit specific clusters of borderline symptoms. The use of medication with borderline patients, however, may introduce special complications particular to borderline pathology. These must be considered, balanced against the potential benefits of pharmacotherapy, and managed when the decision is made to go forward with drug treatment. Medication may be employed in association with either expressive or supportive psychotherapy of borderline patients. This chapter will examine how medication may be used in conjunction with supportive psychotherapy in an overall treatment program. It will review the rationale for pharmacotherapy in treating borderline patients and evidence favoring specific drugs, and will discuss the integration of pharmacotherapy with psychotherapy.

RATIONALE FOR PHARMACOTHERAPY

Since Borderline Personality Disorder (BPD) is marked by profoundly disturbed interpersonal relationship patterns, predominant use of the more maladaptive defenses, and the lack of an integrated identity, psychological interventions have been called upon to play a central role in treatment. Several lines of evidence suggest, however, that psychobiological factors may influence the development of borderline pathology or complicate its expression. Medication may moderate these influences.

On the basis of the current state of knowledge, five different clinical perspectives support the use of medication with borderline patients. The first model suggests that biologically influenced personality traits may determine or intensify the borderline disorder. The second model posits that BPD may be a milder, more chronic variant of a major psychiatric syndrome. Third, even if biological factors play a negligible role in influencing borderline pathology per se, BPD often co-occurs with a medication-responsive Axis I disorder. Thus medication is called for to treat the comorbid condition. Fourth, medications may be conceptualized as symptom-specific agents and may be indicated to treat prominent symptoms. Finally, from a purely atheoretic position, drug trials and anecdotal experience indicate that medication can reduce clusters of borderline symptoms. These different frames of reference imply somewhat different strategies for the use of medication, the selection of specific drugs, and the target symptoms of choice.

The Biological Trait Model

Prominent features of borderline pathology include impulsive self-destructiveness, affective instability, and a tendency to misperceive the social field. Each of these features has been associated with an hypothesized biologically mediated personality trait (Seiver, Klar, & Coccaro, 1985). Studies of aggressiveness in animals and of the brains of patients who have chosen violent methods of suicide suggest that self-harm may be associated with a functional decrease in serotonin activity (Asberg et al., 1987; Mann et al., 1989). Siever and collegues have noted a correlation between a decreased responsiveness of the serotonin system to a fenfluramine challenge and higher levels of aggression on various clinical rating scales. Thus an underactivity of the serotonin system may predispose toward an increased tendency to act out self-destructively. Seiver et al. call this trait "impulsiveness." Cloninger (1986), too, emphasizes the role of the serotinergic system in subduing self-destructive impulses. He considers "harm avoidance" to be an heritable trait that may be impaired in persons with impulsive personality disorders.

Seiver et al. identify a second trait, affective instability, an increased tendency to respond affectively to environmental stimuli. This trait is presumed to underly the characteristic borderline rejection sensitivity. Cloninger views rejection sensitivity as a result of a heightened dependence on behavioral reward. He suggests that there is an inherited tendency to respond strongly to reward and to seek to maintain rewarded behavioral situations. Such heightened need for reward could explain the rapid affective shifts, as well as the extreme reactions to losses of reward-bearing relationships, which characterize borderline patients. Cloninger suggests that reward dependence is associated with low basal noradrenergic activity. Cloningers's reward dependence and Seiver's affective instability may represent the same underlying biological trait.

Finally, a third predisposition that may be found in borderline patients is a tendency toward relative detachment from the environment, contributing at times to transient losses of reality testing. Seiver believes this trait, schizotypy, may reflect an impairment in higher level neurointegrative function. Seiver has shown that tasks that require complex neural integration, like pursuing a moving target with one's gaze, are defective in schizotypal patients. Such performance is also defective in schizophrenia. It may be associated with disturbances in the dopaminergic system.

The Subsyndromal Model

The *subsyndromal model* follows from the assumption that BPDs are dilute forms of specific Axis I syndromes. They may be milder varients along a spectrum or baseline states from which full syndromal exacerbations may periodically emerge. Those who focus upon the borderline patients' vulnerability to transient psychotic episodes, their paranoid ideation, their susceptibility to derealization experiences, and their tendency to magical thinking view the borderline disorder as a subsyndromal form of schizophrenia. The BPD precursor constructs "borderline schizophrenia" and "pseudoneurotic schizophrenia" indicate that an assumed connection to schizophrenia was part of the earliest conceptualizations of the borderline state. The affective instability so prominent in borderline patients, however, suggests a link to a bipolar spectrum (Akiskal, 1981). Certain depressive symptoms seen in borderline patients, such as hypersomnia, a "leaden" quality to the feeling state, and increased appetite suggest that the borderline disorder may be a depressive variant, perhaps most closely related to atypical depression (Leibowitz & Klein, 1981). The poor impulse control of borderline patients has suggested a connection to mild forms of organic mental disorders (Andrulonis et al., 1982; Gardner et al., 1987). Borderline Personality Disorder may represent an adult form of attention deficit disorder, a seizure disorder, or an interictal personality in temporal lobe epilepsy (Ellison & Adler, 1984).

Borderline patients may be a heterogeneous group of patients with subsyndromal forms of a number of different Axis I conditions; the borderline domain may have distinct borders with schizophrenic, affective, and organic disorders. A rational pharmacotherapeutic approach derived from the subsyndromal model would identify the syndrome family to which each borderline patient was most likely linked and would treat with medications effective for that syndrome. On this basis, borderline patients might be treated with neuroleptics, lithium, MAO inhibitors, heterocyclic antidepressants, anticonvulsants, or stimulants.

The Comorbidity Model

The *Comorbidity Model* derives from the observation that BPD often coexists with an affective disorder. In their review, Gunderson and Elliott (1985) report rates for Comorbid Affective Disorder in borderline patients of 14%-83%. Major Depression has been diagnosed in 39%-62% of borderline patients, and typical or atypical Biploar Disorder in 9%-17% of borderlines. Pope et al. (1983) report that, in some patients with Major Affective Disorder and BPD, some symptoms of BPD remitted along with improvement in the affective symptoms, suggesting that an affective syndrome may exacerbate a borderline disorder. This line of reasoning suggests that treatment of any coexisting affective disorder would ameliorate the borderline pathology, while relieving the affective syndrome. Without making assumptions about any underlying etiology, the comorbidity model suggests a medication strategy aimed at treating any identified concurrent Axis I depression or Bipolar Disorder.

The Symptom-Focused Model

The *Symptom-Focused Model* eschews any etiological conceptualization of borderline pathology, but recognizes that borderline patients have sets of symptoms that are known to respond to various medications. Treatment is tailored toward target symptoms. Depression is treated with heterocyclics or MAO inhibitors, transient psychoses with neuroleptics, anxiety with anxiolytics, and impulsivity with anticonvulsants, lithium, or propranolol.

Empirical Models

Anecdotal clinical experience (see, for example, Brinkley et al., 1979) and recent double-blind placebo-controlled studies, suggest that certain classes of psychotropic medication reduce the intensity of a broad spectrum of borderline symptoms. Low doses of neuroleptics, for example, have been reported to not only affect psychoticism, but also to reduce depression, anxiety, interpersonal sensitivity, and impulsive behavior (Cowdry et al., 1988; Goldberg et al., 1986; Soloff et al., 1986). Similar broad-spectrum effects have been reported for MAO inhibitors and carbamazepine (Cowdry et al., 1988). Why classes of medication that have specific effects in particular Axis I disorders should have broad-spectrum effects with borderline patients remains unclear.

CONTROLLED STUDIES

While anecdotal reports as well as open-label studies have pointed to beneficial effects for low-dose neuroleptics, lithium, and antidepressants in the treatment of borderline patients, the use of a double-blind, placebo-controlled design is especially important with the borderline population for several reasons. First, the characteristic instability of borderline symptoms makes it difficult to differentiate medication-induced change from spontaneous symptom fluctuations. Second, borderline patients are especially vulnerable to distortions in their own perceptions of the effects of medication because of the intensity of their transference reactions. In addition, reports about the medication by the borderline patient may be consciously or unconsciously slanted to have an effect upon the therapist.

Low-Dose Neuroleptics

Several placebo-controlled studies have examined the effect of low-dose neuroleptics in treating borderline patients. Montgomery (1987) treated a group of 30 patients hospitalized for self-destructive behavior, who had made at least three prior suicide attempts, with monthly depot injections of 20 mg of flupenthixol or placebo. Two thirds of these patients met DSM-III criteria for BPD. During the 6-month treatment period, patients in the flupenthixol group made fewer suicide attempts at each monthly rating point. The difference became significant by the 4-month point ($p < .05$). By the sixth month, 12 of 16 placebo-treated patients had made a fourth suicide attempt, while only 3 of 14 flupenthixol patients had.

Goldberg et al. (1986) compared low-dose thiothixine (average dose 8.67 mg) to placebo in a group of 50 nonhospitalized DSM-III Borderline and Schizotypal Personality Disorder patients recruited by newspaper advertisement. All patients also had a history of at least one psychotic or quasipsychotic symptom. During the 12-week study period, 42% of placebo subjects and 54% of the neuroleptic patients dropped out. Among those who remained on medication for at least 2 weeks, thiothixine was significantly superior to placebo in reducing illusions and ideas of reference, and in reducing scores on the SCL-90 Psychoticism, Phobic Anxiety, and obsessive–compulsive scales. No significant drug/placebo difference was identified for a cluster of borderline symptoms, a schizotypal symptom cluster, anger–hostility, paranoid–suspiciousness, delusions–hallucinations, or overall GAS score. Although depressive mood was not directly reduced by the medication, there was an improvement in such depressive symptoms as difficulty concentrating, feeling that everything is effortful, and indecisiveness, which were included in the obsessive–compulsive scale. Patients receiving placebo showed a clinically significant improvement over baseline in observer-rated overall borderline score and in patient-rated interpersonal sensitivity and anger–hostility scores. Overall, patients who were most symptomatic at baseline benefitted most from the medication.

Soloff and colleagues (1986, 1989) carried out a 5-week trial, comparing low-dose haloperidol, amitriptyline, and placebo in a group of 90 inpatients meeting Gunderson's Diagnostic Interview for Borderlines (DIB) criteria and DSM-III criteria for Borderline Personality Disorder, Schizotypal Personality Disorder, or both. They reported a broad-spectrum effectiveness of haloperidol in treating depressive, behavioral, cognitive, and interpersonal symptoms. Haloperidol (average dose 4.8 mg per day) was superior to placebo in treating impulsive behavior, interpersonal sensitivity, hostility, schizotypal symptoms, and depression. The effect upon depression, however, appeared most in the expansion items of the 24-item Hamilton Depression Scale, reflecting improvement in feelings of worthlessness, hopelessness, helplessness, paranoia, depersonalization, obsessive–compulsive features, and diurnal variation.

Overall, they report that 70% of haloperidol-treated patients showed improvement in a constellation of hostile–depressive symptoms, and 65% showed improvement in a constellation of schizotypal symptoms. Those most likely to respond to the medication were those most highly symptomatic and most anxious at baseline. Medication effects were of clinical as well as statistical significance, but the clinical effect size was modest— characteristically reflecting shifts from severe to moderate symptomatology by the 5-week point. Medication dropout appeared to be a problem: Approximately one third of the patients in the haloperidol group did not complete the trial in the Soloff et al. (1986) preliminary study, which used a higher mean haloperidol dose of 7.24 mg per day.

Recently Soloff and coworkers (Cornelius et al., 1991) reported a study designed to replicate their initial findings in a new patient sample. They could not replicate the finding of broad-spectrum superiority of haloperidol to placebo. They did, however, continue to find that haloperidol was significantly superior to placebo in reducing interpersonal hostility. The most striking difference from the earlier study was the failure to replicate the antidepressant effect of haloperidol. This may have been due in part to the depressogenic effects of akinesia or akathesia induced by haloperidol.

Cowdry and Gardner (1988) compared the effects of four medications to placebo in a double-blind crossover study. They studied 16 outpatients meeting DIB and DSM-III criteria for BPD, who in addition had symptoms of serious behavioral dyscontrol and met Leibowitz and Klein's (1981) criteria for hysteroid dysphoria. Patients made a commitment to remain in outpatient psychotherapy with the referring physician for the duration of the study. Following a 1-week washout period between drugs, each medication trial lasted 6 weeks. They report that low-dose trifluoperizine (7.8 mg/day mean dose) was superior to placebo in physician-rated suicidality and anxiety, and in patient-rated depression, anxiety, and rejection sensitivity. Cowdry and Gardner suggest, furthermore, that the effect of the low-dose neuroleptic may have been underestimated in their study, because their patient sample contained BPD patients with fewer schizotypal relative to affective/interpersonal symptoms.

MAO Inhibitors

Cowdry and Gardner (1988) studied the MAO inhibitor tranylcypromine as another medication in their crossover design. At an average dose of 40 mg per day, it was superior to placebo in physician-rated depression, anger, rejection sensitivity, capacity to experience pleasure, impulsivity, suicidality, and in a global rating. Patients rated it superior to placebo in controlling depression, anxiety, and rejection sensitivity. Tranylcypromine produced improvement in more areas, in fact, than any of the other drugs in the Cowdry and Gardner study, and appears to have been the best tolerated, with 75% of the patients completing the 6-week trial.

A double-blind placebo-controlled trial of the MAO inhibitor phenelzine by Liebowitz and Klein (1981) yielded somewhat more equivocal findings. Subjects were 16 outpatients meeting criteria for hysteroid dysphoria. Twelve also met DSM-III criteria for BPD. All patients received twice weekly psychoanalytically oriented psychotherapy. The study employed a double-blind discontinuation design in which all patients were treated with open-label phenelzine (15–75 mg per day) for 3 months, and then half were blindly switched to placebo for a 3-month period. Eleven patients reached the 3-month discontinuation point and five were randomized to continue on phenelzine. All of these patients met DSM-III criteria for BPD. Two showed maintenance of a stable good response by the 6-month point, one showed a moderate response, and two did poorly. Leibowitz and Klein (1981) concluded that such borderline characteristics as impulsivity, self-damaging acts, angry outbursts, unstable relationships, feelings of chronic emptiness or boredom, and difficulty being alone may be more responsive to medication than other borderline symptoms.

While design differences between the studies or suboptimal dosing of some of the phenelzine patients might account for the differences in effect in the two studies, it is possible that pharmacological differences between phenelzine and tranylcypromine may be significant. Unlike phenelzine, tranylcypromine is structurally similar to amphetamine. It might be superior to phenelzine because of a rapid amphetamine-like mood-elevating effect or because of an amphetamine-like effect upon an underlying Attention Deficit Disorder in some of the borderline patients. Further studies are needed to explore these possibilities.

Heterocyclic Antidepressants

Soloff and colleagues' inpatient study (1986, 1989), described above, included amitriptyline as one of the medications to be compared. Patients were maintained on an average dose of 149 mg per day and achieved an average blood level of 240 ng/ml. Amitriptyline was significantly superior to placebo only in its effect upon depression, as measured by the 24-item Hamilton Depression Scale. Even on this scale, however, haloperidol was more effective than amitriptyline. Paradoxically, a substantial number of patients appeared to worsen on the antidepressant. Fifty-eight percent showed an exacerbation on the hostile–depression measure and 64% showed an increase in schizotypal symptoms. Among 15 amitriptyline nonresponders, Soloff et al. (1986b) noted significantly more suicide threats, demanding and assaultive behavior, and paranoid ideation than among 14 placebo nonresponders. The response to amitriptyline was unaffected by the presense or absense of a comorbid major depression.

The poor performance of amitriptyline could be a consequence of the masking of any beneficial effects by strong reactions to its anticholinergic side effects. For this reason, study of a less anticholinergic tricyclic would be of interest. Links et al. (1990) carried out a comparison of 6-week trials of the less anticholinergic tricyclic desipramine, lithium, and placebo in a double-blind, random-order crossover design. Thirteen patients meeting the DIB diagnostic criteria participated in the desipramine arm of the study. No statistically significant difference between desipramine and placebo was detected, but the small sample size may have contributed to the failure to find a difference. For each patient who received more than one drug trial, Links and coworkers compared each patient's response to each drug. Of nine patients receiving both lithium and desipramine, five showed a decrease in anger/suicide symptoms on lithium and no response or a worsening on desipramine. While the authors caution about reaching conclusions from their small sample, their findings are consistent with a lower efficacy of desipramine compared to lithium.

The implication of serotonergic systems in regulating impulsive behavior has heightened interest in the serotonin reuptake inhibitor, fluoxetine. To date, double-blind controlled studies of this drug with borderline patients have not been reported. Norden (1989) described his experience with fluoxetine (5–40 mg per day) in an open-label trial with 12 DSM-III-R borderline patients who did not have concurrent major depression. All patients appeared to benefit according to Norden's global rating of them, with 75% characterized as "much" or "very much" improved. The report by Teicher et al. (1990) of the emergence of marked suicidal preoccupation in six depressed patients treated with fluoxetine has raised some question about the use of this drug with action-prone borderline patients. While the seriousness of this potential risk has not yet been fully evaluated, Fava and Rosenbaum (1991) reported on the incidence of post-treatment emergence of suicidal ideation in 1,017 depressed patients treated with a variety of antidepressants. The rate of such ideation among fluoxetine-treated patients (3.5%) was not significantly different from the rate seen in patients treated by tricyclic antidepressants, either alone or augmented with lithium (1.3%).

Anxiolytics

Cowdry and Gardner (1988) included alprazolam as one of the drugs examined in their double-blind, random-order crossover design. Patients received an average dose of 4.7 mg per day, a relatively high dose of alprazolam. The medication was not superior to placebo on any measure. In fact, patients showed significantly more suicidality on alprazolam than on placebo. This might reflect a disinhibiting effect of the anxiolytic.

Anticonvulsants

Patients in the Cowdry and Gardner (1988) study also received carbamazepine (average dose 820 mg per day). This medication had its greatest effect in reducing behavioral dyscontrol. It was rated as significantly superior to placebo by physicians in reducing anxiety, lowering hostility, decreasing suicidality, reducing impulsivity, elevating mood, and global improvement. Interestingly, on all patient-rated scales it showed no superiority to placebo. Cowdry and Gardner note that carbamazepine appears to introduce a period of "reflective delay" in which patients pause to think rather than act in the face of painful affect and impulses. They speculate that the broad spectrum of benefit noted by the physicians may reflect a "halo" phenomena carrying over from the dramatic improvement in acting-out behavior.

Lithium

Lithium might be expected to be beneficial in treating borderline patients both because it regulates the serotonin system and because it stabilizes mood. Klein (1968) had reported it effective in the treatment of Emotionally Unstable Character Disorder (EUCD) patients who were subject to rapid mood shifts. Such patients may represent a subgroup of BPD patients. The study by Links et al. (1990) compared the effect of lithium (average dose 986 mg per day) to that of desipramine and placebo. At the 6-week point, therapists' global ratings indicated a statistically significant superiority of lithium to placebo. For patients who had received adequate medication trials by the 3-week point, there was a trend for lithium to be superior to desipramine and placebo in reducing anger and suicidality. No differences were noted between placebo, lithium, and desipramine in treating depressive symptoms. The study is, however, limited in terms of generalizability and of the possibility of type II error by its small sample size (11 patients completed adequate trials of each active medication).

A Current Perspective

While knowledge of the pharmacotherapy of BPD has been significantly advanced by double-blind, placebo-controlled studies of virtually all classes of psychotropic medications, it remains too early for definitive conclusions. This is because of the small sample sizes, few replication studies, and the brief duration of treatment in these studies. Nevertheless, some preliminary impressions emerge. First, borderline patients exhibit a considerable response to placebo. They show significant additional gains from some medications. While medication effects are clinically significant, they are of modest size; symptoms improve from severe to moderate in intensity.

Low-dose neuroleptics have been most studied and appear to have beneficial effects, especially in reducing anger, self-destructive or impulsive behavior, and psychoticism. The initial antidepressant and broad-spectrum effects reported by Soloff and colleagues (1986, 1989) were not replicated in a more recent study by the same group (Cornelius et al., 1991). Low-dose neuroleptics are not, however, well tolerated by borderline patients, and medication dropout rates are high. Lower doses and the concomitant use of anticholinergics might improve compliance.

MAO inhibitors are better tolerated by the patients and appear to reduce anxiety, depression, suicidality, and rejection sensitivity. A cautionary note is raised by Cowdry and Gardner's observation that 3 of 12 tranylcypromine-treated patients developed severe behavioral dyscontrol. When MAO inhibitors are used, the therapist must ensure that sufficient structure (ranging from a verbal contract with the patient to continuous supervision) is in place to protect the patient from self-destructive violations of the MAO inhibitor dietary restrictions. In patients with severe behavioral dyscontrol, carbamazepine may be the drug of choice. Anxiolytics and tricyclics appear to present more risks than benefits with this patient population. While there is a theoretical basis to expect benefit from fluoxetine, no double-blind controlled studies have been reported. The reports of fluoxetine success in open-labeled studies are difficult to evaluate in this highly placebo-responsive population.

The borderline patients who are most responsive to medication are those who are most symptomatic at baseline. Patients who show a pattern of hostile depression or quasipsychotic symptoms may be most responsive to low-dose neuroleptics. Borderline patients with features of atypical depression may particularly benefit from MAO inhibitors (Parsons et al., 1989). At present, the value of medication in treating nonseverely symptomatic borderline patients has not been established.

INTEGRATING PHARMACOTHERAPY WITH PSYCHOTHERAPY

The physician's act of prescribing a mood- or behavior-regulating drug is always a powerful interpersonal intervention. It elicits strong reality-based as well as transferential feelings in the recipient. Since borderline patients are particularly vulnerable to the activation of intense transferences, the act of prescribing psychotropic medication to a borderline patient can be expected to stimulate especially strong transference reactions. These reactions can affect the patient's relationship to the prescriber and to the medication itself. The prescription of medication to a borderline patient must therefore be carried out within a treatment framework, whether supportive or expressive, that will allow transference developments to be appropriately managed.

If the patient is being treated in expressive psychotherapy, medication-elicited transferences will be managed primarily through clarification, confrontation, and interpretation. The therapist will seek to maintain a position of technical neutrality, aligning himself with the patient's observing ego and remaining equidistant from the patient's acting ego, id, superego, and external reality. When limit setting necessitates a deviation from technical neutrality, the therapist returns to the neutral position via interpretation of the interpersonal process requiring the deviation. The prescription of medication taxes the therapist's ability to maintain technical neutrality. If, for example, medication is prescribed to control self-destructive or impulsive actions, the prescriber may be taking a position *vis à vis* the patient's acting ego, superego, or external reality. In addition, the therapist may need to direct the patient to carry out specific behaviors in relation to the medication (e.g., to follow a specific diet, to obtain blood tests, etc.). Because medication use may force a deviation from technical neutrality in the therapist, some authors recommend that, for patients in expressive psychotherapy, medication prescription be carried out by a separate psychopharmacologist. This, however, introduces a new opportunity for splitting—psychopharmacologist *vis à vis* psychotherapist. It may also encourage a split in the patient's self-representation between a "biological self" and a "psychological self" (Koenigsberg, 1991). Such additional opportunities for splitting argue for a single therapist. Whether the single-therapist or dual-therapist model is used, technical modifications to medication management specific to expressive psychotherapy must be introduced. A further discussion of the integration of medication in expressive psychotherapy is beyond the scope of this chapter.

While the use of medication in supportive psychotherapy is not complicated by a need to maintain technical neutrality, all other complexities remain. These include the influence of strong countertransferences or transferences upon medication decisions, the effect of the act of prescribing upon the underlying therapeutic relationship, the exploitation of medication to serve borderline defensive purposes, and difficulty in assessing the pharmacologic effect of medication relative to its relationship-determined effects.

The Influence of Countertransference and Transference Reactions upon Prescribing

Since borderline patients typically induce powerful countertransference feelings in their therapists, the decision to use medication may be strongly influenced by the state of the countertransference. Therapists who have been made to feel powerless, for example, as a consequence of the patient's use of projective identification to activate a helpless self-representation in the therapist, may be tempted to resort to medication as a means of regaining a sense of control in the treatment. Those who have experienced devaluation in the form of doubt of their psychological skills may introduce medication to move to a terrain where they feel more confident for the moment. The introduction of medication may be a mechanism for distancing from the patient. Medication may be used in an effort to alleviate the therapist's own anxiety or hopelessness about the patient. A sense of urgency about the need to initiate medication is often a useful signal for the therapist to reconsider the state of the countertransference before proceeding.

The patient, too, may look to the introduction of medication in response to strong transferences. Patients with strong dependent transferences often actively seek medication. Those seeking to distance themselves from the therapist or to maneuver the therapist into a domain where they suspect that he will be less confident may ask for medication. Thus close monitoring of the transference is important in making medication decisions, as it is in making other interventions in supportive therapy.

The Effect of Prescribing
upon the Therapeutic Relationship

The act of prescribing medication, or even consideration of medication as an option, can be expected to greatly affect the relationship between patient and therapist. The use of medication may have any of a multitude of interpersonal meanings to the patient. It may be seen as an indication that the therapist is dissatisfied with the patient's progress or that he is alarmed by the patient's symptoms or by material emerging in the sessions. It may be seen as an act of physicianly concern, as a gift, or as a form of feeding. The borderline patient's perception of the act of prescribing is influenced by the array of primitive defenses in her repertoire. The predominant borderline use of projective identification and omnipotent control make it likely that the patient will experience psychotropic medication as an effort by the therapist to attain greater control over her. Borderline patients who use idealization/devaluation defenses extensively may experience the introduction of medication into the treatment as a devaluation—the patient is not capable of change through psychological work and will be treated as a biological preparation. By the same token, the patient may use the therapist's move to medication in the service of devaluing or idealizing the therapist—"he really doesn't know what he's doing psychotherapeutically" versus "he will stop at nothing to help me." The medication itself or the prescription form may symbolize the treatment or may become transitional objects. Medication may also activate identifications with significant others in the patient's life who have been prescribed psychotropic medications or medical treatments in general. The therapist needs to elicit the specific meanings that prescribing may have for his patient.

In order to protect the therapeutic relationship, to achieve compliance with the medication, and to understand shifts in the course of treatment, the therapist should be aware of the patient's predominant transference dispositions prior to prescribing and should clarify the effects of prescribing itself upon the transference. An ongoing awareness of the transference is as important to the supportive psychotherapist as it is to the expressive therapist. As in expressive psychotherapy, the use of questions to clarify the patient's experience of the therapist are helpful in assessing the state of the transference. The therapist's countertransference can also be a useful guide to the activated transference. Transference derivatives activated with the introduction of medication may also be identified by eliciting the patient's specific feelings and fantasies about the prescribed medication.

Medication in the Service of Borderline Defenses

In introducing medication, the therapist is endorsing the notion that the patient's behavior or mood states are influenced by biochemical processes. Effective supportive psychotherapy, on the other hand, requires that the patient ultimately assume responsibility for her actions and feeling states. While these two models are not incompatible, their coexistence in treatment provides a fertile ground for splitting. Assumption of responsibility can be denied as the patient maintains a split-off image of herself as one passively controlled by her neurochemistry. On the other hand, the borderline patient's tendency to use omnipotent control as a defense makes her particularly sensitized to agents of control. She may view pharmacotherapy as mind control, in order to rationalize the projection of a controlling self-representation onto the therapist. She may struggle with the therapist over medication to avoid awareness of her own wishes to control and dominate.

Assessing the Pharmacologic Effects

The therapist who uses medication needs to monitor its pharmacological effects, to regulate dosage, to determine whether its benefits outweigh its drawbacks, and to be aware of side effects. Unfortunately, the borderline patient's report of medication effects and side effects may be strongly shaped by nonpharmacological factors. The patient's defenses of projective identification, omnipotent control, idealization/devaluation, and splitting will influence the patient's report of medication effects to the therapist. Since borderline patients often use reports of their symptoms to elicit particular reactions in others, the patient's report of the medication's effect may be an exaggeration or distortion of any "true" pharmacologic effect. The therapist must attempt to tease apart the pharmacologic effects of the medication from the transference-mediated effects.

The first approach to dissecting apart the pharmacologic from the interpersonally determined effects of the medication is to consider the patient's report in light of the current state of the transference. A patient who is relating to the therapist as a weak victim to an uncaring self-preoccupied mother might unduly emphasize potentially harmful drug side effects, while a patient experiencing herself as a docile child in relation to a strong protective parent might over-rate the drug's beneficial effects. Once again, an awareness of one's countertransference can shed light on the transference and can also permit a more objective assessment of the medication effects.

A second guide to disentangling the transference contribution from the pharmacologic contribution is attending to the time profile of change. Medication effects usually take time to emerge. Furthermore, change in certain symptom areas usually follow a particular pattern. In the pharmacologic response in depression, for example, the patient usually becomes more activated and appears less depressed to others before she reports the subjective experience of a mood improvement. Thus when a depressive borderline patient announces a sudden brightening in mood that was not heralded by a period of increasing activity, and a fuller participation in her life activities, the therapist should be alert to the possibility that important transference elements are prominent in the medication effect.

SUMMARY

Recent placebo-controlled studies suggest that medication may have a role to play in the supportive psychotherapy of borderline patients. The most fully studied medications to date are low-dose neuroleptics and MAO inhibitors. These medications appear to reduce borderline impulsivity, hostility, depression, and interpersonal sensitivity over the short range. Their effectiveness beyond 6–12 weeks has not been well studied. While medications appear beneficial, their clinical effects are modest. The patients most likely to benefit are those who are initially most symptomatic. The introduction of medication into the treatment can provide a focus for such borderline defenses as splitting, as well as for therapist countertransference enactments. Thus the use of medication with borderline patients requires special vigilance to the state of the transference and countertransference, as well as clarification of the specific psychological meaning of the medication to the patient.

CHAPTER 13

Supportive Elements of Inpatient Treatment with Borderline Patients

CHARLES SWENSON

B orderline patients are, with rare exceptions, admitted to hospitals primarily for supportive purposes. The regressive, self-destructive spiral; the relationship(s) in crisis; the brief psychotic episode; the paranoid regression in the transference can all be understood as manifestations of increased impairment of an already weakened ego. An effective hospitalization improves functions of the ego by removing the destabilizing forces of external reality, organizing instinctual chaos, taking over for and reducing pressures from harsh superego factors, facilitating a shift from primitive to more mature defenses, deactivating the predominant and distressing primitive object relations, and integrating a fragmenting self. The goal is rarely to make unconscious conflict conscious, and the strategies are not primarily or ultimately interpretive. Some specialized long-term hospital units have been designed to facilitate expressive psychotherapy, but even in those settings the goals and strategies of the hospital staff other than the therapist are supportive. The emphases are on control, suppression, and adaptation, which in the long-term unit promotes effective participation in the psychotherapeutic task.

So the goal of this chapter is not to distinguish supportive from expressive elements in inpatient treatment; the entire multimodal operation is

The author wishes to acknowledge the valuable suggestions for this chapter of Ann Appelbaum and Lawrence Rockland.

presumed to be supportive. The goal is to categorize and to discuss the various supportive elements in a coherent framework that illuminates and organizes them for the student and practitioner of inpatient treatment. The categories to be discussed first, such as removal from the destabilizing environment, could be considered "nonspecific" supportive features, bearing no obvious relationship to a psychoanalytic theory of treatment. Others, to be discussed later, such as the noninterpretive modification of primitive defenses or the cultivation of an observing ego, do arise from psychoanalytic theory. As borderline pathology arises from a mixture of genetic, constitutional, early developmental, and later socializing influences, the language and concepts of psychoanalytic theory do not encompass our notion of etiology or treatment. As you will see, a range of approaches will be considered potent possibilities in inpatient treatment of the borderline.

The writings of several theoreticians and clinicians form the background for the ideas presented here. Winnicott's concepts of the holding environment (Winnicott, 1965), the transitional object (Winnicott, 1953), and the use of an object (Winnicott, 1969) have provided rich ideas about the inpatient unit as a holding environment, as has Bion's concept of the container and the contained (Bion, 1977). Inpatient models presented by Kernberg (1984), Masterson (1972), Adler (1985), and Appelbaum and Munich (1986) have included extensive discussions of various supportive aspects and how they can set the stage for exploratory psychodynamic work. Gunderson (1984) has discussed the contrasting and overlapping goals and techniques of long-term versus short-term inpatient treatment of borderlines. Ogden (1982) and Kernberg (1987) have provided us with the best discussions of the therapeutic metabolism of projective identification in inpatient treatment. Stern (1986) gave an extended, lucid example.

Levine and Wilson (1985) beautifully discussed the inpatient holding environment, its relationship to the developmentally supportive processes of family life, and its ability to contain projective identification. In the course of their article, they distinguished between two connotations of "holding" in the inpatient holding environment: containing/restraining and facilitating/nurturing. As you will see, I have borrowed from their distinction in two of my categories, framing and holding. Similar to my efforts in this chapter was Gunderson's (1978) delineation of five types of therapeutic processes in inpatient psychiatric milieus: containment, structure, support, involvement, and validation. One who reviews that work will see its influence here.

Although the supportive elements of inpatient treatment do not coincide with the strategies of psychodynamic supportive psychotherapy per se, my efforts in this chapter are heavily colored by the work on supportive therapy by Rockland (1989), Kernberg (1984), Appelbaum (1989), and Werman (1984).

Finally, my proposals follow from my work over the past 10 years in running two inpatient units for borderline patients, and particularly from comments made by former borderline patients in hundreds of conversations about what did and what did not help them in their inpatient stays.

I would suggest that the following seven categories provide a useful framework for discussion:

1. *Retreat*: Removal from the destabilizing environment
2. *Framing*: Imposition of control and restraint
3. *Holding*: Provision of direct ego support
4. *Involvement*: Promotion of interpersonal involvement
5. *Detoxification*: Metabolism of destructive scenarios
6. *Identification*: Presence of models for identification
7. *Supportive Aspects of Specific Therapies*:
   a. Pharmacotherapy
   b. Family Therapy
   c. Rehabilitation and Therapeutic Activities
   d. Cognitive–Behavioral Therapy
   e. Psychodynamic Therapy

By no means does this listing imply that each borderline patient benefits from each category of support, nor of course are all inpatient units equally effective at offering each category. Some patients, for instance, probably only need a retreat and may do as well or better at a health spa or resort as at a hospital. Other patients benefit most from peer involvement or from pharmacotherapy. The value of categorization lies in the chance to think, in a rational and organized manner, about what a particular patient needs or what a particular inpatient unit does and does not do well.

RETREAT

For the borderline patient in crisis, the hospitalization can serve as a retreat from a destabilizing situation. The ego, temporarily relieved of the pressures of what has become an intolerable external reality, is given a rest. The pressures may be those of a too-intense relationship, with its oscillations between engulfment and abandonment; of a growing dreaded sense of isolation; of an all-too-tempting daily exposure to a wide range of vehicles of self-destruction, or of a psychotherapeutic relationship mired in a paranoid regression.

Whatever the particular constellation of pressures, the hospitalization provides an immediate, radical retreat, providing enough distance to allow the ego to set restorative processes in motion. It sets the stage for recovery from the affective and impulsive storm, and for a reassessment of the predicament. It allows, at times, for a spontaneous recovery of reality testing, clearer thought processes, more accurate interpretations of reality, and better decision making. From a slight distance, with the advantage of a revived ego, the patient can effect desired modifications and, if wanted, a titrated reentry to the situation.

Amidst all the other processes set in motion by entering the hospital, it may be difficult to see that this retreat is in some cases exactly what is needed and all that is needed. These are the cases where less is best, where the hospital is a substitute for a spa, a monastery, a hotel, or a house in the woods, and where more ambitious interventions are contraindicated. Mental health professionals who work with halfway houses and supportive apartments are very familiar with examples of borderline patients, having graduated from their programs, needing to reenter the halfway house for a few days or weeks as a restorative retreat amidst a crisis. Patients who don't have such an option, or can't afford the vacation option, at times enter the hospital simply for retreat and then, much to their dismay and detriment, are given overly active treatment. We would be wise with the newly admitted borderline patients, once we have provided a secure, safe situation, and while we proceed with our evaluation, to allow for a period of retreat during which we may witness a remarkable recovery unfettered by our well-intended but too-invasive efforts.

FRAMING

While the retreat by itself may provide relief for the ego from external reality, it does not necessarily provide sufficient surcease from continuing instinctual chaos and sadistic superego elements. Under pressures to discharge unbearable affect and to act out perfectionistic and self-punitive superego trends, the borderline patient suffers impaired impulse control. The patient neglects or over-rides some of the usual rules and boundaries of familial, social, interpersonal, and personal life, at times including the skin boundary. The inpatient unit can provide a firm, indestructible, incorruptible frame that can interrupt impulsive behavioral episodes, absorb and contain assaults on boundaries, reinforce responsible and appropriate behavior, and through it all remain intact and consistent.

It is this aspect of inpatient treatment that I am calling the "framing function," and for borderline patients it is extremely important. It provides the skeleton, the backbone, the structure of the treatment. It encourages delay and restraint, and in conjunction with expressive verbal modalities, helps to create a gradient that transforms action–expressions to thought and verbalization. It corresponds to what Levine and Wilson (1985) called the "restraining/containing" connotation of holding in the inpatient holding environment and to the therapeutic processes of "containment" and "structure" in Gunderson's scheme (1978). It represents the lending of superego elements to the beleaguered ego, and in fact provides possible material for the internationalization of a more effective capacity to control impulsivity, the capacity to say "no" to immediate gratification or relief.

I have found it useful to classify the strategies and interventions that constitute the frame of inpatient treatment into three types, represented in the following diagram by three concentric rectangles:

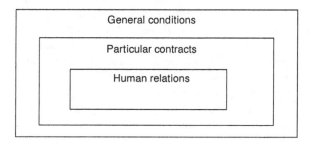

The outer rectangle represents all the rules, boundaries, schedules, agreements, and behavioral expectations that make up that unit's "legal code." It includes the lines of authority and accountability, the specification of consequences of violated rules, and the choice of limit-setting techniques. These general conditions, applicable to all patients, are most effective if applied very consistently, firmly, objectively, nonpunitively, promptly, and crisply. A business-like, matter-of-fact tone is set that conveys to everyone a background expectation of responsibility, collaboration, and behavioral appropriateness. It can be helpful if the unit's rules and expectations are written up and posted for both patients and staff to refer to, and are discussed with each patient on admission.

The atmosphere that I am trying to describe is reinforced by setting discharge dates as soon as possible and by discharging patients who persistently refuse to respect the frame. This type of discharge should be done after a warning and a "probationary" period, and should not be done as punishment but simply as a recognition that this patient does not agree to adhere to these conditions.

The middle rectangle represents those particular contracts or rules applied to a particular case, in addition to the general conditions. The suicidal patient may have a suicidal behavior contract with the staff, which may include approaching the nursing station hourly to state a commitment not to commit suicide. A patient with an eating disorder may have an eating management plan prescribing a target weight, bathroom visits, daily weights, amount of exercise, and a meal plan. These special contracts should be detailed, with clear and consistently applied consequences, and they need to be written and available to the patient and to the staff of all disciplines and all shifts. It would be better not to have a contract like this than to have it applied without consistency.

The inner rectangle represents the expectation that patients and staff members will treat one another with courtesy, respect, and with a collaborative, responsible spirit. This, of course, is an ideal regularly honored in the breach, but it still should be kept as a background expectation. For instance, the patient who addresses a nurse demeaningly, as if talking to a slave, should be addressed by that nurse regarding the demeaning tone before responding to the content of the patient's request.

The maintenance of the frame is a crucial matter; keeping it in a healthy condition can markedly diminish acting-out behavior. Not only can it help patients bring instinctual chaos and harsh superego trends under control, it can restore order to their management of time, of conflicting priorities, and of mixed feelings. It sets a work-oriented tone, encouraging frustration tolerance, delay of gratification, definition of task, and avoidance of excesses. In addition to relieving strain on the ego from drive and superego pressures, it reinforces the executive, synthetic, and organizing functions of the ego.

A former borderline inpatient with a long history of self-mutilation and suicide attempts, having been out of the hospital for 2 consecutive years, was sitting next to a lake, prepared to take a lethal overdose of medication. As she was about to do it, she recalled a mental health worker from her last inpatient stay. In her memory, he told her not to do it, that he gave a damn about her and she should give a damn about herself. She threw the pills in the lake. She told me that this mental health worker had been tough with her, very consistently confrontative, and made her feel that she mattered.

Staff members, in maintaining and reinforcing the frame, have to take it very seriously; have to take patients' behavioral excesses very seriously; have to be firm, clear, and even tough; but the effect will merely be a harsh reinforcement of sadistic superego trends unless it is delivered with caring, concern, and some warmth toward the patient.

In fact, if there is a clear, comprehensive, and relatively unambiguous frame, the staff member is freed from being in a personal battle with the patient. The patient's battle is with the frame, and the staff member is more of a referee than an adversary. This may make it possible for the staff member to be not only clear and firm in applying the framing function, but to be able to be openly supportive and validating as well.

HOLDING

If the framing function provides the structure, the restraint, the skeleton of inpatient treatment, the holding function provides the direct support, the nurturance, the warmth. If the framing addresses impulse, holding addresses affect. If the framing activities provide the ingredients for the internalization of impulse control, the holding activities provide the ingredients for internalization of the capacity to soothe the distressed self.

If the patient is expected to relinquish impulsive discharge and preferred extreme forms of behavioral solutions, we should expect her to feel, perhaps more directly, the painful affects that were fueling that behavior, and we should be prepared to "hold" that distressed patient.

So, one set of activities that I include in the holding functions are those that are designed to comfort, soothe, empathize, and validate. Careful listening; careful attention; direct expressions of concern, reassurance, and hope can bolster the flagging ego, improve self-esteem, and reinforce the presence of an insufficiently available and nurturant object.

In the service of holding, the staff adopts a tolerant, receptive, respectful attitude. They act as "real" people, gratifying the patient's needs for connection. The combination of therapeutic impatience for behavioral excesses with considerable tolerance for affect is the mixture needed by the borderline patient at this stage. I am referring here to the inpatient unit equivalent of Winnicott's good-enough mother.

By "holding" I also mean to refer to the staff's more active posture of offering guidance, advice, encouragement, praise, and feedback toward helping the patient to solve problems and to achieve the most adaptive possible position. Although the literature includes little discussion of the value of such interventions, the ordinary stuff of which friendships are made, patients regularly cite the importance of this kind of help, usually coming from nursing staff, social workers, and therapeutic activities personnel. These "holding" interventions have a direct parallel with similar ones in individual supportive psychotherapy.

The recent trends toward self-help groups, psychoeducation, informed consent, and the involvement of patients in treatment planning are all consistent with an effort to provide patients education about their illnesses and their treatment, and these trends are becoming increasingly common on inpatient units. Borderline patients are being educated about borderline pathology. In my experience this often has an important effect on the borderline patients, providing a sense of mastery and organization that counters trends toward fragmentation and confusion.

The total effect of the holding function seems to be the bolstering of the patient's capacity to tolerate painful affective states, to give up self-destructive behavior, to make sense of what was a confusing reality, to feel hope, and to begin to solve problems in reality. According to Adler and Buie (1979), the central problem of the borderline patient is the near absence of a stable holding–soothing introject and the loss of the evocative memory of caring objects under stress. The holding function assists in the construction and stabilization of such introjects and object–memories.

INVOLVEMENT

Coming into the hospital means forced contact with a variety of strangers, many of whom are in crisis. An unappealing prospect at the sound of it, involvement with other patients and with staff members on the unit can be supportive and educative in a number of ways. An awareness of these by the staff can help them to maximize the patient's uses of involvement.

First of all, of course, the patients and staff are the agents for the delivery of the framing and holding functions.

Secondly, the forced involvement, while it may feel unwelcome, may for many patients come to counter a sense of isolation and emptiness, even at times catalyzing a reinvestment in an object world that has been almost abandoned. Sitting around the television together, playing board games, having talks in and out of group meetings, going on walks together, sleeping in the same room as other patients—all can serve to counter isolation, to catalyze interest in people, and for those who have been in a painful whirlwind of involvement with highly charged figures, these relatively benign contacts can bring a sense of perspective, a reminder of the comforting mundane of benign relatedness.

Thirdly, many borderline patients talk of having been jarred by the recognition that others in the unit were more unfortunate, more severely impaired or traumatized, or were just like them, only more advanced on the path of self-destruction. The impact of these recognitions can be beneficial, as if they suddenly saw their comparative advantages or suddenly saw themselves as they might be further down the road of unchecked pathology. This motivating effect parallels the transformation of Scrooge in "A Christmas Carol" after he was acquainted with his life trends from an observer's perspective.

Fourth, involvement with other patients who have had similar experiences or carry similar symptomatology offers the opportunity to learn from one another a wider range of possible points of view, options, and successful solutions. This goes on in informal chats, task-oriented and supportive groups, and multiple family groups. The borderline patient often has become so consumed with her pain and chaos that other people and other solutions hardly exist, so that the impact of this aspect of involvement can be quite striking.

Fifth, although the erratic and self-destructive behavior of the borderline patient usually has considerable impact on others, the borderline patient often is unaware of it or surprised to hear it. The experience of an activated primitive internal object world, and the effects of primitive defenses, impair the patient's capacity to empathize with people with whom she is interacting. So the opportunity to hear from others what the impact was of a recent angry outburst, suicide attempt, elopement, episode of lying or stealing, or of a pattern of controlling or erratic behavior, is at times quite dramatic. I have spoken to many borderline patients who cite that experience as one of the most painful, memorable, and educational ones of their inpatient stay. It can lead to taking the other into account in a new way. This is reinforced and amplified by their own experiences of having strong negative feelings toward another patient who acts out an episode similar to their own. Unpleasant as it may be for a borderline patient to be around others who act as she does, the opportunities for learning and for future behavioral change are multiple.

Finally, it has been interesting to see how many borderline patients develop relationships on the inpatient unit that last for years. This is especially true, of course, on long-term units, but it also happens on shorter term units. The emotionally heightened state, the mutual sharing of very personal and intimate information, the traversing of crises together, the need for and capacity for intense bonds all combine to create a special and lasting tie that can be called upon in the future when a patient needs sustaining during a crisis. One former inpatient spoke of her "war buddies." Several units have begun periodic reunion groups of former patients to help them capitalize on this avenue of support.

DETOXIFICATION

While I have been emphasizing the supportive possibilities of the functions of retreat, framing, holding, and involvement, a given borderline patient may find any or all of these to feel more noxious than supportive.

The removal from the destablizing environment may feel like an anguishing separation. The confrontational quality of the framing activities may lead her to feel persecuted and controlled, contributing to a paranoid state. The provision of concern, support, and advice as part of the holding function may feel too solicitous, too close, even engulfing, requiring angry or acting-out behavior to interrupt the fear of merger. The multifaceted involvement with others can be an interpersonal nightmare, in which people on the unit come to feel like the figures in the patient's more dreaded internal scenarios. While intended to provide relief and support to a weary ego, the same functions can provide their own dangers, and therefore mobilize the ego's continuing need for primitive defenses.

So it is not uncommon for the borderline patient to enact the same kinds of pathological interpersonal scenarios on the unit as she has used to defend against pain elsewhere. As Ogden (1982), Kernberg (1987), Swenson (1986), and others have shown, these reenactments, executed through the mechanisms of projective identification and splitting, are often congruent both with the patient's internal world and with patterns of interaction in the family. Another supportive function of inpatient treatment of the borderline is the metabolism and "detoxification" of these kinds of scenarios.

These phenomena can range from relatively simple dyadic situations to highly complex scenes. They are organized unconsciously and enacted automatically. For example, a young borderline woman keeps avoiding and putting off the young female occupational therapist who is supposed to identify the patient's rehabilitation and activity needs and to devise that part of the treatment plan. Furthermore, the patient handles the occupational therapist in a subtly demeaning way, making her feel as if she is ineffectual and has nothing of value to offer. The occupational therapist, feeling devalued, useless, and angry, begins to act harshly. Meanwhile, the same patient has quickly involved herself in a mutually gratifying relationship with an inexperienced female mental health worker, who is pleased to have a patient who makes her feel needed and effective. The patient complains convincingly to the mental health worker about the harsh, unsympathetic style of the occupational therapist.

In a team meeting regarding this patient, the occupational therapist complains about the patient's avoidance and mistreatment of her, and the mental health worker suggests that her style is too harsh and unsympathetic for this sensitive, fragile patient. The pathological scenario, brought about by projective identification and splitting, is in full bloom. An understanding of the primitive defensive mechanisms and of the concept of interpersonal enactments of intrapsychic scenarios could lead here to an effective supportive intervention that might return the projections to the patient in metabolized, less toxic form.

For instance, after a team discussion in which the patient is understood as recruiting a gratifying, benign object to join with her against one that she has endowed with sadism, the two women agree to sit down together with the patient. They present jointly to the patient, in a nonaccusatory, collaborative manner, their perception that she seems to see one of them as supportive and the other as harsh and unhelpful, and they communicate their wish that since they each see the other as valuable in her treatment, they'd like to see if the misunderstanding can be addressed and perhaps resolved.

While no one episode like this will "clear up" primitive defensive operations, this kind of approach can nullify the destructive impact of the pathology on the staff's relationships, and can help the patient to feel that her destructiveness is limited. The common denominator of the various ways to accomplish this kind of detoxification is the staff's refusal to fall into the trap of playing out the patient's pathological scenarios. It has its parallel in the supportive individual therapist's noninterpretive undermining of splitting of the transference and distortions of reality.

IDENTIFICATION

The importance of the role of internalization, even in relatively brief inpatient treatments for borderline patients, bears repeating and emphasizing. During the hospitalization, the patient's battered ego is "borrowing" ego functions from the staff: management of instinctual pressure; deintensification of harsh superego trends; synthetic, executive, organizing functions; and so on. The patient gradually resumes more autonomous functioning.

But the style, the attitude, and the communications of certain staff members often remain with the patient, having "stuck," having "fit" somehow. It has been my impression that certain staff members are recalled over and over again, valued in memory, internalized by these patients. They are typically people who combine a capacity for being "real" (as the patients put it) and who stay clearly within the appropriate professional role—confrontational in style but with obvious concern or compassion for the patient. Months and even years later, patients recall certain staff members and certain comments, and use those memories to control themselves, to soothe themselves, and to resurrect hope. It is truly as if the internalization is providing a nidus for the creation of a new, more constructive internalized object relation.

In addition to the internalization of certain aspects of certain individuals, the patient is affected by the way in which the key staff members in her care deal with one another. The tendencies toward splitting self and object representations are, in a sense, confronted by a staff group that works collaboratively, especially if that group includes certain staff members loved and others hated by the patient. The internalization of a collaborative relationship can have a modifying, integrating effect.

SUPPORTIVE ELEMENTS OF SPECIFIC THERAPIES

In addition to the impact of all those ubiquitously present "nonspecific" supportive features discussed up to this point, the specific therapies being applied each bring to bear their own particular supportive effects.

Pharmacotherapy, of course, is directly supportive by virtue of its amelioration of emotional pain or enhanced regulation of impulse and affect. In addition, the meaning of receiving medication as experienced by the borderline inpatient can include the sense of being cared about by a concerned doctor and nurse, the instillation of hope, and the filling of an emptiness inside. The actual distribution of the medication at regular intervals can give the patient a vehicle for predictable contact and involvement. Of course, the entire procedure can alternatively be experienced as a feared form of intrusion and control by untrustworthy, even sadistic, figures. The management of pharmacotherapy requires attention to the balance among these factors so that the supportive elements can be maximized.

The treatment of the family of the inpatient is a supportive form of therapy in several ways. First, the patient can get help in coming to see the family more accurately, more realistically. For instance, the patient may learn that all pathology does not reside in herself, that her behaviors are meaningful in the family context, and that she comes by her difficulties understandably. Second, with the structure and distance provided by the inpatient setting, the patient can try to interact in a new manner. Third, with the help of the family therapist, the relationships can be restructured, manipulated in a way more in concert with the patient's needs. Fourth, the family can be directly educated in understanding the pathology, the treatment, and their own role in the treatment. The inpatient setting can provide a more secure frame for the broaching within the family of previously unspeakable secrets.

The entire gamut of strategies used by occupational therapists, recreational therapist, and vocational counselors are supportive in nature. These professionals are "ego coaches," helping with problem-solving, education, environmental manipulation, mastery, and sublimated drive discharge, all with an active approach that in itself counters the typical borderline passivity in addressing obstacles.

The narcissistic patient who feels too humiliated to work in the canteen, humiliated due to the functional and interpersonal deficits that are underlined, requires a firm hand, considerable encouragement, and a chance to talk periodically with the occupational therapist in order to do it. Her self-esteem, at first wounded, ends up elevated as she becomes increasingly confident at the work, eventually teaching others to do it.

While little further need be said about psychoanalytically oriented psychotherapy, I would simply highlight three features that have stood out over the years on inpatient units that include it. First, one can see palpable growth of an observing ego as the patient comes to "carry" her therapist with her into milieu interactions. Second, even amidst all the supportive interventions of the inpatient unit, it is obvious that there is nothing much more supportive in its effect than the accurate interpretation of a patient's psychological predicament. Third, the therapist seems regularly to serve an auxiliary function in helping the patient to sort out milieu interactions, to clarify her feelings about the players involved, and to internalize features of positively regarded staff members and patients. For instance, a therapist that I was supervising helped a patient to recognize that she admired and wanted to emulate an outspoken, somewhat provocative, but very constructive nurse. The patient, herself meek and fearing that her admiration was ill placed, felt understood and confirmed. In her behavior she gradually took on some of the outspokenness of the nurse, altogether to her benefit.

Many inpatient units have begun to include cognitive–behavioral approaches for their borderline patients. The manualized approach described by Marsha Linehan (1983) as Dialectical Behavior Therapy offers a systematic method of identifying and addressing deficiencies that characterize all hospitalized borderline patients: skills deficits in emotion regulation, distress tolerance, interpersonal effectiveness, and self-management. In our own program, we have borrowed from Linehan's treatment in systematizing the supportive work on one of our units. The approach helps to make goals more explicit, behaviorally defined, and measurable.

The nursing staff plays an active role in teaching and reinforcing the learning of new skills, and in helping patients to apply them on a daily basis. The structure provided by this model to the nurse–patient collaboration is a support for both parties, countering the regressive pulls so common in inpatient treatment.

The patients attend didactic groups in which the skills are taught. This classroom atmosphere helps to frame the task as a collaborative one in which coping skills can be acquired. The cognitive-behavioral therapist on the unit very explicitly uses the unanalyzed positive transference as a reinforcement, as an inducement to give up self-destructive behaviors. Patients leave the unit with additional coping skills, manualized in a workbook, to apply toward better emotion regulation under stress. This active, problem-solving, coping-skills approach can have the effect of fostering greater autonomy. As one discharged patient said, "When I'm in a panic at 3 A.M. and I don't want to bother my therapist or a friend, I go through my notebook and try different skills until something works."

Finally, a word about the supportive nature of the evaluation process for borderline patients. If thoughtfully used, this process can provide considerable support. The patient can be invited into a collaboration; she plays the active part of being an expert on her self, writing a history; filling out self-report inventories; charting daily changes in mood, impulse, relationships, suicidality, eating patterns, and other chosen parameters. The patient can find the process collaborative, comforting, and organizing, and it can contribute significantly to a more competent ego.

NONSUPPORTIVE ELEMENTS
OF INPATIENT TREATMENT

The chapter would not be complete without mentioning that the hospital stay can be nonsupportive, moving the patient further from effective adaptation, in a number of ways and for a number of reasons. These need to be identified, monitored, and addressed.

The removal from the environmental situation can be more destabilizing than stabilizing. This is especially true when the patient derives a sense of mastery, self-esteem, and responsibility from her role as a parent, a student, or on the job, or when the patient is suffering unmitigated separation distress.

The giving over of large sectors of functioning and control to the hospital unit can reinforce passive, dependent trends characteristic of borderline patients beyond the point of usefulness.

The framing function can cause some patients, especially those with narcissistic and paranoid trends, to feel dangerously controlled and manipulated. These patients typically project their own harsh superego elements onto the staff and fight them for control. The patient can easily feel that the unit is a more intense danger situation than anywhere else; elopements and AMA discharges result.

The holding function, as has been mentioned, can psychologically endanger those patients who have tendencies toward merger followed by annihilation terror once closer contact takes place. Certain patients are best supported from a distance. The point should be clear here that "supportive" is not synonymous with close and warm; supportive is whatever it takes in each case to increase adaptive functioning, and this often means allowing the patient to use reasonably useful defensive maneuvers, including distance, control, and intellectualization.

Involvement with others is not necessarily supportive. It can be over-stimulating and overwhelming, can lead to further perceptual and cognitive distortions regarding other patients and staff, and can provoke further impulsive discharges out of anger or desire. Feedback from others at the wrong stage can be felt to be quite an attack, hardly aiding in adaptive functioning. As with framing and holding, involvement has to be titrated and modified according to the assessment of the patient's current ego state, especially according to the current defensive functioning. It is up to the sophisticated inpatient clinician to individualize the ingredients of a given unit to a given patient in order to maximize what for that patient is genuinely supportive.

SUMMARY

The inpatient unit can be conceptualized as an all-encompassing, multifaceted supportive intervention in the longer term treatment of the borderline patient. The patient presents with the manifestations of severe ego weakness, including intolerance of affect, dyscontrol of impulses, and brief lapses in reality testing. The hospital offers a range of functions from which the ego of the patient can temporarily "borrow" in the service of regaining stability and control. This chapter has categorized and discussed the various supportive features of the inpatient unit: retreat, framing, holding, involvement, detoxification, identification, and supportive aspects of specific therapies.

Most borderline patients can indeed regain significant control in a relatively brief inpatient stay, utilizing the structure, support, involvement, and so on. As discharge approaches, the patient is again at risk for regression for a variety of reasons, not the least of which is the sense of being abandoned by the staff and patients. Special attention needs to be given to negotiating this at times hazardous step. The unit staff needs to find the balance between encouraging considerable autonomy while still offering active support and validation. Too much support can be over-protective and infantilizing, while too little as discharge approaches makes the patient feel that she only gets support if she is acting maladaptively. Some system of follow-up, such that the inpatient staff regularly learns of the experiences of discharged patients, can be useful in this regard.

Afterword

Several issues in the book deserve reiteration or further discussion. In addition, I want to include some thoughts stimulated by the other authors. These "afterthoughts" constitute this brief final chapter.

PSYCHOTHERAPY FOR BORDERLINE PERSONALITY DISORDER (BPD)

Dr. Braun reviews the history of psychotherapeutic approaches to the borderline patient in Chapter 2. Initial recommendations for a supportive treatment gave way to an emphasis on exploratory therapies, strongly influenced by the Menninger Psychotherapy Research Project and several charismatic theoretician/writers. But the treatment recommendations that derived from the Menninger Project, particularly the advocacy for exploratory rather than supportive approaches to sicker (borderline) patients, have been subjected to strong criticism, while Wallerstein's follow-up studies have raised further questions about the downgrading of supportive therapy.

As noted in the Introduction, there is an abundant literature on exploratory and psychoanalytic treatments for these patients but almost none about supportive approaches. This, in spite of the fact that many dynamic therapists are treating these patients with a primarily supportive therapy, while others, as Dr. Francis notes in the Foreword, are applying exploratory therapies to inappropriate patients and without the requisite expertise.

Thus, there is a marked discrepancy between the guidance available in the literature and the realities of the treatments currently employed. This book addresses that discrepancy. It offers a guide to the dynamic therapist who, after careful evaluation and treatment planning, decides that a primarily supportive psychotherapy is most appropriate for his patient, either initially or throughout the treatment. The treatment described lies at the opposite pole of the supportive/exploratory continuum from psychoanalytic and exploratory approaches, but the technical interventions of psychoanalytically oriented supportive therapy (POST) can be combined with exploratory strategies to produce various gradations of supportive and exploratory therapies across the continuum.

Both supportive and brief psychotherapies are currently receiving increasing attention due to the convergence of a number of professional and financial issues. Thus, I am particularly intrigued with Dr. Perry's intermittent/continuous supportive therapy for BPD patients. He compares the therapy to treatment for the patient with a chronic medical illness with periodic exacerbations; that is, a lifelong commitment to the patient, with limited periods of treatment at times of crisis.

Perry sees intermittent/continuous treatment as the treatment of choice for most BPD patients, with exploratory psychotherapy or no treatment as the main alternatives. But many BPD patients do not present periodic exacerbations and are characterized rather by chronic severe difficulties and continual crises. Thus, it seems more reasonable to me to view Perry's intermittent/continuous supportive treatment, POST, exploratory psychotherapy, and psychoanalysis as treatments of equal value, so long as each is applied to patients who are appropriate for that modality. In line with that approach, I consider arguments about whether supportive or exploratory therapies, or cognitive–behavioral therapy or psychoanalysis, for that matter, are the treatment of choice for borderline patients to be straw men. The patients subsumed within BPD are too variegated across many parameters to imagine that any single therapy would be the treatment of choice for all of them. The question is more reasonably addressed, as in Chapter 4, by asking what general patient qualities and what specific BPD characteristics suggest which treatment for which patients.

THE CLINICAL CASE

Chapters 5, 6, 7, and 8 present the 2½-year, twice-weekly supportive treatment of a borderline female, with accompanying commentary and discussion. Several issues merit further elaboration.

Mental Status Data

Level A (History) and Level B (Mental Status) data are discussed at the beginning of Chapter 5. Here I want to emphasize that the Mental Status examination is both more comprehensive and more subtle in its detail than the usual categories of Appearance, Affect, Cognitive Processes, etc. might suggest. It also encompasses how the patient relates, her major character traits, defensive style, and so on. The countertransference (broad definition) reactions of the evaluator are important sources of data. The evaluator should not be inhibited about confronting contradictory historical data, inappropriate affects, confusing interview behaviors, and other more subtle aspects of the interaction. When these types of comments are introduced tactfully, they lead to an enriched understanding of the patient (and usually cause the patient to also feel better understood). For example, confusion in the evaluator often reflects identity diffusion in the patient. When this observation and hypothesis are shared with the patient, they can dramatically move the interview onto a deeper level of understanding for both participants.

Educating the Patient

Education of the BPD patient in supportive therapy is discussed early in Chapter 6; here I want to expand the issue. Educating the patient about her pathology and the therapeutic process to be employed is desirable in all psychotherapies for all patients. The patient deserves a detailed explanation for the choice of therapeutic modality, plus basic information about how the treatment is structured and the reasons for the structures.

By contrast, patients are sometimes instructed to lie down on the couch and say what comes to mind, without any rationale offered for the use of the couch, the frequency of visits, the use of free association, the role of the therapist, and so forth. Appropriate educational information helps to cement the therapeutic alliance and decreases early dropouts from treatment. It also furnishes an effective reality backdrop against which the patient's transferences and resistances can later be effectively highlighted. Regressive transferences and resistances will often negate the early educational efforts, but that too is noteworthy.

Termination

As discussed in Chapter 8, termination is less definitive in supportive therapy than in exploratory therapy or psychoanalysis. The supportive therapist emphasizes his continued availability to the patient and may even encourage periodic returns, letters, postcards, and so on. What I wish to stress here is that continued therapist availability does not license social relationships, business arrangements, or other questionable contacts. This is worth mentioning because at least one author (Easson, 1971) has written about the positive aspects of therapist/patient friendships following psychotherapy. I totally disagree. They are setups for exploitation of the patient, including the possibility of overt sexual exploitation.

This is particularly important regarding the termination of supportive treatments of borderline patients, who often are attractive and seductive young women whose intense neediness furnishes fertile soil for therapist misdemeanors. Transferences to the therapist persist for long periods of time, particularly in supportive psychotherapy where positive transferences are relatively ignored. Therapist/patient relationships continue to be asymmetric, loaded with transference and countertransference significance. To promote patient/therapist friendships after any psychotherapy of any patient is a serious error, but the error is particularly destructive to both participants in the supportive psychotherapy of the borderline patient.

COUNTERTRANSFERENCE

I want to, once again, warn the therapist about the temptations and dangers of countertransference acting out during the supportive psychotherapy of the BPD patient. I have seen therapists who certainly knew better defend very unusual (for them) behaviors with BPD patients by such rationalizations as "the patient needs unconditional acceptance" or "the patient needs a corrective emotional experience." These are not incorrect statements, but they address only one aspect of the patient. What primarily drives such behaviors are the wishes, frustrations, rescue fantasies, and so forth of the therapist, and the needs that are being met belong more to the therapist than to the patient. Supportive therapy, because of its wide range of acceptable interventions, offers myriad opportunities and temptations for the acting out of countertransference. Nowhere is this greater than with BPD patients; for example, those who enact the deprived and abused waif role with consummate skill. Guidance, advice, suggestion, gratification, praise, limits, etc.—all are employed *only when the ego deficits of the patient require them.*

A second issue—countertransference (broad sense) reactions in the psychotherapy of BPD patients—are too often attributed totally to projective processes from the patient. Interestingly, analysts who treat primarily neurotic patients tend to discuss countertransference reactions primarily in terms of their own irrational countertransferential enactments (Jacobs, 1991). Both views are understandable, because the intense, primitive behaviors of BPD patients do invoke powerful counter-reactions in their therapists, as compared to the more modulated and integrated transferences of neurotic patients.

But no matter how powerful are the patient's projective processes, or how fragile are her self/nonself boundaries, the therapist's mind is not a black box. There are always two people involved in the relationship, each with irrational aspects and childhood residua, however more powerful, primitive, and chaotic may be the patient's irrationality. The therapist constantly monitors his internal experiences in order to better understand subtle aspects of the patient and the interaction, but he will do so more accurately and with more conviction after he separates out his own irrationalities, his own contributions to his emotional reactions. At best, attributing everything to the patient is an oversimplification; at worst it can be destructive to the patient.

SUPPORTIVE THERAPY AND PSYCHOPHARMACOLOGY

Just as there is no "best" psychotherapy for all borderline patients, there is no best psychopharmacologic treatment (nor is there likely to be). Almost every psychopharmacologic agent has been tried, without convincing evidence for any one drug of choice. As discussed by Koenigsberg in Chapter 10, Soloff and others have demonstrated the widespread positive effects of low-dose neuroleptics. But in Cowdry's study, half of the patients were not able to tolerate low-dose neuroleptics, and the MAO inhibitor and the anticonvulsant agent appeared to be most effective.

Soloff's subjects were inpatients with a heavy schizotypal overlay, while Cowdry's were outpatients and primarily affective. These two studies, when viewed together, suggest a promising direction for further psychopharmacology/BPD research. A differential therapeutics of pharmacologic interventions is needed, as there is beginning to be a differential therapeutics of psychotherapies. This will likely require further advances in the subtyping of BPD patients, because valid subtypes should provide data that are relevant to differential drug effectiveness. On the other hand, differential pharmacologic responses can also provide clues to subtyping, the "pharmacologic dissection" of Donald Klein (1973).

INPATIENT TREATMENT OF BPD

I am struck by the parallels between the inpatient treatment described by Swenson and the major supportive strategies described in this book and designed for outpatients. Although we work in the same institution, the parallels developed quite independently.

THE STRESSES OF POST WITH BPD PATIENTS

If it is not already obvious, I want to emphasize the difficulties and stresses of treating BPD patients with POST. No therapist should attempt more than two or three of these therapies at the same time. In addition, the therapist who treats such patients supportively needs to be particularly concerned about the adequacy of his own support systems. Supervision should be freely utilized, as well as open discussions with colleagues about troublesome cases. Hopefully, the therapist is fortunate enough to have a satisfactory and supportive nonprofessional life that will help buttress him against the stresses of these treatments. BPD patients are difficult when treated with any modality, but the stresses are multiplied in POST by less frequent sessions, less clear guidelines for interventions, and the dangers of countertransference acting out, which I suspect the reader, by now, is getting tired of hearing about.

Finally, addressing myself to my readers, the therapists of these patients, I hope you have found the book helpful and that it has provided you with a theoretical frame and an organized set of strategies, techniques, guidelines, and practical suggestions for treating these very difficult patients supportively. Thank you for reading it, and I wish you luck.

References

Abend, S. M., Porder, M. S., & Willick, M. S. (1983). *Borderline patients: Psychoanalytic perspectives*. New York: International Universities Press.

Adler, G. (1981). The borderline-narcissistic personality disorder continuum. *American Journal of Psychiatry, 138*, 46–50.

Adler, G. (1985). *Borderline psychopathology and its treatment*. New York: Jason Aronson.

Adler, G. (1989). Psychodynamic therapies in borderline personality disorder. *Review of Psychiatry, 8*, 49–65.

Adler, G., & Buie, D. (1979). Aloneness and borderline psychopathology: The possible relevance of child development issues. *International Journal of Psychoanalysis, 60*, 83–96.

Akiskal, H. S. (1981). Subaffective disorders: Dysthymia, cyclothymia and bipolar II disorders in the "borderline" realm. *Psychiatric Clinics of North America, 4*, 25–46.

Alexander, F. (1954). Psychoanalysis and psychotherapy. *Journal of the American Psychoanalytic Association, 2*, 722–733.

Alexander, F. (1961). *The scope of psychoanalysis*. New York: Basic Books.

Alexander, F., & French, T. M. (1946). *Psychoanalytic therapy: Principles and applications*. New York: Ronald Press.

American Psychiatric Association. (1987). *Diagnostic and statistical manual of mental disorders* (3rd ed., rev.). Washington, DC: American Psychiatric Association.

Andrews, G., & Harvey, R. (1981). Does psychotherapy benefit neurotic patients? *Archives of General Psychiatry, 38*, 1203–1208.

Andrulonis, P. A., Glueck, B. C., Stroebel, C. F., Vogel, N. G., Shapiro, A. L, & Aldridge, D. M. (1981). Organic brain dysfunction and the borderline syndrome. *Psychiatric Clinics of North America, 4*, 47–66.

Andrulonis, P. A., Glueck, B. C., Stroebel, C. F., & Vogel, N. G. (1982). Borderline personality subcategories. *Journal of Nervous and Mental Disease, 170*, 670–679.

Appelbaum, A. H. (1989). Supportive therapy: A developmental view. In L. R. Rockland, *Supportive therapy: A psychodynamic approach* (pp. 40-57). New York: Basic Books.

Appelbaum, A. H., & Munich, R. (1986). Reinventing moral treatment: The effects upon patients and staff members of a program of psychosocial rehabilitation. *The Psychiatric Hospital, 17,* 11-19.

Asberg, M., Schalling, D., Traskman-Bendz, L., & Wagner, A. (1987). Psychobiology of suicide, impulsivity and related phenomena. In H. Y. Meltzer (Ed.), *Psychopharmacology: The third generation of progress* (pp. 655-668). New York: Raven Press.

Balint, M. (1965). *Primary love and psychoanalytic technique.* London: Tavistock.

Barasch, A., Frances, A., Hurt, S., Clarkin, J., & Cohen, S. (1985). Stability and distinctness of borderline personality disorder. *American Journal of Psychiatry, 142,* 1484-1486.

Bellack, J., & Small, L. (1978). *Emergency psychotherapy and brief psychotherapy* (2nd ed.). New York: Grune & Stratton.

Bergin, A. E., & Lambert, M. V. (1978). The evaluation of psychotherapeutic outcomes. In S. L. Garfield & A. E. Bergin (Eds.), *Handbook of psychotherapy and behavior change: An empirical analysis.* New York: Wiley.

Bibring, E. (1954). Psychoanalysis and the dynamic psychotherapies. *Journal of the American Psychoanalytic Association, 2,* 745-770.

Bion, W. (1977). Attention and interpretation: Container and contained. In W. Bion (Ed.), *Seven servants: Four works.* New York: Jason Aronson.

Boyer, L. B., & Giovacchini, P. L. (1967). *Psychoanalytic treatment of schizophrenic, borderline, and characterologic disorders.* New York: Jason Aronson.

Brenner, C. (1979). Working alliance, therapeutic alliance and transference. *Journal of the American Psychoanalytic Association, 27*(Suppl.), 137-157.

Brinkley, J. R., Beitman, B. D., & Friedel, R. O. (1979). Low-dose neuroleptic regimens in the treatment of borderline patients. *Archives of General Psychiatry, 36,* 319-326.

Buie, D. H., & Adler, G. (1982). Definitive treatment of the borderline personality. *International Journal of Psychoanalytic Psychotherapy, 9,* 51-87.

Butcher, J. N., & Koss, M. P. (1978). Research on brief and crisis-oriented psychotherapies. In S. L. Garfield & A. E. Bergin (Eds.), *Handbook of psychotherapy and behavior change* (2nd ed.). New York: Wiley.

Caplan, G. (1964). *Principles of preventive psychiatry.* New York: Basic Books.

Castelnuovo-Tedesco, P. (1965). *The twenty minute hour.* Boston: Little, Brown.

Chessick, R. D. (1977). *Intensive psychotherapy of the borderline patient.* New York: Jason Aronson.

Chessick, R. D. (1982). Intensive psychotherapy of a borderline patient. *Archives of General Psychiatry, 39,* 413-419.

Cloninger, R. C. (1986). A unified biosocial theory of personality and its role in the development of anxiety states. *Journal of Psychiatric Developments, 3,* 167-226.

Cornelius, J. R., Soloff, P. H., & Anselm, G. (1991, May 11-16). Phenelzine versus haloperidol in borderline personality. *New Research Abstracts.* Presented at the 144th Annual Meeting of the American Psychiatric Association, New Orleans.

Cowdry, R. W., & Gardner, D. L. (1988). Pharmacotherapy of borderline personality disorder: Alprazolam, carbamazepine, trifluoperazine, and tranylcypromine. *Archives of General Psychiatry, 45,* 111–119.

Davanloo, H. (1978). *Basic principles and techniques in short-term dynamic psychotherapy.* New York: Spectrum.

Deutsch, H. (1942). Some forms of emotional disturbance and their relationship to schizophrenia. *Psychoanalytic Quarterly, 11,* 301–321.

Dewald, P. A. (1971). *Psychotherapy: A dynamic approach.* New York: Basic Books.

Easson, M. (1971). Patient and therapist after termination of psychotherapy. *American Journal of Psychotherapy, 25,* 635–642.

Ellison, J. M., & Adler, D. A. (1984). Psychopharmacologic approaches to borderline syndromes. *Comprehensive Psychiatry, 25,* 255–262.

Ewing, C. P. (1978). *Crisis intervention as psychotherapy.* New York: Oxford University Press.

Fava, M., & Rosenbaum, J. F. (1991). Suicidality and fluoxetine: Is there a relationship? *Journal of Clinical Psychiatry, 52,* 108–111.

Frances, A. (1982). Categorical and dimensional systems of personality diagnosis: A comparison. *Comprehensive Psychiatry, 23,* 516–527.

Frances, A., Clarkin, J., & Perry, S. (1984). *Differential therapeutics in psychiatry: The art and science of treatment selection.* New York: Brunner/Mazel.

Frank, J. D. (1974). *Persuasion and healing.* New York: Schocken.

Freud, S. (1957). The future prospects of psychoanalytic therapy. In J. Strachey (Ed. and Trans.), *The standard edition of the complete psychological works of Sigmund Freud* (Vol. 11, pp. 139–151). London: Hogarth Press. (Original work published 1910)

Freud, S. (1958). The dynamics of transference. In J. Strachey (Ed. and Trans.), *The standard edition of the complete psychological works of Sigmund Freud* (Vol. 12, pp. 97–108). London: Hogarth Press. (Original work published 1912)

Frosch, J. (1960). Psychotic character. *Journal of the American Psychoanalytic Association, 8,* 544–551.

Frosch, J. (1964). The psychotic character. *Psychiatric Quarterly, 38,* 81–96.

Frosch, J. (1970). Psychoanalytic considerations of the psychotic character. *Journal of the American Psychoanalytic Association, 18,* 24–50.

Gardner, D., Lucas, P. B., & Cowdry, R. W. (1987). Soft sign neurological abnormalities in borderline personality disorder and normal control subjects. *Journal of Nervous and Mental Disease, 175,* 177–180.

Gill, M. M. (1964). Psychoanalysis and exploratory psychotherapy. *Journal of the American Psychoanalytic Association, 2,* 771–797.

Giovacchini, P. (1984). *Character disorders and adaptive mechanisms.* New York: Jason Aronson.

Glover, E. (1931). The therapeutic effect of inexact interpretations: A contribution to the theory of suggestion. *International Journal of Psychoanalysis, 12,* 397–411.

Goldberg, S. C., Schulz, S. C., Schulz, P. M., Resnick, R. J., Hamer, R. M., & Friedel, R. O. (1986). Borderline and schizotypal personality disorders treated with low-dose thiothixene vs. placebo. *Archives of General Psychiatry, 43*, 680–686.

Gomes-Schwartz, B. (1978). Effective ingredients in psychotherapy: Prediction of outcome from process variables. *Journal of Consulting and Clinical Psychology, 46*, 1023–1035.

Graham, S. R. (1958). Patient evaluation of the effectiveness of limited psychoanalytically-oriented psychotherapy. *Psychological Reports, 4*, 231–234.

Greenson, R. R. (1967). *Technique and practice of psychoanalysis* (Vol. 1). New York: International Universities Press.

Grinker, R. R. Sr., & Werble, B. (1977). *The borderline patient.* New York: Jason Aronson.

Grinker, R. R. Sr., Werble, B., & Drye, R. (1968). *The borderline syndrome: A behavioral study of ego-functions.* New York: Basic Books.

Gunderson, J. G. (1977). Characteristics of borderlines. In P. Hartocollis (Ed.), *Borderline Personality Disorders* (pp. 173–192). New York: International Universities Press.

Gunderson, J. G. (1978). Defining the therapeutic processes in psychiatric milieus. *Psychiatry, 41*, 327–335.

Gunderson, J. G. (1984). *Borderline personality disorder.* Washington, DC: American Psychiatric Press.

Gunderson, J. G. (1989). Borderline personality disorder. In A. Tasman, R. E. Hales, & A. J. Frances (Eds.), *The American Psychiatric Press Review of Psychiatry* (Vol. 8, pp. 3–125). Washington, DC: American Psychiatric Press.

Gunderson, J. G., & Elliott, G. R. (1985). The interface between borderline personality disorder and affective disorder. *American Journal of Psychiatry, 142*, 277–288.

Gunderson, J. G., Frank, A. F., Ronningstam, E. F., Wachter, S., Lynch, V. J., & Wolf, P. J. (1989). Early discontinuance of borderline patients from psychotherapy. *Journal of Nervous and Mental Disease, 177*, 38–42.

Gunderson, J. G., & Kolb, J. E. (1978). Discriminating features of borderline patients. *American Journal of Psychiatry, 135*, 792–796.

Gunderson, J. G., Kolb, J. E., & Austin, V. (1981). The diagnostic interview for borderline patients. *American Journal of Psychiatry, 138*, 896–903.

Gunderson, J. G., & Singer, M. T. (1975). Defining borderline patients: An overview. *American Journal of Psychiatry, 132*, 1–10.

Heilbrunn, G. (1966). Results with psychoanalytic therapy and professional commitment. *American Journal of Psychotherapy, 20*, 89–99.

Heinicke, C. M. (1969). Frequency of psychotherapeutic sessions as a factor affecting outcome analysis of clinical ratings and test results. *Journal of Abnormal Psychology, 74*, 553–560.

Hoch, P. H., & Polatin, P. (1949). Psychoneurotic forms of schizophrenia. *Psychiatric Quarterly, 23*, 248–276.

Horowitz, M. J., Marmar, C., Weiss, D., DeWitt, K., & Rosenbaum, R. (1984).

Brief psychotherapy of bereavement reactions. *Archives of General Psychiatry, 41,* 438–448.

Howard, K. I., Kopta, S. M., Krause, M. S., & Orlinsky, D. E. (1986). The dose-effect relationship in psychotherapy. *American Psychologist, 41,* 159–164.

Hurt, S. W., & Clarkin, J. F. (1990). Borderline personality disorder: Prototypic typology and the development of treatment manuals. *Psychiatric Annals, 20,* 13–18.

Imber, S. D., Frank, J. D., Nash, E. H., Stone, A. R., & Gliedman, L. H. (1957). Improvement and amount of therapeutic contact: An alternative to the use of no-treatment controls in psychotherapy. *Journal of Consulting Psychology, 21,* 309–315.

Jacobs, T. J. (1991). *The use of the self: Countertransference and communication in the analytic situation.* New York: International Universities Press.

Kaufman, I., Frank, T., Friend, J., Heims, L. W., & Weiss, R. (1962). Success and failure in the treatment of childhood schizophrenia. *American Journal of Psychiatry, 118,* 909–913.

Kernberg, O. F. (1965). Notes on countertransference. *Journal of the American Psychoanalytic Association, 13,* 38–56.

Kernberg, O. F. (1967). Borderline personality organization. *Journal of the American Psychoanalytic Association, 15,* 641–685.

Kernberg, O. F. (1971). Prognostic considerations regarding borderline personality organization. *Journal of the American Psychoanalytic Association, 19,* 595–635.

Kernberg, O. F. (1975). *Borderline conditions and pathological narcissism.* New York: Jason Aronson.

Kernberg, O. F. (1977). The structural diagnosis of borderline personality organization. In P. Hartocollis (Ed.), *Borderline personality disorders* (pp. 87–121). New York: International Universities Press.

Kernberg, O. F. (1984). *Severe personality disorders.* New Haven: Yale University Press.

Kernberg, O. F. (1987). Projective identification, countertransference and hospital treatment. *Psychiatric Clinics of North America, 10,* 257–272.

Kernberg, O. F., Burstein, E. D., Coyne, L., Appelbaum, A., Horwitz, L., & Voth, H. (1972). Psychotherapy and psychoanalysis: Final report of the Menninger Foundation's psychotherapy research project. Part I. *Bulletin of the Menninger Clinic, 36,* 1–277.

Kernberg, O. F., Selzer, M. A., Koenigsberg, H. W., Carr, A. C., & Appelbaum, A. H. (1989). *Psychodynamic psychotherapy of borderline patients.* New York: Basic Books.

Kety, S. S., Rosenthal, D., Wender, P. H., & Schulsinger, F. (1968). The types and prevalence of mental illness in the biological and adoptive families of adopted schizophrenics. In D. Rosenthal & S. S. Kety (Eds.), *The transmission of schizophrenia* (pp. 345–362). Oxford: Pergamon Press.

Klein, D. F. (1968). Psychiatric diagnosis and the typology of clinical drug effects. *Psychopharmacologia, 13,* 359–386.

Klein, D. F. (1973). Drug therapy as a means of syndromal identification and nosological revision. In J. O. Cole & A. J. Friedhoff (Eds.), *Psychopathology and Pharmacology* (pp. 143-160). Baltimore: The Johns Hopkins University Press.

Knight, R. P. (1953a). Management and psychotherapy of the borderline schizophrenic patient. *Bulletin of the Menninger Clinic, 17,* 139-150.

Knight, R. P. (1953b). Borderline states. *Bulletin of the Menninger Clinic, 17,* 1-12.

Knight, R. P. (1954). Management and psychotherapy of the borderline schizophrenic patient. In R. P. Knight & C. R. Friedman (Eds.), *Psychoanalytic psychiatry and psychology.* New York: International Universities Press.

Koenigsberg, H. W. (1991). Borderline personality disorder. In B. D. Beitman & G. L. Klerman (Eds.), *Integrating pharmacotherapy and psychotherapy.* Washington, DC: American Psychiatric Press.

Kohut, H. (1971). *The analysis of the self.* New York: International Universities Press.

Kohut, H. (1977). *The restoration of the self.* New York: International Universities Press.

Lebenluft, E., Gardner, D. L., & Cowdry, R. W. (1987). The inner experience of the borderline self-mutilator. *Journal of Personality Disorders, 1,* 317-324.

Levine, I., & Wilson, A. (1985). Dynamic interpersonal processes and the inpatient holding environment. *Psychiatry, 48,* 341-357.

Liebowitz, M. R., & Klein, D. F. (1981). Interrelationship of hysteriod dysphoria and borderline personality disorder. *Psychiatric Clinics of North America, 4,* 67-87.

Linehan, M. M. (1983). *Dialectical behavior therapy for treatment of parasuicidal women: Treatment manual.* Seattle: University of Washington.

Linehan, M. M. (1987a). Dialectical behavior therapy: A cognitive behavioral approach to parasuicide. *Journal of Personality Disorders, 1,* 328-333.

Linehan, M. M. (1987b). Dialectical behavior therapy for borderline personality disorder: Theory and method. *Bulletin of the Menninger Clinic, 51,* 261-276.

Linehan, M. M., & Wasson, E. (in press). Behavior therapy for borderline personality disorder. In A. S. Bellack & M. Hersen (Eds.), *Handbook of comparative treatments.* New York: Wiley.

Links, P. S., Steiner, M., Boiago, I., & Irwin, D. (1990). Lithium therapy for borderline patients: Preliminary findings. *Journal of Personality Disorders, 4,* 173-181.

Lorr, M., McNair, D. M., Michaux, W. W., & Raskin, A. (1962). Frequency of treatment and change in psychotherapy. *Journal of Abnormal Psychology, 64,* 281-292.

Luborsky, L., Singer, B., & Luborsky, L. (1975). Comparative studies of psychotherapy: Is it true that "everyone has won and all must have prizes"? *Archives of General Psychiatry, 32,* 995-1008.

Malan, D. H. (1976). *The frontier of brief psychotherapy.* New York: Plenum Press.

Mann, J. (1973). *Time limited psychotherapy.* Cambridge, MA: Harvard University Press.

Mann, J. J., Arango, V., Marzuk, P. M., Theccanat, S., & Reis, D. J. (1989). Evidence for the 5-HT hypothesis of suicide: A review of post-mortem studies. *British Journal of Psychiatry, 155*(Suppl. 8), 7-14.

Marziali, E., Marmar, C., & Krupnick, J. (1981). Therapeutic alliance scales: Development and relationship to psychotherapy outcome. *American Journal of Psychiatry, 138,* 361–364.

Masterson, J. F. (1972). *Treatment of the borderline adolescent: A developmental approach.* New York: Wiley.

Masterson, J. F. (1976). *Psychotherapy of the borderline adult: A developmental approach.* New York: Brunner/Mazel.

Masterson, J. F. (1978). The borderline adult: Transference acting out and working through. In J. F. Masterson (Ed.), *New perspectives on the treatment of the borderline adult* (pp. 121–148). New York: Brunner/Mazel.

Masterson, J. F. (1981). *The narcissistic and borderline disorders.* New York: Brunner/Mazel.

McGlashan, T. H. (1983). The borderline syndrome: Is it a variant of schizophrenia or affective disorder? *Archives of General Psychiatry, 40,* 1319–1923.

Meissner, W. W. (1980). A note on projective identification. *Journal of the American Psychoanalytic Association, 28,* 43–67.

Modell, A. (1963). Primitive object relationships and the predisposition to schizophrenia. *International Journal of Psychoanalysis, 44,* 282–292.

Montgomery, S. A. (1987). The pharmacology of borderline personality disorders, *Acta Psychiatrica Belgica, 87,* 260–266.

Moore, B. E., & Fine, B. D. (1968). *A glossary of psychoanalytic terms and concepts.* New York: American Psychoanalytic Association.

Norden, M. J. (1989). Fluoxetine in borderline personality disorder. *Progress in Neuropsychopharmacology and Biological Psychiatry, 13,* 885–893.

Ogden, J. (1982). *Projective identification and psychotherapeutic technique.* New York: Jason Aronson.

Orlinsky, D. E., & Howard, K. I. (1978). The relation of process to outcome in psychotherapy. In S. L. Garfield & A. E. Bergin (Eds.), *Handbook of psychotherapy and behavior change: An empirical analysis* (2nd ed.). New York: Wiley.

Orr, D. W. (1954). Transference and countertransference: A historical survey. *Journal of the American Psychoanalytic Association, 2,* 621–670.

Parsons, B., Quitkin, F. M., McGrath, P. J., Stewart, J. W., Tricamo, E., Ocepek-Welikson, K., Harrison, W., Rabkin, J. G., Wager, S. G., & Nunes, E. (1989). Phenelzine, imipramine, and placebo in borderline patients meeting criteria for atypical depression. *Psychopharmacology Bulletin, 25,* 524–534.

Perry, J. C., & Klerman, G. L. (1978). The borderline patient. *Archives of General Psychiatry, 35,* 141–150.

Perry, S. (1987). The choice of duration and frequency for outpatient psychotherapy. In R. Hales & A. Frances (Eds.), *American Psychiatric Association Annual Review* (Vol. 6, pp. 398–414). Washington, DC: American Psychiatric Press.

Perry, S., Cooper, A. M., & Michels, R. (1987). The psychodynamic formulation: Its purpose, structure and clinical application. *American Journal of Psychiatry, 144,* 543–550.

Perry, S., Frances, A., & Clarkin, J. (1985). *A DSM-III casebook of differential therapeutics: A clinical guide to treatment selection.* New York: Brunner/Mazel.

Perry, S., Frances, A., Klar, H., & Clarkin, J. (1983). Selection criteria for individual dynamic psychotherapies. *Psychiatric Quarterly*, *55*, 3–16.

Pope, H. G. Jr., Jonas, J. M., Hudson, J. I., Cohen, B. M., & Gunderson, J. G. (1983). The validity of DSM-III borderline personality disorder. *Archives of General Psychiatry*, *40*, 23–30.

Pruyser, P. (1975). What splits in "splitting"? *Bulletin of the Menninger Clinic*, *39*, 1–46.

Racker, H. (1953). A contribution to the problem of countertransference. *International Journal of Psychoanalysis*, *34*, 313–324.

Racker, H. (1957). The meanings and uses of countertransference. *Psychoanalytic Quarterly*, *26*, 303–357.

Reich, A. (1951). On countertransference. *International Journal of Psychoanalysis*, *32*, 25–31.

Rinsley, D. (1982). *Borderline and other self disorders*. New York: Jason Aronson.

Rockland, L. (1989). *Supportive therapy: A psychodynamic approach*. New York: Basic Books.

Rosenbaum, M., Friedlander, J., & Kaplan, S. (1956). Evaluation of results of psychotherapy. *Psychosomatic Medicine*, *18*, 113–132.

Schlesinger, H. J. (1969). Diagnosis and prescription for psychotherapy. *Bulletin of the Menninger Clinic*, *33*, 269–278.

Schmideberg, M. (1947). The treatment of psychopaths and borderline patients. *American Journal of Psychotherapy*, *1*, 45–55.

Seiver, L. J., Klar, H., & Coccaro, E. (1985). Psychobiologic substrates of personality. In H. Klar & L. J. Seiver (Eds.), *Biologic response styles: Clinical implications*. Washington, DC: American Psychiatric Press.

Selzer, M. A., Koenigsberg, H. W., & Kernberg, O. F. (1987). The initial contract in the treatment of borderline patients. *American Journal of Psychiatry*, *144*, 927–930.

Sifneos, P. E. (1972). *Short-term psychotherapy and emotional crisis*. Cambridge, MA: Harvard University Press.

Skodol, A. E., Buckley, P., & Charles, E. (1983). Is there a characteristic pattern to the treatment history of clinic outpatients with borderline personality? *Journal of Nervous and Mental Disease*, *171*, 405–410.

Smith, M. L., Glass, G. V., & Miller, T. I. (1980). *The benefits of psychotherapy*. Baltimore, MD: The Johns Hopkins University Press.

Soloff, P. H., Anselm, G., Nathan, R. S., Schulz, P. M., Ulrich, R. F., & Perel, J. M. (1986). Progress in pharmacotherapy of borderline disorders: A double-blind study of amitriptyline, haloperidol, and placebo. *Archives of General Psychiatry*, *43*, 691–697.

Soloff, P. H., Anselm, G., Nathan, R. S., Schulz, P. M., Cornelius, J. R., Herring, J., & Perel, J. M. (1989). Amitriptyline versus haloperidol in borderlines: Final outcomes and predictors of response. *Journal of Clinical Psychopharmacology*, *9*, 238–246.

Spitzer, R. L., & Endicott, J. (1979). Justification for separating schizotypal and borderline personality disorders. *Schizophrenia Bulletin*, *5*, 95–100.

Spitzer, R. L., Endicott, J., & Gibbon, M. (1979). Crossing the border into borderline personality and borderline schizophrenia: The development of criteria. *Archives of General Psychiatry, 36,* 17–24.

Sterba, R. (1934). The fate of the ego in analytic therapy. *International Journal of Psychoanalysis, 15,* 117–126.

Stern, A. (1938). Psychoanalytic investigation of and therapy in the borderline group of neuroses. *Psychoanalytic Quarterly, 7,* 467–489.

Stern, A. (1945). Psychoanalytic therapy in the borderline neuroses. *Psychoanalytic Quarterly, 14,* 190–198.

Stern, D., Fromm, M., & Sacksteder, J. (1986). From coercion to collaboration: Two weeks in the life of a therapeutic community. *Psychiatry, 49,* 18–32.

Stone, M. H. (1987). Psychotherapy of borderline patients in light of long-term follow-up. *Bulletin of the Menninger Clinic, 51,* 231–247.

Stone, M. H. (1990). *The fate of borderline patients: Successful outcome and psychiatric practice.* New York: The Guilford Press.

Stone, M. H., Hurt, S. W., & Stone, D. K. (1987). The PI-500: Long-term follow-up of borderline inpatients meeting DSM-III criteria. I. Global outcome. *Journal of Personality Disorders, 1,* 291–298.

Strupp, H. H., Hadley, S. W., & Gomes-Schwartz, R. (1977). *Psychotherapy for better or worse: An analysis of the problem of negative effects.* New York: Jason Aronson.

Swenson, C. (1986). Modification of destructiveness in the long-term inpatient treatment of severe personality disorders. *International Journal of Therapeutic Communities, 7,* 153–163.

Teicher, M. H., Glod, G. A., & Cole, J. O. (1990). Emergence of intense suicidal preoccupation during fluoxetine treatment. *American Journal of Psychiatry, 147,* 207–210.

Ticho, E. A. (1972). Termination of psychoanalysis: Treatment goals, life goals. *Psychoanalytic Quarterly, 41,* 315–333.

Tower, L. E. (1956). Countertransference. *Journal of the American Psychoanalytic Association, 4,* 224–255.

Van Stambrouck, S. (1973). Relation of structural parameters to treatment outcome. *Dissertation Abstracts International, 33,* 5528.

Volkan, V. D. (1987). *Six steps in the treatment of borderline personality organization.* Northvale, NJ: Jason Aronson.

Waelder, R. (1936). The principle of multiple function. *Psychoanalytic Quarterly, 5,* 45–62.

Waldinger, R. J., & Gunderson, J. G. (1984). Completed psychotherapies with borderline patients. *American Journal of Psychotherapy, 38,* 190–202.

Waldinger, R. J., & Gunderson, J. G. (1987). *Effective psychotherapy with borderline patients: Case studies.* New York: Macmillan.

Wallerstein, R. S. (1975). *Psychotherapy and psychoanalysis: Theory, practice, research.* New York: International Universities Press.

Wallerstein, R. S. (1981). The bipolar self: Discussion of alternative perspectives. *Journal of the American Psychoanalytic Association, 29,* 377–394.

Wallerstein, R. S. (1986). *Forty-two lives in treatment: A study of psychoanalysis and psychotherapy.* New York: The Guilford Press.

Werman, D. (1984). *The practice of supportive psychotherapy*. New York: Brunner/Mazel.

Winnicott, D. W. (1953). Transitional objects and transitional phenomena. In *Collected Papers* (pp. 229-242). London: Tavistock, 1958.

Winnicott, D. W. (1960). Countertransference. *British Journal of Medical Psychology, 33*, 17-21.

Winnicott, D. W. (1965). *The maturational process and the facilitating environment*. New York: International Universities Press.

Winnicott, D. W. (1969). The use of an object. *International Journal of Psychoanalysis, 50*, 711-716.

Zetzel, E. R. (1971). A developmental approach to the borderline patient. *American Journal of Psychiatry, 127*, 867-871.

Zilboorg, G. (1941). Ambulatory schizophrenia. *Psychiatry, 4*, 149-155.

Zirkle, G. A. Five-minute psychotherapy. *American Journal of Psychiatry, 118*, 544-546.

Index